NAVAMSA

A Practical Treatise on Prediction

NAVAMSA

A Practical Treatise on Prediction

by

Ranjan Pal

MS, PhD

Research Scientist and Faculty Member
Massachusetts Institute of Technology, USA

The author is formally trained in *jyotish* (and its research) by Dr. Richa Shukla, equivalent to the requirement of titles *Jyotish Alankara* and *Jyotish Acharya*.

Foreword by

Gayatri Devi Vasudev

MOTILAL BANARSIDASS
INTERNATIONAL
DELHI

First Edition : Delhi, 2025

ISBN : 978-93-48911-18-6

Also available at
MOTILAL BANARSIDASS INTERNATIONAL
H. O.: 41 U.A. Bungalow Road, (Back Lane) Jawahar Nagar, Delhi - 110007
4261 (Basement) Lane # 3, Ansari Road, Darya Ganj, New Delhi - 110002
12/1A, 2nd Floor, Bankim Chatterjee Street, Kolkata - 700073
Shop #. 6, 241, Luz Ginza Complex, Luz Corner, Mylapore, Chennai - 600004
Stockist : Motilal Books, Ashok Rajpath, Near Kali Mandir, Patna - 800004

Printed in India by
MOTILAL BANARSIDASS INTERNATIONAL

॥ ॐ श्री गणेशाय नमः ॥

Dedication

Ranjan Pal dedicates this work to his supportive parents and his undying spirit.

Ranjan Pal dedicates this work to his revered Guru Richa Shukla for her love and support.

Ranjan Pal dedicates this work to all the brilliant logical minds who simply do Vedic astrology for a hobby and to whom the subject comes very easily with the grace of Almighty.

The book is written without salutations to conform with global writing norms. The author uses salutations uniformly in the 'Acknowledgements' section to honor his Guru, astrology masters, and colleagues helping the author in his journey.

Foreword

Interest in *jyotisha* or astrology has been growing in leaps and bounds with highly qualified enthusiasts making a beeline to study the subject methodically, and in addition, share their understanding of this science. The trend for such a happening began with the *Father of Modern Astrology* Dr. B. V. Raman's books on just about every aspect of astrology taking it to the educated public. It is to this trend that the academically highly qualified author Dr. Ranjan Pal has contributed his understanding of *Navamsa, a subject that has so far not received the treatment it rightly deserves.* The importance of *Navamsa* is evident from its inclusion in any horoscope alongside the *Rasi* chart. The present work, therefore, may be said to do yeoman's service to the cause of *jyotisha* and opening new vistas in the understanding of this (probably the most important) *varga* chart. Case studies that are included in this title are a lesson in practical application of the *Navamsa*.

The author's stance, and rightly so, that there should be a certain degree of replicability if astrology is to be accepted as a science is well supported by his treatment of the content of the text. I am sure the book will be received with enthusiasm by the astrology community and students.

I wish the author all success in his future literary endeavors in this ancient science.

Bengaluru **Gayatri Devi Vasudev**
April 30, 2025

Testimonials

"Ranjan has written an absolute masterclass for the educated, astrologically aware, but principally ignorant audience. He has shown us the importance of predicting events and native characteristics using the Navamsa (D9) chart alongside the birth chart (D1) by necessarily using proper principles laid down by the sages. Most astrology beginners and enthusiasts often go blank when given the D9 chart and have virtually no clue of how to look at the D9 for every event in a native's life. Ranjan has unlocked that mystery for readers in this magnum opus effort."

A Professor, and Doctor of Medicine in Social and Preventive Medicine, All India Institute of Medical Science.

"The author has rekindled my interests in Vedic astrology simply by the sheer power and clarity of his writing. As a student at IIT Delhi, I took up astrology in my senior year but could not go beyond the very easy and marketing videos astrologers put up on the Internet. These videos do not allow you to learn astrology deeply. I follow Dr. Richa Shukla's videos that are great in building concepts but do not help me to go deeper into the logic of why things happen. After reading Dr. Pal's pre-published manuscript, I could not stop appreciating his depth of understanding of the subject, and the crystal-clear way he presents his ideas. Combining this with Dr. Shukla's videos, I am now doing much better in my self-studies of knowing depths of Vedic astrology."

A beginner in Vedic astrology and an engineering student at the Indian Institute of Technology Delhi.

"I am not surprised Ranjan wrote a classic like this on the Navamsa. I am fairly knowledgeable in Vedic astrology with more than 15 years of experience, and I can safely say (knowing Ranjan) that the jyotish community will scarcely find such clear writing. The mind of this guy is brilliant and extremely clear in whatever subject he touches, be it math, engineering, business, or jyotish. He does not get into complexities but is a master of explaining complex ideas in a stepwise clear manner using very basic principles. Such a logical talent is a rarity. Ranjan has used a part of this talent in astrology apart from using most of it in what he does in his day-to-day profession. If astrology is to be ever taught at India's best schools and colleges, textbooks should be written like what Ranjan has done."

A top-level banking executive at HSBC with 15+ years of jyotish experience.

"Astrological analysis is incomplete without combining D9 analysis along with D1. This exceptionally well-written book with immaculate logic and loads of worked out examples will immensely help budding astrologers learn the nuances of analysing a chart in totality by combining D9 analysis along with D1 for finer results."

A retired Professor of Nagpur University; practicing astrologer for over 20 years, and a businessman.

"I have been learning astrology online and offline and feel this book is a must read for all astrology students to be able to refine their analysis by using D9 charts. Most schools don't teach in-depth D9 analysis and that's where this book will help students. The concepts are superbly explained with a clear thought process and follow-up examples. There has never been a book like this"

A senior student of Vedic astrology with a celebrity astrologer in West India.

" Being an arduous student of Vedic astrology I can say with utmost confidence that this book will prove to be a game changer for both the serious astrology student, and the beginner keen on getting his/ her concepts cleared on the Navamsa. Dr. Pal has written this book in a very scientific manner and with extreme precision taking the reader step by step through the various elements of D9 in a systematic manner. The book covers the entire gamut of the D9, and I believe it is the only book available in the market space that covers the entire D9 spectrum in such a logical way! The book has ample examples and case studies for students to understand and practice. Having read this book, I strongly recommend this book for serious astrology students as a go to bible for D9. "

A senior student (from the USA) of Vedic astrology with celebrity astrologers in North and South India.

"The author is nothing short of a logical genius. Knowing him well from years and being a student of Vedic astrology with Dr. Richa Shukla, I can safely say that this book will clear all the doubts of every student, be it the toddler, the novice, or the expert on the subject of the D9."

Professor and Ex-Dean at the Indian Institute of Management Calcutta, Ex-IITian, and a student of Vedic astrology with Dr. Richa Shukla.

"This is simply the best book ever written on the Navamsa (D9). Dr. Pal has covered all the bases with depth and clarity, unlike most of the confusing material available on the market. Everyone puts a D9 chart in books – no one explains how it works. Dr. Pal does it to perfection."

Professor at the Indian Institute of Management Ahmedabad, a celebrity author in management, and a Vedic and Western philosopher.

"Some write astrology books on D9 for putting in charts (without explaining concepts to depth), some write books to confuse students, some write books for the sake of writing, and some (like Dr. Ranjan Pal) write a book that cares for the student investing in time and money on astrology. This book on the Navamsa is a masterpiece to say the least – for the beginner, and also for confused."

A student (from the USA) of Vedic astrology with a celebrity astrologer in North India.

"After C. S. Patel's D9 classic, this stands out as the best book ever written on the Navamsa (D9). The book is complete in concepts, has tons of examples that make all concepts easily understandable, and is a reader's delight. The book goes beyond C. S. Patel's classic by the sheer quality of exceptional writing so much in demand by students of Vedic astrology. No wonder, Ranjan is the standout disciple of Dr. Richa Shukla out of 1000s."

A student of Vedic astrology with Dr. Richa Shukla.

"A legendary Vedic astrology author in the making. The author has taken Navamsa understanding to a standard never seen before. Marvellous!"

A Vedic astrology enthusiast from the Indian Institute of Technology Madras.

"Simply a masterpiece in Vedic astrology. This book will, without a doubt, stand out as one of the best pieces of astrological pedagogy for schools and centers of jyotish."

A student (from the USA) of Vedic astrology with a celebrity astrologer in South India.

Preface

The *Navamsa* chart (D9) in Vedic astrology is the most important divisional chart as per all our revered sage astrologers and modern masters. In addition, it is the second most important chart (after the birth chart) that needs to be necessarily used along with the birth chart (D1) to make predictions. The *Navamsa* chart is so important that virtually no practicing astrologer makes predictions on clients without looking at the *Navamsa* chart. Alternatively, any practicing astrologer not only needs the birth chart but also the *Navamsa* chart of a client, as the set of necessary and sufficient charts, to make most (if not all) predictions on the client. Simply using the birth chart for predictions is grossly ineffective.

However, the irony is that there are only a handful of modern Vedic astrology books that deal with the *Navamsa* (D9) chart, given the huge importance of this topic. There are numerous classics that have dealt with the D9 chart. Most important of these include *Sarvartha Chintamani*, *Jataka Tatva*, *Saravali*, *Phaladeepika*, *Jataka Parijata*, *Uttara Kalamrita*, *Deva Keralam*, *Dhruva Nadi*, *Vidya Madhaviyam*, *Prasna Marga*, and *Hora Sara*. Now, why should this be a problem given that one could simply read the sages and masters who authored such revered classics and use the D9 to make predictions? The simple answer to this question is that in the modern day and age, students and novice practitioners of the subject of Vedic astrology (*jyotish*) hardly ever read and absorb classics. Most of them take the easier (but not necessarily the most effective) route of either listening to online videos/lectures by teachers of astrology. Only a few read topic related books written by modern-day astrology masters and by revered sages.

P.1 - The Issues with Online Learning

Let's face it that the first and foremost issue with paid online learning is that they arc cxpcnsive. While one can buy any book on a topic in *jyotish* for at most USD 20, people are paying hundreds of USD to learn the subject today. Statistics have it that nearly 80% of Vedic astrology enthusiastic students around the globe are learning the subject online (paid or unpaid). None of the online videos/lectures talk about D9-related *shlokas* from these above-mentioned classics. While this may not be a problem, the problematic thing is that there are hardly any systematic principles (churned from the classics) about the application of D9 being taught to students that will allow them to use both the D1 and the D9 chart to make effective predictions. Even courses that focus on divisional charts give such D9 principles a miss.

Most of the available general courses cover the D9 chart tangentially where the essence of the D9 and what it stands for is mentioned, but a thorough analysis and use of both the D1 and D9 together for predictions, is not taught. Most of the time, I have observed chart readers (usually the novice student or the perceived knowledgeable student) only work with the D1 chart and are immensely tired using their logical thinking simply on the D1 or the birth chart. In other words, barely have they scratched the surface of making effective predictions by analyzing the D1, their "mediocre" minds (a term introduced by the great sage *Parashara* to his brilliant student *Maitreya*, for the average modern student of astrology in the *Kaliyuga*) cannot dig deeper to analyze multiple charts at a time.

My revered *jyotish Guru* Richa Shukla had once told me that *"online courses have no entry bar and as a result not everything can be taught as in a classroom setting and that too one where the students have not been basic screened. The interested student should show enough motivation to ask the right questions and only then the Guru will open the secrets of D9 and Jyotish in general to him/her"*. There could be nothing closer to this truth. The only problem with this system is that most of the astrological talking parrots who control the social media and blogs today are "graduating" from these online courses and giving the *maya* (illusion) to the readers that the D1 chart is enough to make predictions, and this leads to a downward spiral of the ever-growing astrology enthusiasts believing that D1 (and not D9) analysis is sufficient.

The truth here is that a D1 analysis is 'probably' sufficient only for an expert and brilliant astrologer with at least 10000 charts of experience. Every other astro enthusiast/professional should always see the D9 for every aspect of a native's life along with the D1 chart. As the legendary astrologer K. N. Rao (roughly) puts it *"No astrological comment should be made on any birth chart without a further analysis on the relevant divisional charts that necessarily should always include the D9"*.

P.2 – Drawbacks of Existing Books on the D9

If one Google's books (not classics) on the D9, there are many. Most of them (as of December 2024) are not very useful (convey no meaningful information on predictive aspects – leave alone principles) or are incremental addition of existing books of modern renowned and respected authors of Vedic astrology who have dealt with the *Navamsa*.

I list below some important drawbacks of D9-related books (having versions in the English language) that I personally feel have added to important knowledge and applications that the modern student and practitioner of Vedic astrology has benefitted from over the years.

1. The legendary astrologer C. S. Patel has written two excellent books on the *Navamsa*: *Navamsa in Astrology*, and *Navamsa and Nadi Astrology*. Most will find these two books to be exceptionally insightful (for the non-beginner) and I have no hesitation in calling each of them a modern classic. However, they are quite theoretical (without much practical worked out examples) and overload the practitioner (and surely the beginner) student with too much information. Moreover, many Vedic *sutras* (borrowed from the *Suka Nadi* literature) are lacking a logical and exemplar footing on how

they can be used in complement to non-Nadi approaches. In other words, these masterpieces lack practical bones and are not for the budding student/practitioner (or the "mediocre"), who look out for worked out case studies. As the popular and wise saying goes: *an ounce of practice is worth 100 ounces of theory*, it is imperative to educate Vedic astrology students to use the necessary minimum theory by examples to make good predictions using the D9 chart.

2. The multiple books of greats like K. N. Rao, B. V. Raman (especially *How to Judge a Horoscope*), and Gayatri Vasudev have made use of the D9 chart to make predictions in multiple arenas of a native's life and well worth the read. However, these books lack the fundamentals on *how, what*, and *why* of applying the D9 chart in complement to analysing the D1 chart in making predictions. The defence here is that these books did not focus on the *Navamsa* chart. It is fair to say that an enthusiastic student should combine the D9 masterpieces by C. S. Patel alongside the books by Rao, Raman, and Vasudev to be thorough in both theory and practice of the use of D9. The modern online-savvy student/enthusiast is unwilling to invest in such diligent and persevering efforts. In the age of *WhatsApp* and *ChatGPT* hardly anyone wants to buy and read a book, leave alone read three to four books just to understand the workings of the D9 chart.

3. Seminal efforts on the theory and applications of divisional (*varga*) charts have been laid down by revered astrologers Seshadri Iyer, K. N. Rao, and Suresh Chandra Mishra (among others) in their books and research papers. These books have covered concept-building theory and applied them to charts in a tangential form without much focus on a stepwise application of D9 (and other relevant divisional charts) concepts to case studies. Students only look for

applications via detailed worked out examples, and hence these seminal books are not very popular in the popular age or 'pop-age' of Vedic astrology. Moreover, it is the art of great writing and teaching that case studies be discussed in depth (even if a few) to ensure students get to the depth of concepts and their applications.

4. In the very recent past, there has been some efforts by the renowned V. P. Goel, on the practical applications of using the D9 chart complementing a D1 analysis to arrive at holistic predictions and assessments via the use of case studies. The books by V. P. Goel commendably provide us with multiple charts to analyse – however, the analysis is not in-depth and structured enough to explain salient concepts and its applications (much in contrast to the great general writings by the revered B. V. Raman Gayatri Vasudev, Krishna Kumar, T. S., Vasan, and A. K. Gaur – though they have not written on divisional charts). Alternatively, the books by V. P. Goel do not detail out a replicable structured approach for the student of astrology.

The Need of the Hour – There is the need of a book on *Navamsa* that is light on the pockets of readers (when compared to the 75-odd USD one pays for a webinar or course on the same topic) and hits the bull's eye in teaching enthusiasts a replicable structured way of analyzing the D1 and D9 charts together. To the best of my knowledge such a two-pronged benefit is missing from books and courses.

Whenever I see any astrologer speaking of the D9 (that too the respectable ones), there is hardly much replicability. If you call astrology a science (as we all know it is, along with it being an art) and demand global respect (and not ridicule), there should be a certain degree of replicability in the stepwise logic being applied to the D9 for every chart. Special intuitions do better for predictive analysis on every chart, but the most important first step is basic logical structure that is replicable across all native charts. Without this, every smart beginner of the subject is bound to lose interest in D9 analysis (or astrology in general) as concept application will appear too random and unstructured.

Without a stepwise application of *jyotish* principles on the combination of D1 and D9 charts to answer queries pertaining to common life events mentioned above, no D9 book serves the correct purpose of the modern (online) learning of predictive astrology. Such a book approach is a must in teaching predictive astrology to the huge population of the "D1 is enough" mindset students who have an (renewed) interest in Vedic astrology and who will potentially affect the lives of citizens approaching them for astrological advice in years to come.

Disclaimer on Drawbacks: The author respects all the authors of the above-mentioned texts and has learned immensely from all of them. The purpose of the constructive criticism of the works of some (not all) is to simply state what lacks in their books in terms of a pedagogical mastery for the next generation of budding astrologers. The last thing they would avoid is making hurried and vaguely incorrect predictions by single line *sutras* coming out of existing literature from respected authors. These authors, excellent *jyotishis*, often do not have the time or take up moral responsibility to teach students in the most rigorous logical manner. They have mostly with lot of effort translated the language and knowledge of the sages (into English or in local languages) form for us. However, they sometimes forget that less but logically and well-explained information is much better than too much information not coherently and logically linked together that does not help but harm a person's ability to analyze and predict on horoscopes. As my revered *Guru* Richa Shukla says for her students – *"only 1 out of 100 get the essence of the subject."*

P. 3 – The Main Contribution of the Book

This book addresses the need of the hour. It takes a direct approach to lay down in the simplest, logical, and practically illustrative flavor the bare conceptual and predictive elements of the *Navamsa* chart.

Alternatively, the book first borrows D9 concepts/axioms from the sages and masters that are reflective of multiple classics and modern well-documented textbooks but adds on the highly in-demand practical bone to illustrate each important concept in a logical and more importantly principled essence (to make the reader avoid rote learning) with practical worked out examples. **The book does not mix Jaimini astrology while discussing the fundamentals of the D9 chart.** The author considers Jaimini a separate and advanced application focus.

The book then takes the reader on a journey to predict in a structured replicable manner the static elements and life events of a native using a combination of the D1 and D9 charts via the application of house/dispositor concepts, the *Vimshottari dasha* system, and planetary transits.

Finally, as a unique feature, the **book provides unsolved practice case studies on the use of D1 and the D9 charts** to predict on the most popular arena of a native's life, i.e., education, career, marriage, wealth/fortune, illness, and children. These unsolved case studies **can be used by students and faculty alike as discussion studies in class.**

We have not bothered about laying down the "unnecessary" and repetitive details regarding, for example, the effect of different planets in different *Navamsas*, or predictive *sutras* of divisional charts (in this case the D9). Such information is publicly available in plenty, and in addition can easily be gleaned from existing books written by sages and the modern masters. The author recommends books by C. S. Patel and H. R. Seshadri Iyer in this regard. This book does repeat the most important concepts from these books necessary for predictions and analysis and tops them up with illustrative usage examples.

P. 4 - How is the Book Written?

The author is an engineer and philosopher by graduate education with elite higher education and research credentials. In addition, he holds an academic position in a leading institution on the globe. While these points might be perceived as being "pompous", there is no denying the fact that there are three things that most engineers and philosophers (if not all) love and live by: (i) infallible logic to construct arguments, (ii) validation of arguments using a well-founded data (*sutras* by our Vedic sages and modern masters) and/or statistical analysis, and (iii) extending theory to practice by repeated application and validation. In this book, we have tried our best as possible to adhere to these logical principles in every piece of analysis.

The author is non-professional but an expert Vedic astrologer (hobbyist) with a storehouse of astrology principles piled up on his mind. That is a prerequisite for writing this book. However, he admits that he might not have that brilliance of insight characteristic of great and God-gifted astrologers. The irony here is that such insights are not needed when it comes to lucidly teaching the building blocks of D9 (or any astrological concept) to the mass of budding astrology enthusiasts and students. What is needed is stepwise scientific application and integration of principles to case studies for any astrological query at hand. The author satisfies this need in the book.

There is another salient and unique point about this book. It is one of the very few (if not only) books that is written by a rigorously trained but non-pecuniary astrologer. Such is the openness of Richa Shukla (the *jyotish Guru* of the author), that she wanted to promote her research student to be an independent author. Alternatively, it also shows that eventually logic and analysis rigor is all that matters, and it can come from anyone having a strong command of argumentative logic, and *jyotish*.

P. 5 - How To Read this Book?

The book is intended for students - both beginners and those that are advanced. In either case, the **student should read the book in sequence** to crystallize their concepts. The simple reason being – according to the author's experience, many students who think they are advanced are actually not. They are often either confused in the meaning of difficult concepts, or take things face value, i.e., rote learning, as mentioned by teachers/books/Internet speakers, without understanding the fundamentals at the grass root level – subsequently making faulty predictions.

This book provides **worked-out examples** after each concept, and the reader should thoroughly redo the examples on their own and then move forward to the next concept. Each worked-out example is loaded with principled arguments. This will improve learning. These examples are detailed unlike one/two line and unclear analysis in most existing books. In purely astrological terms, an interested reader with a weak Jupiter and Mercury in their horoscope usually finds it hard to read and understand Vedic astrology. **This book is methodically written to address such interested students also.** The book also consists of multiple **case study charts** for the students to practice (and for instructor teaching material) by learning from the worked-out examples.

Ranjan Pal
Boston, Massachusetts, USA
December 2024
Massachusetts Institute of Technology

Acknowledgements

(with salutations)

The essence of this book is derived in part from an effort of astrological exposition and pedagogy conducted by Dr. Ranjan Pal under the inspiration of his revered teacher and Vedic astrologer Dr. Richa Shukla; MA, PhD, *Jyotish Acharya*, *Jyotish Alankara*. Ranjan Pal acknowledges that without the fiery inspiration, guidance, and love of Richa Shukla, the book would not have materialized. In this regard, Ranjan Pal acknowledges the countless chats of both encouragement and banter, between himself and Richa, that pushed the author to relentlessly pursue excellence in understanding fundamental concepts in astrology and astrological analysis. The outcome of this beautiful relationship has led to this pedagogical effort. As the popular belief goes: the ardent seeker only needs a seed flame; the author acknowledges Richa Shukla to be the primary source of this flame.

Dr. Ranjan Pal acknowledges his late father Dr. Manabendra Nath Pal (ex-Professor and Acting Director at the Indian Institute of Management Calcutta) for sowing the seeds of *jyotish* in his son from early childhood (beginning in the *mahadasha* of the 8th lord). He taught basic astrology and its logic and mathematics to Dr. Ranjan Pal and always showed him his intellectual and moral limits on how far to go in Vedic astrology (i.e., striving for excellence, but not taking it up as a profession), given his son's primary career aspirations and his way of life. This seed became a tree over the years with self-study and bore fruit when Dr. Ranjan Pal found his *jyotish Guru* in Dr. Richa Shukla after 20 years (in the *mahadasha* of Ketu in his 8th house), who nurtured the talent in a way as the *Guru* should, to help her student walk on the path of excellence.

Dr. Ranjan Pal acknowledges Smt. Mrs. Gayatri Devi Vasudev - Hon. Sr. Vice President of the Indian Council of Astrological Sciences (ICAS), for taking the efforts of reviewing the book and writing a Foreword. She is undoubtedly a living legend and one of the greatest living Vedic astrologers showing many enthusiasts like the author on how to make predictions through rigorous horoscope analysis via her books and rare appearances in online interviews. It thus makes this book on D9 extra special that such a legendary author and daughter of Dr. B. V. Raman - the legendary founding father of modern astrology, decided to write a Foreword. The author could not be more humbled by this gesture and hopes he has done justice to contributing to the very important topic of Navamsa analysis in Vedic astrology.

Dr. Ranjan Pal acknowledges his colleague Mrs. Ekta Jain, a very diligent student of Vedic astrology who is a true friend in need, and someone with a great heart who was always there for the author whenever he wanted to discuss astrology. This is despite her multiple family commitments and constraints. Ekta was instrumental at many times to help the author get his book charts and related data in shape, and proofreading arguments put forward by the author. She also contributed to the text in some important parts of this book. Dr. Ranjan Pal acknowledges this selfless mindset of Mrs. Jain. It was so heartening to see Ekta being more positively excited at times at the author's forward footsteps towards this book than the author himself. It is big-hearted and sacrificing friends like the lovely Mrs. Ekta Jain who always wishes well for their near and dear-ones, and such mindsets make any pedagogical and expository efforts truly meaningful and successful.

Dr. Ranjan Pal acknowledges Mr. Ankit Bhushan, who along with Dr. Richa Shukla, was instrumental in opening some of the authors' mental locks of astrological analysis. The author thanks the Almighty for a chance meeting with Ankit and paving the way for the many relished astro-analysis meetings (*guftagoos*) at cafes around the

Massachusetts Institute of Technology and Harvard University between Ankit and the author.

Dr. Ranjan Pal acknowledges his colleague Dr. Bodhibrata Nag (Professor, Indian Institute of Management Calcutta), a student of Dr. Richa Shukla, to always be there for the author in terms of clearing obstacles related to publishing innovative and insightful ideas, be it in astrology or otherwise. Dr. Bodhibrata Nag is himself a research scholar of repute and recognizes the fact, along with the author, that doing quality work is only half the battle won, the rest of the battle is won via negotiations with leading publishers prior to publicizing the work.

Finally, Dr. Ranjan Pal acknowledges Shri K. N. Rao, being their astro-academic grandfather (the *jyotish Guru* of Dr. Shukla) for his superb and brilliant insights through his many books on analysis, and also especially acknowledges Dr. B. V. Raman, Mrs. Gayatri Vasudev, Shri C. S. Patel, Shri S. C. Mishra, Shri J. N. Bhasin, and Shri A. K. Gaur for the lucid, conceptual, and detailed *Parashari* wisdom they impart through their books. He is indeed an *Eklavya* to these modern masters.

Dr. Ranjan Pal would like to thank Mr. Abhishek Jain and Mrs. Poonam Taneja from the Motilal Banarsidass (MLBD) International for providing him with the opportunity to publish his book in their prestigious and historic publishing house. He also thanks the anonymous editing staff of this esteemed publishing agency.

Table of Contents

*"Everything should be made as simple as possible,
but not simpler"*

- Albert Einstein

*"Here is an essential principle of education:
to teach details is to bring confusion;
to establish the relationship between
things is to bring knowledge"*

- Maria Montessori

Part 1
Fundamental Concepts
(with Examples)

CHAPTER 1

Meaning and Importance of the *Navamsa*

In this chapter we will define a *navamsa*, uniquely connect its meaning to the structure of *nakshatras*, and state the immense and non-negotiable importance of **'the Navamsa chart'** - also synonymously called as the *Navamsa* (note the capital N in *Navamsa*) or D9, in Vedic astrology.

1.1 What is a *navamsa*?

The term *'navamsa'* simply implies one-ninth portion (*amsa*) of a house in the birth chart that is also known as the D1 chart, or alternatively, the D1. Hence for 12 houses of the D1, there are 12x9 = 108 *navamsas*. The 12 houses of the zodiac in total span 360 degrees. Hence each *navamsa* is of span 360/108 = 3d20' (3 degrees and 20 minutes). Technically, any house in any chart - be it the D1 or any divisional chart, can be divided into nine *amsas*. However, the term *'navamsa'* has been reserved by the sages only for the birth chart house divisions. Why the sages have done this is something we will reason in sub-chapter 1.3. We now explain the concept of a *navamsa* via the following example.

Example – Suppose a native is born with the Aries ascendant. Then the first house lies in the Aries *rashi* that spans from 0 to 30 degrees. The nine *navamsas* of this *rashi* (House 1) are:

navamsa #1 - spans from 0d0’ – 3d20’

navamsa #2 – spans from 3d20’+ – 6d40’

navamsa #3 – spans from 6d40’+ – 10d00’

navamsa #4 – spans from 10d0’+ – 13d20’

navamsa #5 – spans from 13d20’+ – 16d40’

navamsa #6 – spans from 16d40’+ – 20d0’

navamsa #7 – spans from 20d0’+ – 23d20’

navamsa #8 – spans from 23d20’+ – 26d40’

navamsa #9 – spans from 26d40’+ – 30d00’

Here the notation ‘+’ implies that the boundary degrees can only belong to a single *navamsa*. In other words, *navamsa* #2 can only start beyond 3d20’ (hence 3d20’+) and not at 3d20’ because 3d20’ belongs to the first *navamsa* of the Aries *rashi*.

Similarly, the second house is in the Taurus *rashi*, that spans from 30+ degrees to 60 degrees of the zodiac. The nine *navamsas* of this *rashi* (House 2) are:

navamsa #1 - spans from 30d0+ – 33d20’

navamsa #2 – spans from 33d20’+ – 36d40’

navamsa #3 – spans from 36d40’+ – 40d00’

navamsa #4 – spans from 40d0’+ – 43d20’

navamsa #5 – spans from 43d20’+ – 46d40’

navamsa #6 – spans from 16d40’+ – 20d0’

navamsa #7 – spans from 50d0’+ – 53d20’

navamsa #8 – spans from 53d20’+ – 56d40’

navamsa #9 – spans from 56d40’+ – 60d00’

It is often the case that in popular lingo, the term *navamsa* is thought to be a chart, i.e., the D9 (the subject of discussion in Chapter 2). Unfortunately, this is not the case. It is because of this lingo and the usually ignorant mass of students making astrology their fashionable discussion/blogging hobby, that the concept of 'a' *navamsa* and its distinction from 'the' *Navamsa* has confused students and even some professionals (i.e., anyone who analyses horoscopes for money) forever. This latter fact has been verified by the author through Internet surveys and interactions with multiple students.

Every birth chart has many *navamsas* (108 to be exact), but there is only one D9 or the *Navamsa* chart for a single birth chart (D1). The long-run impact of this confusion is the well-known lack of conceptual understanding of the D9 chart and its correct use (or lack of use) for assessments and predictions on life matters of a native.

1.2 Connection of *Navamsas* with *Nakshatras*

Simply put, a *navamsa* and a *nakshatra* in the D1 chart (birth chart) are uniquely connected via a direct correspondence. A *nakshatra* spans 13d20' and each *nakshatra* has 4 padas (legs) with each *pada* spanning 3d20' with 4 multiplied by 3d20' totaling to 13d20'. **Hence one *navamsa* corresponds to one *pada* of a *nakshatra*.** The 27 *nakshatras* of the zodiac with 108 padas in total span 360 degrees and corresponds directly to the 108 *navamsas* of any birth chart that also span 360 degrees of the zodiac.

The structural equivalence of a single *nakshatra pada* with a single *navamsa* is the most important thing to remember for anyone reading this book. This is the most salient concept while using *navamsas* for assessments and predictions using the *Navamsa* chart along with the D1 chart. We now explain this concept via the following example.

Example – Suppose a native is born with the Aries ascendant. The nine *navamsa -nakshatra pada mappings* of this *rashi* (House 1) are:

navamsa #1 - 0d0' – 3d20', *Ashwini, Pada* 1

navamsa #2 – 3d20'+ – 6d40', *Ashwini, Pada* 2

navamsa #3 – 6d40'+ – 10d00', *Ashwini, Pada* 3

navamsa #4 – 10d0'+ – 13d20', *Ashwini, Pada* 4

navamsa #5 – 13d20'+ – 16d40', *Bharani, Pada* 1

navamsa #6 – 16d40'+ – 20d0', *Bharani, Pada* 2

navamsa #7 – 20d0'+ – 23d20', *Bharani, Pada* 3

navamsa #8 – 23d20'+ – 26d40', *Bharani, Pada* 4

navamsa #9 – 26d40'+ – 30d00', *Kritika, Pada* 1

Similarly, the second house is in the Taurus *rashi*. The nine *navamsa -nakshatra pada mappings* of this *rashi* (House 2) are:

navamsa #1 - 30d0+ – 33d20', *Kritika, Pada* 2

navamsa #2 – 33d20'+ – 36d40', *Kritika, Pada* 3

navamsa #3 – 36d40'+ – 40d00', *Kritika, Pada* 4

navamsa #4 – 40d0'+ – 43d20', *Rohini, Pada* 1

navamsa #5 – 43d20'+ – 46d40', *Rohini, Pada* 2

navamsa #6 – 16d40'+ – 20d0', *Rohini, Pada* 3

navamsa #7 – 50d0'+ – 53d20', *Rohini, Pada* 4

navamsa #8 – 53d20'+ – 56d40', *Mrigshira, Pada* 1

navamsa #9 – 56d40'+ – 60d00', *Mrigshira, Pada* 1

We provide in **Figure 1**, the complete zodiac, *nakshatra*, *nakshatra pada* mapping for the 108 *navamsas* (along with the knowledge of which *pada* of which *nakshatra* goes into which *rashi* in the D9 chart – the latter being a topic of study in Chapter 2). The houses do not matter in this Figure as every *rashi* will have 9 *navamsas*, each a *nakshatra pada*. Take note that Figure 1 is not in a birth chart format, and the *rashis* are in clockwise order. We suggest the ardent student make a study poster to help him/her remember this map over time. This is important to analyze and make predictions without lookups.

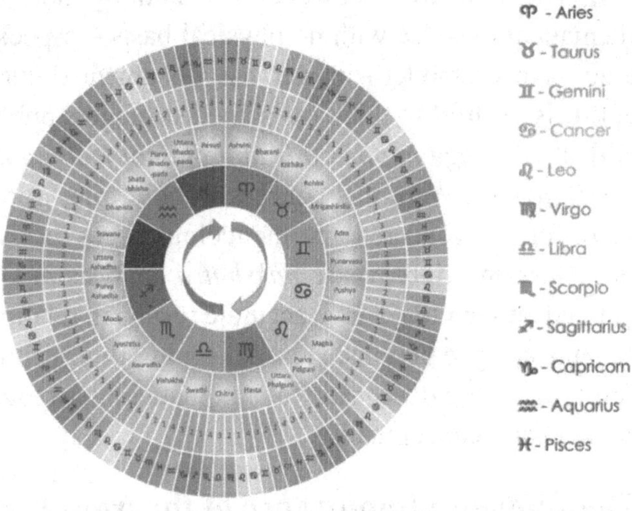

***Figure 1:** Nakshatra, Nakshatra Pada, navamsa Map*

1.3 The *navamsa* is a Concept only for the D1

We can now provide an answer (continuing from Section 1.1) as to why the term *'navamsa'* has been reserved by the sages (as per documentation) only for the birth chart house divisions. It is simply because *nakshatra padas* are only a concept of the D1 (birth chart), as it is the only chart that reflects the physical zodiac, and *nakshatras* are physical star configurations in the zodiac.

There are astrologers who consider *nakshatras* in divisional charts also; however, there is no mention of such a concept in the scriptures and manuscripts by sages, and in books by renowned modern astrologers. Note here that divisional charts that include the D9 are conceptual (non-physical) transformations of the birth chart to provide a microscopic perspective of planetary positions in the birth chart. One could technically extend the concept of *nakshatras* in D1 to that in divisional charts – however, it is nothing more than a mathematical exercise with no physical basis – especially when no sage or modern master has documented such a concept. It is wishful to think (as some astrologers publicly opine) that *"the sage implied this and did not feel the need to write it down"*. Were this concept to hold true, it is too important for our veneered and meticulous sages to give it a miss in writing. Moreover, a *nakshatra* analysis in D1 is fine-grained enough to achieve accurate results in relation to assessments and predictions. Hence, keeping things simple, we don't assume *nakshatras* to automatically extend to divisional charts conceptually.

1.4 The Immense Importance of the *Navamsa*

We now shift our focus to the *Navamsa* chart, also simply called the *Navamsa* (the alphabet *N* written in capital is mandatory as it's a unique single chart), or popularly also known as the D9 (divisional chart 9).

How one can derive the *Navamsa* or the D9 from the birth chart (D1) is left to discuss in Chapter 2. However, before we do that, it is important to know *how important is the D9 to Vedic astrology and why.*

1.4.1. How Important is the D9 Chart?

The first important thing to know is that D9 is one of the *Parashari shodashvarga* divisional charts (along with the D60) from which **every aspect of life** can be analyzed. Hence, intuitively it holds every much as importance as the D1 (birth chart).

The second important thing to know is that in the *Parashari Vimshopak Bala* point system given to divisional chart importance, the D9 uniquely gets second highest (after D1) points (5 out of possible 20) in the *Shadvarga* scheme of 6 divisional charts; uniquely fourth highest (after D1, D3, and D12) points (2.5 out of possible 20) in the *Saptavarga* scheme of 7 divisional charts. joint third highest (after D60 and D1) points (1.5 out of possible 20) in the *Dasvarga* scheme of 10 divisional charts; and uniquely third highest (after D60 and D1) points (3 out of 20) in the *Shodashvarga* scheme of 16 divisional charts. It is evident that in most of the *Parashari varga* schemes, D9 stands out (apart from D1 and D60) as the most important divisional chart from which **all events of a native's life** can be gleaned. While D60 holds more weight than the D9 (and D1), it is extremely difficult to have access or be certain that one has access to the exact D60 chart due to birth time inaccuracies of up to more than a minute that is usual for many natives, especially for charts we find in books and the Internet.

1.4.2 Why is the D9 Chart so Important?

It is easy to understand that a planet (say A) in the D1 chart, i.e., the birth chart, is placed on a *nakshatra* in the zodiac, that implies it is placed in one (out of the 4) *pada* of that *nakshatra*, and the *pada* is ruled by a particular planet (say B). It is in the house lorded by B that planet A will be placed in D9.

While, we will leave the discussion on how the D9 chart is formed till Chapter 2, **it is obvious that the D9 is simply an enlarged microscopic view of the entire D1 chart.** *Nothing less, nothing more.* This point needs to be kept in mind, Hence, the D9 chart is 'equally' important as the D1 chart to glean into all aspects of a native's life for which we look in D1. To re-iterate C. S. Patel's words, *the Navamsa (D9) is the X-ray photo of the birth chart D1 that helps us clearly see the fruits that we can get in this lifetime (on various areas of life) that are 'hidden' in the tree that we call D1.*

We request the reader/enthusiast not to worry at this stage of the book about the fact that the D9 is a divisional chart for spouse/marriage/fortune/dharma. It is indeed true that the D9 chart is a divisional chart that does deal with spouse/marriage/fortune/dharma (and we will take this up in detail in the later chapters of the book) – however, first and foremost the D9 chart is a chart providing a microscopic view of the D1 chart. This is the only line of thought that will help build up strong concepts regarding D9 necessary for accurate assessments and predictions.

CHAPTER 2

How to Derive the *Navamsa* Chart from D1

In the previous chapter, we discussed the role of the D9 chart as acting like a microscope to zoom into the D1 chart. A planet placed in a *nakshatra pada* in the D1 gets placed in D9 in a house that is owned by the lord (excluding shadow planets Rahu and Ketu) of the *pada*. However, each lord (apart from the Sun and the Moon) owns two houses in the zodiac. The question then is: *which of the (two) house(s) in the D9 a planet in the D1 will move to (and why)?*

To answer this question, in this chapter we will discuss how to prepare the D9 chart from the D1 chart. To this end, we will first describe the logic of how the D1 chart is mapped to the D9 chart. This book is the first to provide this logic. *In most books, a simple D1-D9 mapping table is provided without any logic of why this mapping has been proposed by our revered sages.* We will then propose **four** examples of deriving the D9 for ease of exposition.

2.1 How Did Our Sages Design the D9 Chart?

To understand the divine wisdom and highest intelligence of our revered sages, note that each of the 4 *padas* of a *nakshatra* signifies *dharma*, *artha*, *kaama*, and *moksha* in that order. These are the four *purusharthas* of any human born on earth and define all the *karma* (and its nature) the native will expend in a lifetime. Hence, it is popularly said that the *nakshatras* showcase the core personality of a native in all spheres of life, as personality is driven by the nature of *karma*. The sages used this simple and fundamental *purushartha* principle to design the D9. *Nothing less and nothing more*!

Illustrations - Let us illustrate the above point with some examples. Say, that a person (native) has a planet A in the 3rd *pada* of the *Vishakha nakshatra*, i.e., lies between 26d30'+ and 30d00' of Libra. This *pada* is a *kaam pada* ruled by Mercury. However, Mercury rules both Gemini and Virgo *rashis*. Gemini is a *kaam rashi*, whereas Virgo is an *artha rashi*. Hence, in the D9 chart, planet A will occupy the Gemini *rashi*. Say, again that another person (native) has a planet B in the first *pada* of the *Krittika nakshatra*., i.e., lies between 26d40'+ and 30d00' in Aries. This *pada* is a *dharma pada* and ruled by Jupiter. However, Jupiter rules both Sagittarius and Pisces. Sagittarius is a *dharma rashi*, whereas Pisces is a *moksha rashi*. Hence, in the D9 chart, planet B will occupy the Sagittarius *rashi*. Finally, let us do a third example. Say that a native has a planet C in the first *pada* of the *Purva Phalguni nakshatra*, i.e., lies between 13d20'+ and 16d40' in Leo. This *pada* is a *dharma pada* and ruled by Sun. However, Sun, being a luminary, only rules Leo that is a *dharma rashi*. Hence in the D9 chart, planet C will occupy Leo.

2.2 The Table Shortcut to Forming D9 from D1

Having understood the core foundational concept behind the formation of the D9 from D1, it is time for easy and memoizable shortcuts to know the position of any planet in the D1 chart as to where it is placed in the D9 chart. The basic principle here is that:

1. for Fire *rashis* in D1, the planets placed in the first *navamsa* go in the sign of Aries in D9; planets in the subsequent 8 *navamsas* of these Fire signs are placed in the 8 *rashis* starting from Taurus and ending in Sagittarius.
2. for Earth *rashis* in D1, the planets placed in the first *navamsa* go in the sign of Capricorn in D9; planets in the subsequent 8 *navamsas* of these Earth signs are placed in the 8 *rashis* starting from Aquarius and ending in Virgo.
3. for Air *rashis* in D1, the planets placed in the first *navamsa* go in the sign of Libra in D9; planets in the subsequent 8 *navamsas* of these Air signs are placed in the 8 *rashis* starting from Scorpio and ending in Gemini.
4. for Water *rashis* in D1, the planets placed in the first *navamsa* go in the sign of Cancer in D9; planets in the subsequent 8 *navamsas* of these Water signs are placed in the 8 *rashis* starting from Leo and ending in Pisces.

This 4-step principle is illustrated in **Table 1** and **Table 2**. The numbers in the cells denote which *rashi* in D9 will be the destination of a planet placed in a certain *navamsa* of a certain sign (*rashi*) in the D1. Note that the boxed cells in Table 1 denote *vargottama* placements (a placement where a planet in the D1 chart is placed in the same sign as in the D9 chart, and we will cover this important concept in Chapter 3. Also note that the planets in the 1st, 5th, and 9th *navamsa* of any (Fire/Earth/Air/Water) sign in D1 always end up in the *rashi* of the same element (Fire/Earth/Air/Water) in D9 – thereby obtaining its full *tattwa* strength.

We conclude by providing **four** examples of D1 (with planetary degrees) to D9 mapping, using Table 1 or Table 2, and *Parashara Light 9.0.*

Table 1

Table Caption – The D1 to D9 mapping memory chart

Degree in *Rashis*	Ar	Ta	Ge	Cn	Le	Vir	Lib	Sco	Sag	Cp	Aq	Pi
0d00' to 3d20' (*navamsa* #1)	1	10	7	4	1	10	7	4	1	10	7	4
3d20'+ to 6d40' (*navamsa* #2)	2	11	8	5	2	11	8	5	2	11	8	5
6d40'+ to 10d00' (*navamsa* #3)	3	12	9	6	3	12	9	6	3	12	9	6
10d00'+ to 13d20' (*navamsa* #4)	4	1	10	7	4	1	10	7	4	1	10	7
13d20'+ to 16d40' (*navamsa* #5)	5	2	11	8	5	2	11	8	5	2	11	8
16d40'+ to 20d00' (*navamsa* #6)	6	3	12	9	6	3	12	9	6	3	12	9
20d00'+ to 23d20' (*navamsa* #7)	7	4	1	10	7	4	1	10	7	4	1	10
23d20'+ to 26d40' (*navamsa* #8)	8	5	2	11	8	5	2	11	8	5	2	11
26d40'+ to 30d00' (*navamsa* #9)	9	6	3	12	9	6	3	12	9	6	3	12

Table 1

Table Caption – The tattwa-based D1 to D9 mapping

Degree in *Rashis*	F	E	A	W	F	E	A	W	F	E	A	W
0d00' to 3d20' (*navamsa* #1)	1	10	7	4	1	10	7	4	1	10	7	4
3d20'+ to 6d40' (*navamsa* #2)	2	11	8	5	2	11	8	5	2	11	8	5
6d40'+ to 10d00' (*navamsa* #3)	3	12	9	6	3	12	9	6	3	12	9	6
10d00'+ to 13d20' (*navamsa* #4)	4	1	10	7	4	1	10	7	4	1	10	7
13d20'+ to 16d40' (*navamsa* #5)	5	2	11	8	5	2	11	8	5	2	11	8
16d40'+ to 20d00' (*navamsa* #6)	6	3	12	9	6	3	12	9	6	3	12	9
20d00'+ to 23d20' (*navamsa* #7)	7	4	1	10	7	4	1	10	7	4	1	10
23d20'+ to 26d40' (*navamsa* #8)	8	5	2	11	8	5	2	11	8	5	2	11
26d40'+ to 30d00' (*navamsa* #9)	9	6	3	12	9	6	3	12	9	6	3	12

F (Fire Rashi); **E** (Earth Rashi); **A** (Air Rashi); **W** (Water Rashi)

Example #1 (D1 to D9 mapping)

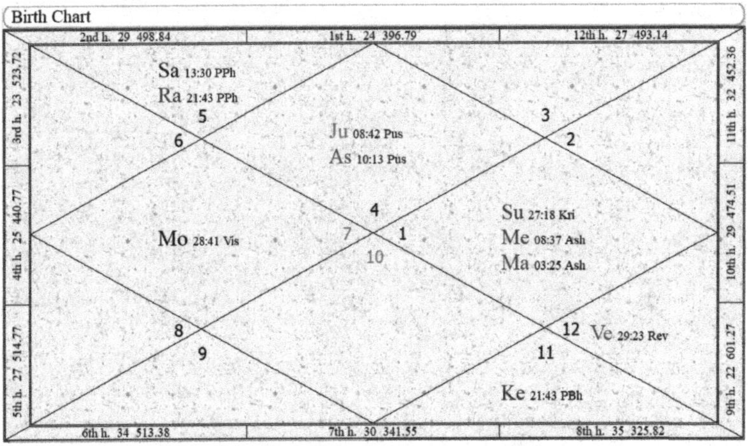

Birth Chart

As	10:13:03	Pushya	Hoh	3,Sa/Ve/Ke
Su	27:18:33	Krittika	Ah	1,Su/Su/Ve
Mo	28:41:12	Vishakha	Tay	3,Ju/Ve/Ke
Ma	03:25:33	Ashwini	Chay	2,Ke/Su/Me
Me	08:37:50	Ashwini	Cho	3,Ke/Ju/Ve
Ju	08:42:22	Pushya	Hay	2,Sa/Ve/Mo
Ve	29:23:16	Revati	Chee	4,Me/Sa/Ma
Sa	13:30:53	P.Phalg.	Moh	1,Ve/Ve/Ve
Ra	21:43:39	P.Phalg.	Tee	3,Ve/Ju/Ra
Ke	21:43:39	P.Bhadra.	Say	1,Ju/Ju/Ra

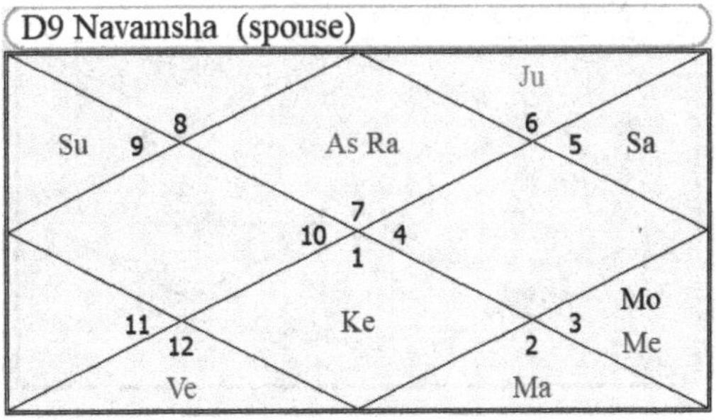

Example #2 (D1 to D9 mapping)

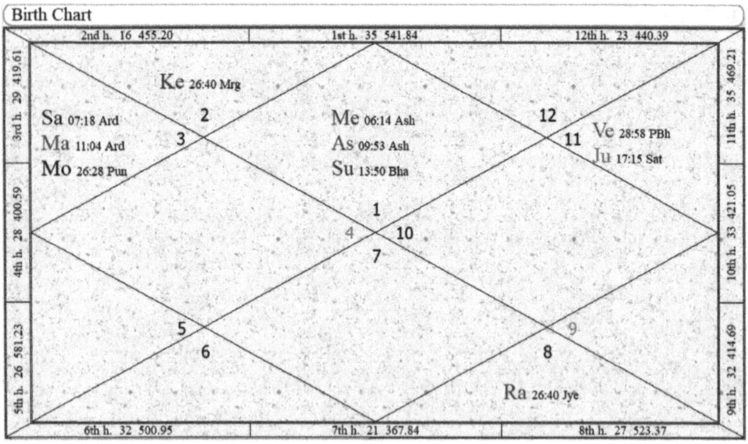

Birth Chart

As	09:53:44		Ashwini	Cho	3,Ke/Sa/Me
Su	13:50:18		Bharani	Lee	1,Ve/Ve/Mo
Mo	26:28:36		Punarvasu	Koh	2,Ju/Ke/Me
Ma	11:04:06		Ardra	Gha	2,Ra/Sa/Me
Me	06:14:11	c	Ashwini	Chay	2,Ke/Ra/Sa
Ju	17:15:05		Satabhi.	Soo	4,Ra/Ve/Me
Ve	28:58:28		P.Bhadra.	Dah	3,Ju/Su/Ra
Sa	07:18:20		Ardra	Koo	1,Ra/Ra/Sa
Ra	26:40:13		Jyeshtha	Yoo	4,Me/Ju/Me
Ke	26:40:13		Mrigashi	Vo	2,Ma/Ju/Me

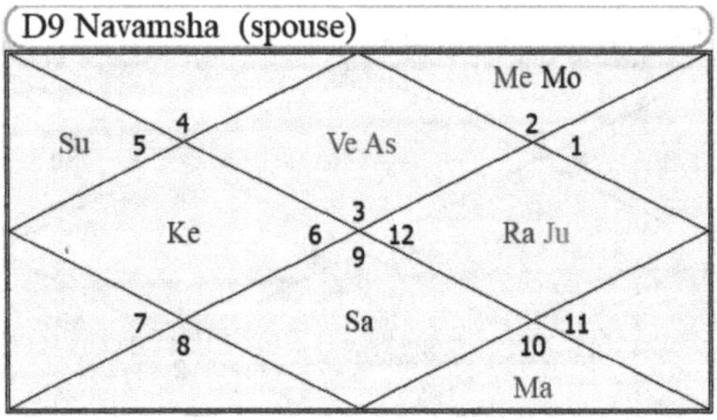

Example #3 (D1 to D9 mapping)

Birth Chart

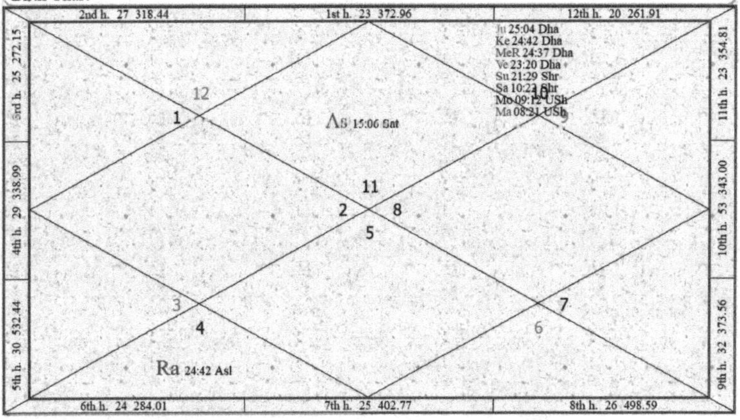

Birth Chart

As	15:06:17		Satabhi.	See	3,Ra/Ke/Sa
Su	21:29:46		Shravana	Kho	4,Mo/Ve/Ra
Mo	09:12:56		U.Shad.	Jee	4,Su/Ve/Sa
Ma	08:21:22	c	U.Shad.	Jee	4,Su/Ve/Mo
Me	24:37:56	Rc	Dhanish.	Gah	1,Ma/Ra/Ju
Ju	25:04:47	c	Dhanish.	Gah	1,Ma/Ra/Me
Ve	23:20:46	c	Dhanish.	Gah	1,Ma/Ma/Ma
Sa	10:22:40	c	Shravana	Khi	1,Mo/Mo/Ju
Ra	24:42:25		Ashlesha	Day	3,Me/Ra/Sa
Ke	24:42:25		Dhanish.	Gah	1,Ma/Ra/Sa

D9 Navamsha (spouse)

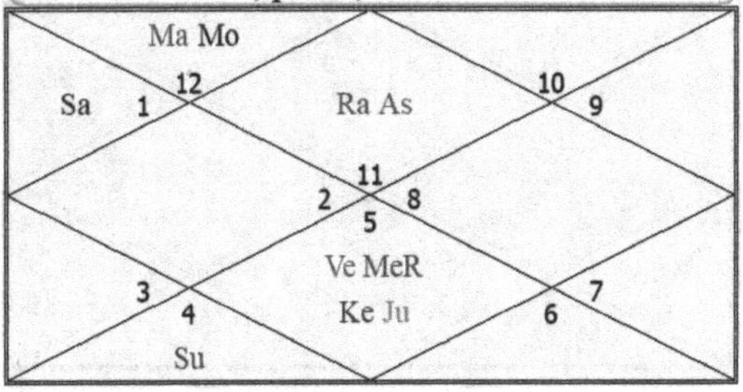

Example #4 (D1 to D9 mapping)

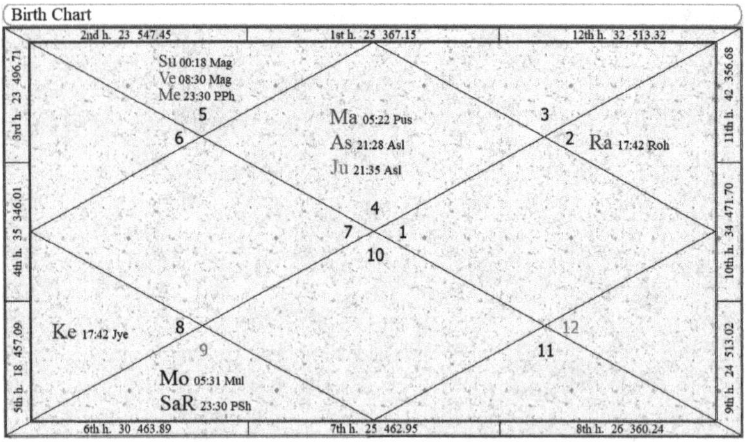

Birth Chart

As	21:28:28		Ashlesha	Doo	2,Me/Ve/Ke
Su	00:18:24		Magha	Mah	1,Ke/Ke/Ma
Mo	05:31:10		Moola	Yoh	2,Ke/Ma/Mo
Ma	05:22:32		Pushya	Hoo	1,Sa/Sa/Ju
Me	23:30:34		P.Phalg.	Too	4,Ve/Sa/Ra
Ju	21:35:00	c	Ashlesha	Doo	2,Me/Su/Su
Ve	08:30:56	c	Magha	Moo	3,Ke/Ju/Ve
Sa	23:30:02	R	P.Shad.	Dah	4,Ve/Sa/Ra
Ra	17:42:39		Rohini	Vee	3,Mo/Sa/Ju
Ke	17:42:39		Jyeshtha	Noh	1,Me/Me/Ma

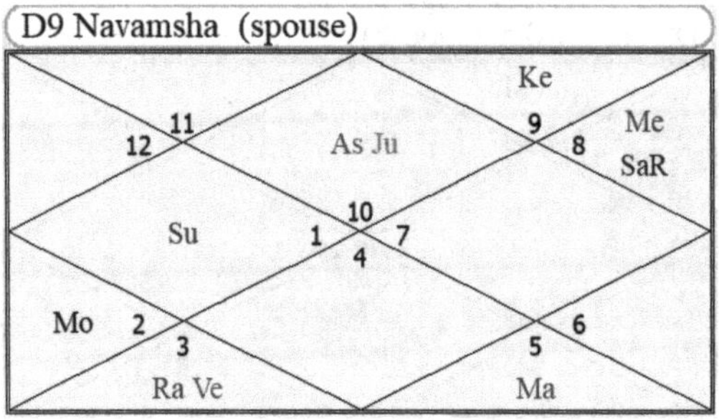

CHAPTER 3

The Key D9 Houses and the *navamsas*

In the previous chapter, we discussed how to form the D9 chart from the D1 chart. In this chapter, we will discuss the key foundational elements of the D9 chart. This will include the key houses of the D9, and the important *navamsas* of the D1 chart (and reflected in the *Navamsa* chart).

However, before we do this, it is important to answer an extremely relevant question as we steadily progress into analyzing the D9 chart: *do planetary aspects and yogas operate in the D9 chart as they do in D1?* After all the (key) houses in the D9 do not stand alone as independent entities – they will need to interact with one another in some manner, else there is no point in having the structure of the D9 or any divisional chart the same as the D1 chart. Our sages simply could not randomly make divisional charts of the same structure as the D1 chart. There must be some sound reasoning behind this. Let us explore this in this chapter.

3.1 Settling the Debate on Aspects, *Yogas* in D9

Ok, so the D9 is chart with 12 signs, and planets along with the ascendant are placed in the signs just like they do in the D1 chart. That is what we saw in Chapter 2. So, *do planets aspect other planets and form yogas in the D9 chart, as they do in D1?* There has been a huge divide in the *jyotish* community for eons on this question. Many (pundits) think that the answer is a 'yes' and many think it is a 'no'.

This book will not take any side – simply because there is no need to take sides. Both classes are correct to some extent, and at the same time they were never crystal clear about to what extent and why they are not correct. This is fair, given that no astrologer will ever have complete cosmic consciousness like our sages did, at the same time they are not physicists and with due respect most get the physics wrong.

Let's clarify one point with confidence – **planetary aspects and *yogas* matter in the D9** (or in any divisional chart). However, *it is not in the way many people think*, i.e., the aspects and *yogas* function in the **same fashion** as they do in the D1. They do not. Let us showcase key logical arguments in this regard.

1. To start with, there has been no explicit mention of planetary aspects in D9 by the sages. Why should it be? The divisional charts are not a physical manifestation of the zodiac and the placement of planets in the zodiac. Divisional charts are conceptual and non-physical extensions of the D1. Aspects only work when one physical body, i.e., a planet, sees another physical body via cosmic rays. Basic physics in operation here. This can only happen in the D1. A planet located in the Aries sign in D1 – the physical zodiac cannot at the same time physically occupy Leo in D9, and physically occupy Taurus in D60 and so on. This is not only basic physics but also

commonsense. Our sages had this in plenty apart from their unconceivable genius.

2. The reality is that a planet is physically located on the zodiac in the D1 and at the same time is conceptually located in another house (correspondingly sign) of the divisional charts, in our case the D9. The planets in the D9 chart 'influence' (not physically aspect) each other (either one way or mutually) via certain planetary placements and these placements are exactly similar (but not same) to physical aspects in the D1 chart (as per the classics). This is precisely the reason two planets may not share any physical relationship, i.e., via aspects and conjunctions, in the D1 but might influence each other in the D9. Put in another way, if there is no physical relationship between two planets in the D1, can there be a physical relationship between the two in the conceptual D9 chart? Obviously, no. It is merely a subtle influence (rooted in their physical placement in D1, say via connection of their dispositors as an example) that was not visible in the D1 chart and gets magnified in the D9 chart. **This 'influence' is often taken 'synonymously' as 'aspect' in D9 by modern authors, without clarification**. On the other hand, it is also possible that two planets share a physical relationship in the D1 chart but an influence between them is absent in the D9 chart. This means that in the D1 chart the planets shared the same house or could see each other's houses, but in the microscopic sense never 'looked' at one another, i.e., the bonding existed in D1 but was not strong enough to reflect in the D9.

3. *Yogas* are simply house-planet placement configurations. When they occur in physical form as in the D1, they are very strong. Similar placement configurations between houses and planets will also form in the D9 (and in every divisional chart), and they are also *yogas* in every sense of the term, but in conceptual non-physical space. These *yogas* of the non-physical D9 chart, in complement with the *yogas* of the physical D1 chart affect the life matters of a native.

Hence, influence/'aspects' and *yogas* are both operative in the D1 and in the D9. What is the difference? They cannot be of the same power in both the charts, because if they would then sage *Parashara* would have given equal importance in the *Vimshopak Bala* point system to the D1 and the D9. He did not in any of the *Shodashvarga* systems. The points in the *Vimshopak Bala* system are a proxy to the actual relative weights one should give to the 'aspects' and *yogas* in the D1 and the D9 charts, but no one knows the ground truth and all established astrologers have their own weight allocation system between the two based on their empirical experience.

3.2 Special Significances of the D9 Chart

We know now that the D9 chart is a microscopic version of the D1 chart gleaning into every aspect of a native's life. However, at the same time D9, i.e., the *Navamsa* chart, holds some special significances **being the chart that can be independently studied to analyze *dharma/spouse/fortune* of a native** according to sage *Parashara,* and all these significances are rooted in *dharma* (not necessarily religion, but righteous values in general). Hence, the *Navamsa* chart is sometimes also called the *Dharmamsa*. An interesting question then is: *why does dharma drive spouse and fortune for a native?*

Dharma of a native is examined from the ninth house of the D1 chart, and the one-ninth division of signs is called a *navamsa*. Hence the D9 chart is alternatively a magnified view of the 9th house of D1, and the implications of the primary 9th house significance (*dharma*) on all aspects of native's life. It is as simple as this. Sage *Parasara* advises us to examine the D9 for spouse as it is the fruit/gains of *dharma*. Why is this the case? This is because the 11th sign from the 9th house is the 7th house (the house of spouse) which shows gains/increase of *dharma* and the 12th sign from the 9th house in the 8th house which shows loss/decrease of *dharma*. Thus, marriage of a native indicates an increase of *dharma* (via the addition of a spouse) while widowhood/loss of wife symbolizes a destruction of *dharma*. Hence, the 8th house also indicates the longevity of the spouse in Vedic astrology. One should carefully observe that in Hindu weddings the son-in-law (or daughter in law) is regarded as Vishnu (Lakshmi) as his (her) coming to the family has led to an increase in *dharma*.

Ok we got why *dharma* drives the spouse for a native. Why does *dharma* drive fortune for a native? One must be aware that Lord Vishnu is the protector of *dharma*. The D9 chart indicates the blessings of Lord Vishnu in this life that reflects our past life *dharma/adharma* **in all arenas of life**. Hence, the D9 showcases the *dharma/adharma phal* (fruits of *dharma and adharma*) in this life in all arenas. These fruits are nothing but the fortune a native is blessed with in this life. As an example, getting a good spouse is a fruit of good *dharma* in previous lives. Since *dharma phal* drives the performance of every arena of a native's life in this birth (covering the 12 houses of a person's D1 chart), the D9 (*Navamsa*) or the *Dharmamsa* is one of the most important divisional charts in Vedic astrology.

3.3 Key Houses of the D9 Chart

We have established that *dharma* is the key seed for getting the results of every arena of a native's life, and the D9 is reflective of *dharma phal* for a native. So, what do the different houses of the D9 represent?

The **first house** of D9 is a *kendra* house and represents *swadharma* and one's commitments to *dharma* (and subsequent fruits) towards the self (not personal self only, but also to people much relying on the self, such as spouse, children etc. Also note that *dharma* is represented in Hindu philosophy as a four-legged animal, and the first house represents the fourth (lowest) *pada* of this animal. Purely from a marriage viewpoint, the first house of D9 controls the promise of marriage.

The first house also denotes the personal self. The *lagna* in the D9 (like in and along with the *lagna* in D1) also indicates looks, appearance, personal nature. One's *dharma* towards the personal self in prior births result in fruits that reflect in this life on the self and are captured in the D9 *lagna* placement.

The **fourth house** of D9 is a *kendra* house and represents *dharma* and one's commitments (and subsequent fruits) to society, motherland, and one's personal comforts within or without marriage. The fourth house represents the third (and third highest) pada of *dharma* that is a four-legged animal.

Purely from a marriage viewpoint, the fourth house of the D9 shows enjoyment/peace in marriage.

It is also mentioned in the scriptures that Lord Vishnu resides in the 4th house of the D9 for a native, and one way to get His blessings is to directly meditate on the planetary mantra corresponding to the avatar associated with the planet(s) placed in the 4th house, or the lord of the 4th house. The 4th house of the D9 is often called the heart of the D9.

The **seventh house** of D9 is a *kendra* house and represents *dharma* and one's commitments (and subsequent fruits) to one's spouse and other family members, where the term 'family' not only refers to one's own family (spouse, children, etc.) but also extended family of the native (e.g., in-laws, parents, other immediate relatives). The seventh house represents the second (and second highest) *pada* of *dharma* that is a four-legged animal.

The seventh house also indicates the spouse of the native. In addition, it is the *streebhoga* house for men and *purushbhoga* house for women; and among other things signifies the gain from *dharma in relationships and marriage* (the 7th house is the 11th from the 9th house).

The **tenth house** of D9 is a *kendra* house and represents *sarwadharma* (universal *dharma*) and one's commitments to the entire world (adhering to the philosophy of *Vasudaiva Kutumbakam*) that includes spouse, parents, children, people in workplace, people external to family but not in workplace, animals, and any possible relationship of the self with the surrounding environment. The tenth house represents the first (and highest) *pada* of *dharma* that is a four-legged animal. Purely from a marriage viewpoint, the 10th house of the D9 denotes the actions in a marriage by the native.

The tenth house also indicates the peace/comfort house of the spouse (the 10th house being 4th from the 7th house). Sri Lakshmi resides in the 10th house of the D9 as Lord Vishnu resides in the 4th house. The 10th house of D9 also signifies the *karma* of marriage and relationships.

While the *kendras* of the D9 denote where the *dharma* activities (and is nature depending on planetary placements) of a native is going to be focused, the **trine** (*trikon*) **houses** 1, 5, 9 of the D9 from the *lagna* in the D9 reflect the permanent natures and abilities of the native. These houses are the sustaining forces of the *Navamsa* chart. This is because the *Navamsa* chart is the accumulation of *dharma* from past births and reflects the blessings of Lord Vishnu as fruits of *dharma* to experience in the current birth. Hence, the *trikon* houses show the natural abilities that come to a native due to the accumulation of *dharma* from prior births, and this primarily depends on the planets that are placed in the trines. In specific relation to marriage/relationships (that the D9 chart also signifies), the 5th house indicates the creativity/intelligence in marriage/relationships whereas the 9th house indicates the *dharma* in marriage/relationship. Note here that the D9 aspects are not physical aspects as in D1, and hence are not as strong in terms of planetary rays and/or exchange of rays. **Hence placements carry most importance in the D9 (and in divisional charts in general)**. Hence, a question that arises here is: *what are the primary abilities that a native is blessed with if certain planets are placed in the trines?* We list a few important signature abilities for each planet. In addition, we list the deity of each planet – praying/worshipping who will result in blessings related to the significances of the planet, an increase in natural abilities, and protection from ill effects.

Sun – activities that need routine/habit and rhythm. The deities are Lord Shiva, *Agni*, and *Surya*.

Moon – activities involving a mental push such as emotional, *bhakti*, and inspirational outlets of effort. The deities are *Gauri Maa* and *Parvati Maa*.

Mars – activities involving fighting, protection, defense, and culinary skills. The deity is *Kartikeya*.

Mercury – activities involving speech, intelligence, communication, business, accounting, compromise, and reasoning. The deity is Lord Vishnu.

Jupiter – activities involving intelligence, wisdom, supreme knowledge, *dharma*, general knowledge, knowledge of Vedas, astrology, advising, and (philosophical) debating. The deities are Lord Narayana, Lord Vishnu, Lord Shiva, *Indra*.

Venus – activities involving the arts, traveling for pleasure, relating to details, bed pleasure activities, sexual activities, and good decision making. The deities are Lakshmi, *Radha*, *Sachi*.

Saturn – activities involving patience, knowledge of traditional things, maintaining rigid structures, maintaining historical traditions, and influencing masses of society. The deities are Lord Narayana, Lord Brahma, *Yama*.

Rahu – activities involving cunningness, planning, mastering hard/heavy things easily, scheming, strategy, knowledge of weapons and poison, alchemy, tantric/tamasic practices, devious and outlier types of intelligence. The deities are *Durga*, *Chandi*, *Chamunda*.

Ketu – activities involving computers and small machines, intuition, self-emancipation and its knowledge, secrecy, and astrology. The deity is *Ganesha*.

We state here that meditating upon and chanting of Vishnu *Sahasranama* is also sufficient for appeasing all planets.

3.4 Other (Key) Houses of the D9 Chart

Having covered the *kendras* and the *trines* of the D9 chart, it is time we discuss its 2nd, 3rd, 6th, 8th, 11th, and 12th houses. It is not that these houses are not key – they are also key houses. **However, the best way to analyze such houses is to express these houses as *kendra* or *trine* to either other houses or the key houses** mentioned in Section 3.3., i.e., the *kendra* or *trine* house from the D9 *lagna*. Hence, we discuss these houses after the quadrants and trines of the D9.

The **second house** of the D9 to start with is the wealth and speech house of marriage/relationships, and wealth due to good (*dharmic*) deeds of self (seen from the D9 *lagna*). Then, it reflects the natural ability of the native to gain benefits on *karma* related matters of the 10th house (i.e., *dharmic* and spousal *karma*) of the D9 is the Lakshmi *sthana*, and the 2nd house of the D9 is the 5th house (*trine*) from the 10th house (*kendra*). The second house of the D9 is also the 8th house (of secrecy) from the 7th house and indicates secret affairs in the marriage.

The **third house** of the D9 is the effort and communication house of marriage/relationships. It is also the house of the father-in-law as it is the 9th house from the 7th house of spouse. Consequently, it is also the natural abilities of the spouse due to the fruits of *dharma* acquired in past lives. The significance of this house in D9 gives better results over time as it is an *upachaya* house.

The **sixth house** (also an *upachaya* house) of the D9 to start with is the daily mundane grind house of marriage/relationships, along with being the house of marriage enemies (and discord). It is also the 12th house from the 7th house of spouse and indicates the loss of the spouse. The 6th house of the D9 is also the 4th from the 3rd house of the father-in-law and indicates peace/harmony place for the father-in-law. Hence, it is also possible that the spouse goes to her father (or native's father-in-laws' house) for a short time and separates from the husband of the spouse temporarily, hence this house stands for short-term physical separations in marriage. The 6th house of the D9 is also the *dharmic* commitments (and its fruits) of the father-in-law to his society, home, and motherland, as the 6th house is the 4th house from the 3rd house of the father-in-law.

The **eighth house** of the D9 is the house of uncertain/sudden events in marriage/relationships, and of inheritances from the marriage. Note that the 8th house is the 2nd from the 7th house of the D9 and is thus a *maraka* house for spousal matters. Marriage/relationship breaks (in other words, longevity of marriage) are seen from this house of the D9 chart. The 8th house is also the 4th house from the 5th house of the D9. The 5th house of the D9 chart indicates intelligence in marriage/relationships. Hence the 8th house indicates the peace from the intelligence in marriage, and the *dharmic* commitments (and its fruits) in relation to the marital/spouse intelligence applied at home. Bad intelligence use will lead to break of relationships and vice versa.

The **eleventh house** (also an *upachaya* house) of the D9 signifies gains from marriage/relationships. The term 'gain' also implies lust (but in a negative sense of gain). Note that the 11th house is the 2nd house from the 10th house of Lakshmi *sthana* – indicating gains from the Lakshmi *sthana* and all matters signifying that *sthana* in the D9 chart. The 11th house of the D9 is also the 3rd house from the 9th house and indicates the courage house for ensuring *dharma* in marriage and relationships. The 11th house of the D9 also indicates the creative abilities of the spouse (as 11th house is the 5th from the 7th house).

The **twelfth house** of the D9 indicates relationship distancing, loss and expenditures, and *moksha* (emancipation) in marriage/relationships. On the other hand, it also shows the sexual pleasures of marriage/relationships. The 12th house is the 4th from the 9th house, and the 5th house from the 8th house. Since the 8th house is in trine with the 12th house, all the natural abilities in relation to the 8th house transfer over to the 12th house (i.e., secret affairs, loss due to sudden breaks in relationships). The 12th house of the D9 being the 4th from the 9th house indicates the *dharmic* commitments (and its fruits) in relation to ensuring *dharma* applied in marriage (that can lead to *moksha* in marriage), *Guru* affairs, and father affairs.

3.5 Chart Example to Understand the D9 Houses

We take an example chart to describe in considerable detail how the D9 affects the significance of some of the individual D9 houses in the native.

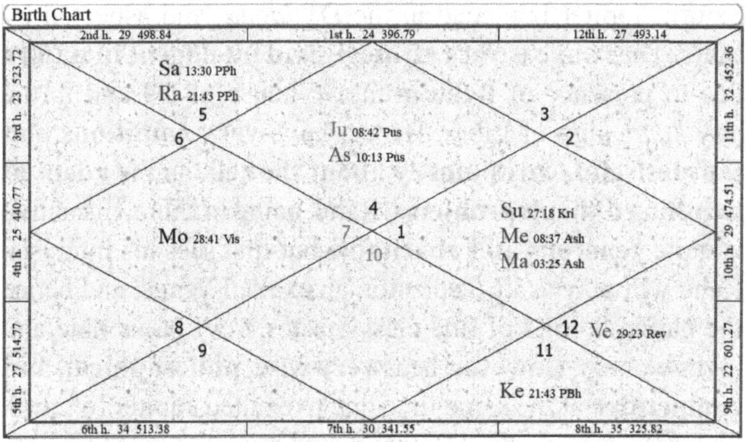

Consider the native whose chart you see above. The D9 chart of the native is shown below.

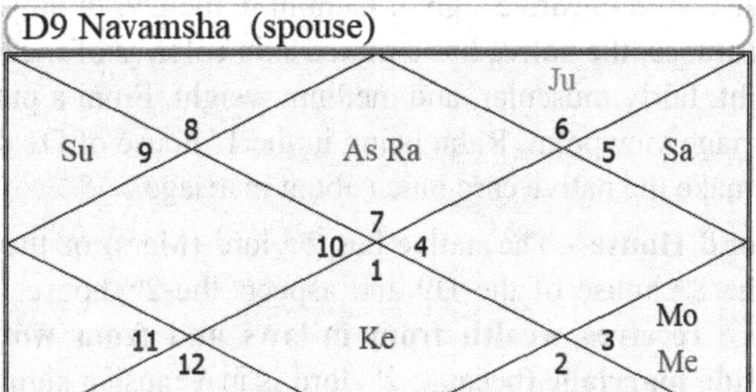

The first thing to notice is that 6 out of the 9 planets in the D1, and 4 out of the 9 planets in the D9 are in *kendras* and *trikon* houses. Hence, the pillars and natural ability propensities of the native are strong.

First House - The native has Rahu in the first house of the D9. However, in D1, Moon the *lagna* lord is fortified by multiple strong aspects from Mars, Sun, Mercury, and

Saturn. Jupiter is placed in the D1 *lagna*, and aspected by Mars. The native is **very strategic and intelligent in nature** due to presence of Rahu in the 1st house of D9 and in the airy *kaam* sign of Libra. Hence, he is **very ambitious and self-desireful, cares mostly about the self,** and is **adept at handling difficult problems**. Rahu, being in Libra, the native is quite **generous and charitable** but first sees his interests. Rahu will play as its dispositor, an exalted Venus, and hence the native is fond of fine classy tastes, very passionate and loves women. However, he is **very wise, philosophical, and competitive** at the same time due to exalted Jupiter (6th lord, 9th lord) sitting in the D1 *lagna*, and aspected by Mars who also mutually aspects *lagna* lord Moon. The native is **quite communicative** also as the *lagna* lord in D1 is with Mercury in the communicative sign of Gemini in the D9. In physical appearance, the native has a mixed skin color, is of medium height, fairly muscular, and medium weight. From a purely marriage viewpoint, Rahu being in the 1st house of D1 does not make the native care much about marriage.

Second House - The native has 2nd lord (Mars) of the D9 in the 8th house of the D9 and aspects the 2nd house. The native **receives wealth from in-laws and from women outside marriage** (because 2nd lord is in Venusian sign and in an *artha rashi*). The wealth from marriage/relationships can come to this native in transformative ways such as by inheritance. Mars, aspected by Saturn is in the sign of Venus in D9 and **causes challenges and tough situations in marital life and with revengeful in-laws** (as Mars is in the house of marital benefits), but the native fights and wins over the challenges because Mars is a *yogakaraka* planet for the native in the D1 chart and is aspected by wisdom planet Jupiter in the D9 chart.

Fourth House - The native has no planet in the fourth house of the D9. However, the 4th lord is Saturn (a separative planet) that goes to the 8th position from its own house (placed in an enemy sign) and is aspected by hot and separative planet Mars from the 8th house with Mars being the *maraka* house lords. **The native finds less peace at home in married life and enjoys more peace from secretive feminine alliances** (Mars placed in Venus's house). However, Jupiter aspecting the 4th house of the D9 ensures necessary peace at home. In addition, due to Mars being *yogakaarak* in the D1, there are benefits and gains accrued from these alliances with the 4th lord placed in the 11th house of the D9. **The in-laws and the alliances (signified by the 8th house) create an environment for the native to gain**, but the gain does not give enough peace of mind (though it gives some amount) to the native due to the ill placement of Saturn in the D9. The *dharma phal* of the native from previous births does not give the native a platform (or the need) in this birth to contribute to good/*dharmic* deeds towards motherland and nearby society, or marriage life at home. However, it is strongly emphasized that the native does not do *adharmic* deeds towards motherland, and society, due to the positive aspect of Jupiter on the 4th house.

Ninth House - The native has Moon and Mercury in the ninth house of the D9. The Moon in a *trikon* house has given the native **very good natural singing abilities, and the natural ability to emotionally inspire people (and students) with whom he interacts.** Mercury in the 9th house and in its own house has given the native **exceptional intelligence and a strong natural ability to communicate, do business, write, do mathematics, and conduct logical reasoning**

on a wide variety of topics. The native is a computer scientist, decision scientist, and an applied mathematician in a premier institution of the world and is also adept in the occult sciences. The combination of the Moon and Mercury in trine with strategic and intelligent Rahu in Venus's *kaam rashi* in the D9 *lagna* has **given the native a communicative personality that mesmerizes others around him and attracts females.** This quality also helps the native in doing business with others and fulfilling his desires, and the native has many collaborative ventures in his work and hobby place (Mercury is a primary significator of the 10th house and is the lord of hobbies for the native being the 3rd lord in D1). The 9th house hosting Moon and Mercury is mutually aspected by Sun who is the 11th lord in the D9, and the 2nd lord in D1. Hence **the significances of gains and wealth via communication and emotional stirring is much boosted for the native.** The 9th house being the *dharma* house of marriage is fairly strong contributed by an aspect of Sun from a *dharma rashi* providing a large force in the D9 chart to ensure that *dharma* is being upheld in marriage/ relationships.

Tenth House - The native has no planet in the tenth house of the D9. However, the 10th lord is Moon that goes to the 12th position from its own house, and is aspected by hot and separative planet Sun. Hence, the **native does not do enough *karma* for married life at home**, i.e., there is a lack/loss of homely married life *karma*. Even the spouse does not feel very comfortable at home in a married life setting (as the 4th lord from the 7th house of D9 goes to the 9th house of D9). However, the 10th lord of the D9 (driving the good/*dharmic* deed for the world) in the 9th house and being in conjunction with Mercury (9th lord) in a communicative *rashi* **leads to a transfer of the married-life *karmic* potential to the outside world in terms of communication that is inherently natural in the native** on topics of spirituality, philosophy, and higher learning in IT/cyber, and also forms a *dharma-karma adhipati yoga* **giving fame/name to the native**. In relation to *dharma phal* from past births, the native gets the platform to sufficiently contribute to good deeds for the world through communication on higher learning (including post graduate education) and philosophy.

3.6 *Vargottama navamsa*

We will now discuss one of the most central concepts in relation to the *Navamsa* chart - a *vargottama navamsa.* Many details of this *navamsa* can be found in the classic and some modern texts. In this text, we briefly describe the salient points in relation to this *navamsa* and most importantly follow it up with an analysis on a practical chart to understand the use.

One must note that the term *'vargottama'* implies an *uttam varga*, i.e., a very good divisional placement of a planet. A *vargottam* planet in relation to the D9 is one that is placed in the same *rashi* in both the D1 and the D9 charts. This implies that the dispositor of the *vargottam* planet in the D1 and the D9 charts are the same. As an example, the Moon in Aries in D1 and in D9 makes Moon a *vargottama* planet. So, the important question is: when is a planet *vargottama*?

Any planet (and the birth ascendant) in the first *navamsa* (between 0d00' and 3d20') of a movable sign is *vargottama* (e.g., Mars in 1st *navamsa* of Aries). Any planet in the 5th *navamsa* (between 13d20' and 16d40') of a fixed sign is *vargottama* (e.g., Sun in the 5th *navamsa* of Leo). Similarly, any planet in the 9th *navamsa* (between 26d40' and 30d00') of a dual sign is *vargottama* (e.g., Venus in the 9th *navamsa* of Pisces). A native born in a *vargottama lagna* often rises very high in life.

As earlier mentioned, *vargottama* a very good divisional placement of a planet. *What are the extents of 'very good'?* A *vargottama* planet can be in an *uccha* state (exhibiting superlative power of the very good division) if the planet is exalted in D1 and D9; in an ordinary state (exhibiting very high power of the very good division) if the planet is placed in non-exalted and non-debilitated in D1 and D9; and in a *neecha* state (exhibiting high power of the very good division) if the planet is debilitated in D1 and D9.

If a *vargottama* planet (or ascendant) is in *rashis* 2,3,4,6,7,9,12 that are owned by natural benefic planets then from a sign (*rashi*) viewpoint, the planet (or ascendant) is *subha vargottama*. If on the other hand, a *vargottama* planet (or ascendant) is in *rashis* 1,5,8,10,11 that are owned by natural malefic planets then from a sign (*rashi*) viewpoint, the planet (or ascendant) is *paapa vargottama*. For this classification, the *lagna* (ascendant) and Moon *vargottamas* are given most importance, as they represent the quality and nature of mind and body.

We illustrate the concept and use of the *vargottama navamsa* via studying the earlier chart in this chapter.

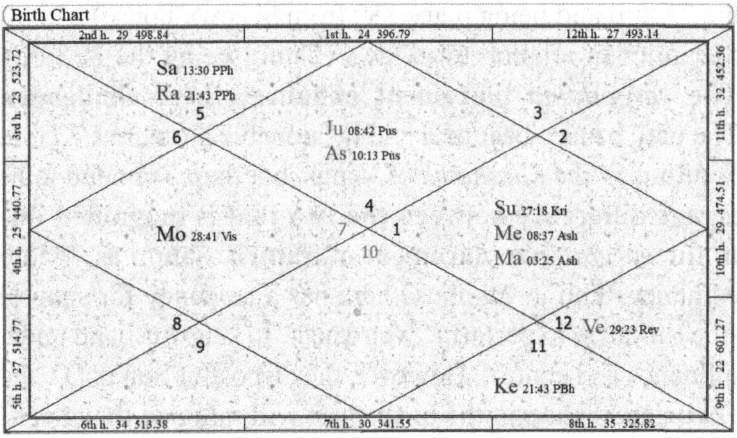

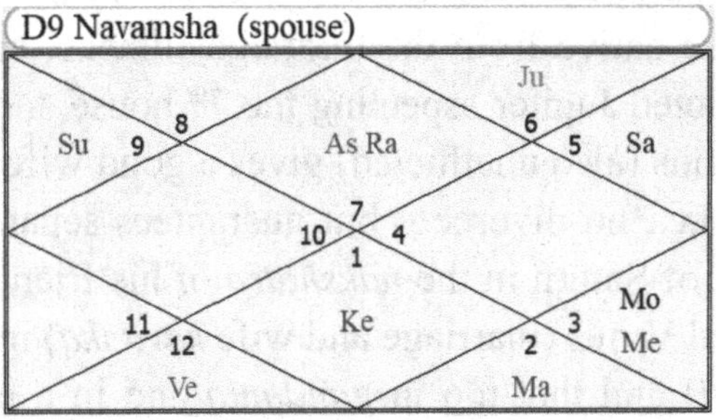

The native has two *vargottama* planets: Saturn acting as 7th and 8th lord in D1 and 4th lord, and 5th lord in the D9 that makes it a *yogakaaraka*; and Venus acting as 4th lord, and 11th lord in D1 and Lagna lord and 8th lord in the D9. Venus is *uccha vargottama.*

Saturn - Saturn is sitting in a *paapa vargottama* in D9 from a *rashi* viewpoint, and in an enemy sign. It is needless to say that Saturn is not comfortably placed both in the D1 and in the D9. In D1, Saturn is the 7th lord and the 8th lord, placed in the 2nd house, and aspects the 8th house, the 4th house, and the 11th house in the D1. The native faces a lot of distance and challenges in his married/relationship life (Saturn being the 7th lord and being placed 8th from his own house) and his dynamics in relation to in-laws (Saturn being the 8th lord). **The *vargottama* placement enhances these challenges.** The native has a beautiful and fashionable partner as 7th lord Saturn is in the *nakshatra* of Venus, but there is bound to be an **age difference between the two that is magnified due to the *vargottama* placement of Saturn.** Saturn as 7th lord conjunct Rahu in 2nd house here has a tendency for spousal side (in-laws) to perform "weird acts" to keep husband under influence and control. However, the dispositor Sun in D1 and D9 being exalted in the birth chart will mitigate the effects. However, Saturn placed in the 11th house in the D9 brings gains to the native from the marriage/alliance, and exalted and unafflicted Jupiter aspecting the 7th house and marriage *karaka* Venus (also unafflicted) gives a good wife and saves marriage, i.e., no divorce – but guarantees separation. The placement of Saturn in the *nakshatra* of his friend and very well-placed Venus (marriage and wife *karaaka*) in a *moksha* sign (*rashi*) and that too in *gandanta* and in a mutual 6/8 axis, gives a spiritual marriage/relationship.

The native is always away from his mother and homeland both by distance and in the number of interactions over speech in the modern Internet age as Saturn aspects the 4th house in D1 and is *vargottama* – **the latter also contributing to why there is both a physical and speech distance rather than simply a physical distance.** However, since the dispositor of Moon (Venus) in D1 is exalted, there is a very good and spiritual relationship between the mother and the native, despite the distance. The native is separated from his homeland and home, but with the 4th lord exalted, the native feels homely wherever he settles.

Saturn being placed in the house of wealth in D1 and with Rahu will delay the native getting wealth in life, and **this delay will magnify more with Saturn being *vargottama* in D9**. The native works very hard to earn his wealth. However, the dispositor Sun being exalted in D1, and *karaka* of wealth Jupiter being exalted in D1, wealth will eventually come in plenty to the native but with lots of patience and hard work. This is in addition to the fact that Saturn in D9 in the 11th house will guarantee gains eventually. Saturn, also being a *yogakaaraka* in the D9 along with being *vargottama*, will result in lasting gains, power, and achievements for the native but with delay and hard work. Also note in the D9, Mars as 2nd lord aspects Saturn from the 8th house, and results in the native getting secretive gains from the feminine class.

Saturn being in the 2nd house of Leo with Rahu will give a royal, mesmerizing, and fiery speech capabilities to the native **that is amplified with the *vargottama* placement of Saturn,** in addition to speech *karaka* Mercury in a fiery sign conjunct Mars and Sun. The native is bold beyond a point in speech. However, Saturn has given these qualities later in life (post 35 years) due to its *vargottama* placement in a *paapa vargottama* sign – as a matter of fact that native was quite shy in childhood.

The native will likely benefit in longevity as the dispositor of the house of longevity is the *karaaka* of longevity and aspects the house of longevity. **Saturn being *vargottama* is likely to enhance the longevity of the native.** This is precisely why things will come late in this life to the native as longevity usually controls how much and how the native will experience all good (and not so good) promises of the D1 chart – *yogas* and *dashas* permitting.

Venus - Venus is sitting in a *subha and uccha vargottama* in D9 from a *rashi* viewpoint, and in his exalted sign. Here again, it is needless to say that Venus is extremely well and comfortably placed in the D1 being aspected by an exalted Jupiter, and very well placed in the D9 also being aspected by Jupiter – but in the 6th house of the D9.

Exalted Venus is the 4th lord and 11th lord in D1 and placed in the 9th house, **hence significances with respect to these three houses will be much amplified (due to the *vargottama* placement of Venus and due to the aspect of exalted Jupiter)**, and, and especially in the *dasha* periods of Venus.

The 4th lord, a natural benefic, goes to 6th from his own house and **being *vargottama* results in non-malicious but 'frequent' clashes of the native opinions with his mother** who is extremely religious and pious (4th lord in 9th house in a *moksha rashi* and unafflicted). However, the mother brings very good fortune to the native. Such soft clashes will also be there with the feminine class in general, who will also bring fortune to the native. The natural significances of Venus will get a boost and more so in the *dasha* periods of Venus. However, also note that the placement of Venus in *gandanta* and in a *moksha rashi* position can result in some emotional turmoil in the Venus *mahadasha* in relation to the significances of Venus in the chart. Venus being the 11th lord goes to 11th from his own house, becomes exalted and aspected by exalted Jupiter, **and is *vargottama*, indicating immense gain of the native from good and learned women.**

Also note that Venus is the Chandra Lagna lord of the native in D1 of a *kaam rashi*, and the Lagna lord of the native in the D9. Hence the mind of the native is extremely fine (very meticulous and elite and luxury loving), artistic (a connoisseur of music, movies), desire loving, and is a good weigher of the pros and cons of anything – especially matters related to women. **These characteristics get more pronounced due to the *vargottama* properties of Venus.** The native is a perfectionist with regards to these significances of Venus and does not want to settle for anything less, even if it means trying many things before achieving 'perfection' in ideality. In addition, note that Venus is the *nakshatra* lord of Saturn (7th lord and 8th lord) and Rahu in the second house. Being *vargottama*, this Venus will make the native drive only for elite food choices (be it *sattwik* or *non-sattwik*), elite and very wise and learned women partners of 'foreign' (different religion/caste/culture) nature (due to 9th aspect of an exalted Jupiter on Venus, both of which are placed in a *moksha rashi*).

In terms of D9 special significances only in relation to Venus, Lagna lord (acting as relationship lord) Venus being exalted in the 6th house of the D9 leads to mundane ego clashes between the native and his partner – however, the mutual aspect of Jupiter on Venus (both being *Gurus* leads to egos, but wisdom prevails) dampens the impact of the clashes, for the good. **However, Venus being *uccha vargottama* results in ego clashes and spousal cold war that lasts long spoiling the sweetness of the relationship.** The 8th lord Venus in the 6th house also results in a *Vipareeta Raja Yoga*, and cancels/ mitigates the ill effects of *maraka* house lord for spousal matters and helped by Jupiter being 6th lord aspecting Venus in its own house. This *yoga* eventually benefits the native in marriage derived from challenging circumstances. The longevity of marriage is sustained among challenges/clashes with both native and partner being patient on detachment.

3.7 *Pushkar navamsa*

We will now discuss another central concept in relation to the *Navamsa* chart - a *Pushkar navamsa.* These *navamsas* have been somewhat "secret" in Vedic astrology given that *Chandra Kala Nadi* and *Jataka Parijata* are only a few classic texts where they have been mentioned. It was the legendary C. S. Patel that brought the concept to light in a modern textbook for the first time. However, the use of these *navamsas* results in deep and fine horoscope assessment. In this text, we briefly describe the salient points in relation to this *navamsa* and most importantly follow it up with an analysis on charts to understand the use like we did in Section 3.5.

A *Pushkar navamsa* is a special *navamsa* of length 3d20' in particular signs (*rashis*) and this *navamsa* is auspicious. The term 'Pushkar'carries this meaning in the sense of a *navamsa* that nourishes. While a *vargottama navamsa* may give powerful effects (both positive and negative) of a planet (or ascendant) placed there; in contrast planets (or ascendant) placed in the *Pushkar navamsa* either give auspicious/high status results or curtails the negative effects of a malefic (natural or functional) planet placed in that *navamsa.* A question one may ask is: *what are the Pushkar navamsas in the zodiac?*

The 7th and 9th *navamsas* **(20d00' to 23d20' and 26d40' to 30d00')** of signs Aries, Leo, and Sagittarius in D1 are

Pushkar navamsas and occupy signs Libra (ruled by Venus) and Sagittarius (ruled by Jupiter) in the D9 chart. The 3rd and 5th *navamsas* **(6d40' to 10d40' and 13d20' to 16d40')** of signs Taurus, Virgo, and Capricorn in D1 are *Pushkar navamsas* and occupy signs Pisces (ruled by Jupiter) and Taurus (ruled by Venus) in the D9 chart. The 6th and 8th *navamsas* **(16d40' to 20d00' and 23d20' to 26d40')** of signs Gemini, Libra, and Aquarius in D1 are *Pushkar navamsas* and occupy signs Pisces (ruled by Jupiter) and Taurus (ruled by Venus) in the D9 chart. Finally, the 1st and 3rd *navamsas* **(0d00' to 3d20' and 6d40' to 10d00')** of signs Cancer, Scorpio, and Pisces in D1 are Pushkar *navamsas* and occupy signs Cancer (ruled by Moon) and Virgo (ruled by Mercury) in the D9 chart.

Table 3

Sign Element	Signs	Pushkar Degrees	Nakshatra	Pushkar Navamsha
Fire Signs	Aries (Mesha)	20° 0' to 23°20'	Bharani 3rd Pada	Libra
		26°40' to 30° 0'	Krittika 1st Pada	Sagittarius
	Leo (Simha)	20° 0' to 23°20'	Purva Phalguni 3rd Pada	Libra
		26°40' to 30° 0'	Uttara Phalguni 1st Pada	Sagittarius
	Sagittarius (Dhanu)	20° 0' to 23°20'	PurvaShadha 3rd Pada	Libra
		26°40' to 30° 0'	UttaraShadha 1st Pada	Sagittarius (Vargottama)
Earth Signs	Taurus (Vrushabha)	6° 40' TO 10° 0'	Krittika 4th Pada	Pisces
		13° 20' TO 16° 40'	Rohini 2nd Pada	Taurus (Vargottama)
	Virgo (Kanya)	6° 40' TO 10° 0'	UttaraPhalguni 4th Pada	Pisces
		13° 20' TO 16° 40'	Hasta 2nd Pada	Taurus
	Capricorn (Makara)	6° 40' TO 10° 0'	UttaraShadha 4th Pada	Pisces
		13° 20' TO 16° 40'	Sravana 2nd Pada	Taurus
Air Signs	Gemini (Mithuna)	16° 40' TO 20° 0'	Ardra 4th Pada	Pisces
		23° 20' to 26° 40'	Punarvasu 2nd Pada	Taurus
	Libra (Tula)	16° 40' TO 20° 0'	Swati 4th Pada	Pisces
		23° 20' to 26° 40'	Vishakha 2nd Pada	Taurus
	Aquarius (Kumbha)	16° 40' TO 20° 0'	Satabhisha 4th Pada	Pisces
		23° 20' to 26° 40'	PurvaBhadra 2nd Pada	Taurus
Water Signs	Cancer (Kataka)	00° 00' to 3° 20'	Punarvasu 4th Pada	Cancer (Vargottama)
		6° 40' to 10° 0'	Pushya 2nd Pada	Virgo
	Scorpio (Vrishchika)	00° 00' to 3° 20'	Vishakha 4th Pada	Cancer
		6° 40' to 10° 0'	Anuradha 2nd Pada	Virgo
	Pisces (Meena)	00° 00' to 3° 20'	PBhadra 4th Pada	Cancer
		6° 40' to 10° 0'	UBhadra 2nd Pada	Virgo

There are 24 *Pushkar navamsas* in total in the zodiac and each *rashi* in D1 hosts 2 *Pushkar navamsas* **(see Table 3)**. Please observe two interesting patterns – (i) the D9 house lords of the *Pushkar navamsas* are always natural benefic planets, indicating the auspicious nature of these *navamsas* in *muhurta*, natal, *nadi*, and *prasna* astrology; and (ii) three out of the 24 *Pushkar navamsas* are *vargottama navmasas*, i.e., the 5th *navamsa* in the sign of Taurus, the 1st *navamsa* in the sign of Cancer, and the 9th *navamsa* in the sign of Sagittarius. Planets that lie on a *Pushkar navamsa* that is also a *vargottama navamsa* can give immensely positive results to a native.

It goes without saying that the more the number of planets for a native in *Pushkar navamsas*, the more powerful the horoscope is. Usually, 2-3 planets in *Pushkar navamsas* and well placed **(this is necessarily important for best results)** in the D9 chart can make the native a king or equivalent among his/her peers during the right *dasha* periods. We also remind the reader that the trine *navamsas* of any sign (the 1st, 5th, and 9th) are benefic to the native.

Concept Illustration – Let us consider Jupiter - a natural benefic planet. When Jupiter is in a *Pushkar navamsa* and occupies a *kendra* or *trikon* in the D1 chart, the native can be extremely wealthy as Jupiter is the significator of wealth. Likewise other positive significances of Jupiter will get a boost when Jupiter is well placed in a *Pushkar navamsa*. However, if the same Jupiter in a *Pushkar navamsa* is placed in 6, 8, and 12 houses of the D1 chart, the native will still be wealthy but might be disease prone, bereavement, or separation prone. Note here that Jupiter in D1 can be related to 6/8/12 houses and form a *raja yoga* – the boost in wealth will be immense, but not without paying a cost. In addition, if Jupiter is well placed in a *Pushkar navamsa* in D1, but not well placed in the D9 chart, will give mixed results.

On the other hand, if a natural or functional malefic planet is well placed in D1 in a *Pushkar navamsa*, the negative traits of the planet will be curtailed for the native, alongside a boost in the positive traits of the planet. Likewise, if the same malefic planet is not well placed in either D1 or D9, the curtailing effects of negative traits of the planet will be reduced, but the positive traits of the planet will remain intact but achieved through lots of challenges and struggles in life. As a matter of fact, it is a matter of good fortune to have malefic planets (well placed) in *Pushkar navamsas* (conditioned that benefic planets are well placed and strong), as they help curtail the negative effects of these planets on the native, while the benefic planets do their good job anyhow.

We now illustrate the use of the *Pushkar navamsa* via multiple example charts.

Example #1 (*Pushkar navamsa* Analysis)

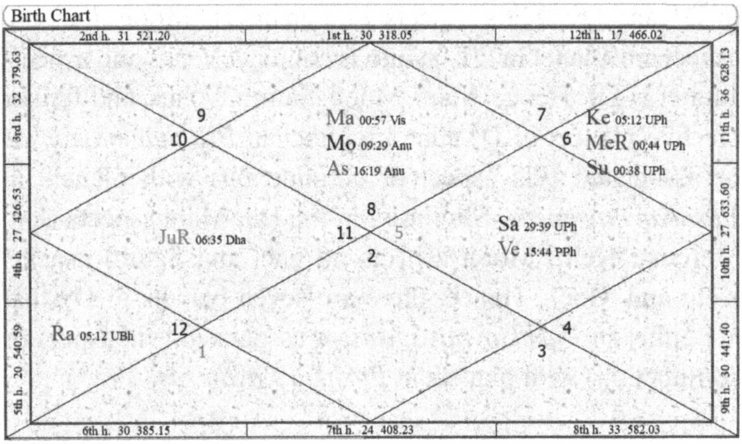

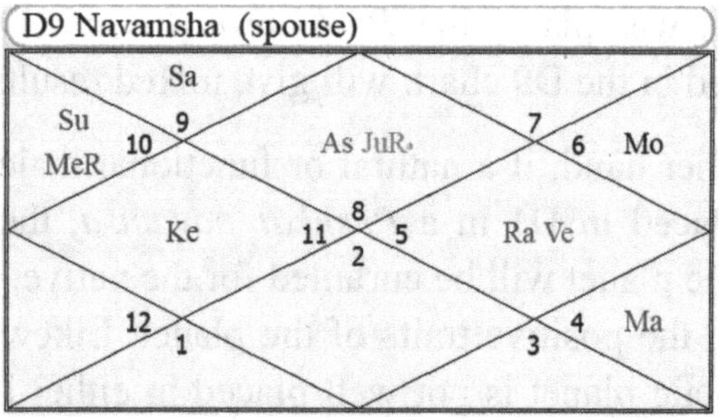

The native has Mars in a *Pushkar navamsa* as it is in the 1st *navamsa* of Scorpio in D1. He also has Moon in a *Pushkar navamsa* as it is in the 3rd *navamsa* of Scorpio in D1. In addition, the native has Saturn in a *Pushkar navamsa* as it is in the 9th *navamsa* of Leo in D1. Here, Mars is a functional benefic and natural malefic; Saturn is neutral being a malefic lord of a *kendra* house (acts as a functional benefic), and naturally malefic. The Moon is both a functional and a natural benefic planet for the native.

Mars is well placed (i.e., not in 6/8/12 houses) in D1 and D9; Moon is well placed in D1 and D9; and Saturn is well placed in D1 and D9. Mars aspects Jupiter in D1. Moon does not aspect any planet in D1. Saturn is conjunct Venus and aspects Jupiter in D1. Hence, Mars, Moon, Saturn, Venus, and Jupiter are five planets in D1 that are either in *Pushkar navamsas* or associated (via aspect or conjunction) with planets in *Pushkar navamsas*. Similarly, in the D9, Mars aspects Sun, Mercury, Ketu; Moon aspects no one; and Saturn aspects Ketu and Moon. Hence, there are seven planets in D9 that are either in *Pushkar navamsas* or associated (via aspect or conjunction) with planets in *Pushkar navamsas*.

The native became a state supremo during the Venus *mahadasha*, the nation supremo in the Moon *mahadasha*, and retained his national leadership in the Moon and the Mars *mahadashas*. See that Venus is the 7th lord of *pada praapti* for the native, and is conjunct Saturn placed (in *Pushkar navamsa*) in the 10th house of career and status. It is aspected by 5th lord Jupiter who is influenced by Saturn and Mars – both placed in *Pushkar navamsas*. Now see that Moon is the 9th lord debilitated (but gets *neechbhanga*) that is conjunct with *lagna* lord Mars who is in a *Pushkar navamsa* and both aspect the 7th house of *pada praapti* for the native. In addition, Mars influences Jupiter in the 4th house of D1, where Jupiter is mutually aspected by Saturn. No wonder, the native is "enjoying" political power for a long period of time at the state and the national levels.

Example #2 (*Pushkar navamsa* Analysis)

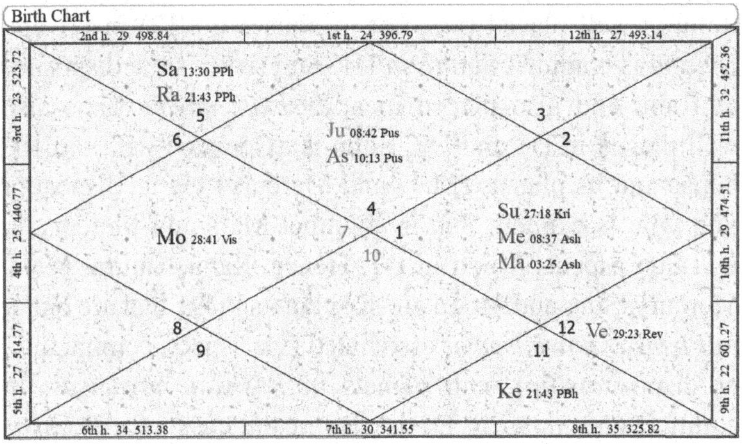

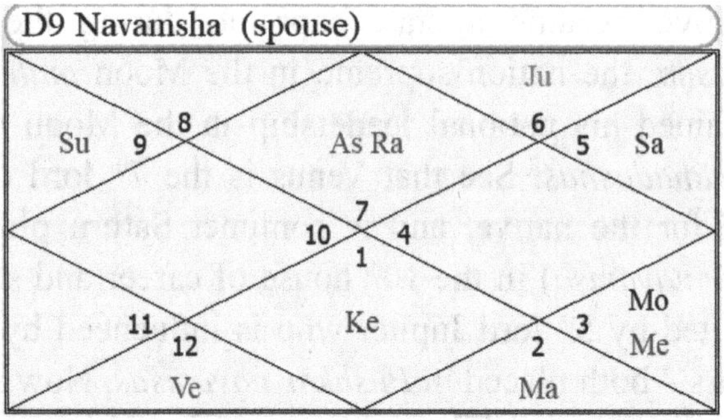

The native has Rahu (a natural malefic) in a *Pushkar navamsa* as it is in the 7th *navamsa* of Leo in D1. The native also has Sun in a *Pushkar navamsa* as it is in the 9th *navamsa* of Aries in D1. Here, the dispositor of Rahu, i.e., Sun, is a natural malefic and functionally neutral (being the lord of second house). Rahu is with Saturn who is the 7th lord and 8th lord and acts as a naturally malefic and functionally benefic (being a malefic lord of a *kendra* house).

Rahu is well placed (i.e., not in houses 6/8/12) in D1 and D9 and is conjunct Saturn in D1. Sun (who is the dispositor of Rahu and also placed in a *Pushkar navamsa*) is also well placed in D1 and D9. Rahu is associated with the 10th house and its planets (Mars and Mercury) via its dispositor Sun who is exalted. Sun is conjunct Mars and Mercury in D1. Sun aspects Moon in D1. Hence, Rahu, Saturn, Mars, Mercury, Sun, and Moon are six planets in D1 that are either in *Pushkar navamsas* or associated (via aspect, conjunction, or dispositorship) with planets in *Pushkar navamsas*. In addition, the *lagna* in D1 is also at the cusp of a *Pushkar navamsa*. Similarly, in D9, Sun aspects Moon and Mercury. Rahu via dispositorship is associated with Venus that mutually aspects Jupiter. Hence, Rahu, Mercury, Moon, Sun, Venus, and Jupiter are six planets in D9 that are either in

Pushkar navamsas or associated (via aspect, conjunction, or dispositorship) with planets in *Pushkar navamsas*.

The native got a very good higher education (PhD) abroad in the Mercury *mahadasha* and obtained during this *dasha* a faculty position in one of the renowned engineering sciences universities in the USA and in the world. Mercury is a *karaka* of the 10th house of career, quantitative fields, teaching, and communication; is placed in the 10th house in D1 with engineering planet Mars who is 10th lord and *yogakaaraka*; is the 12th lord (of foreign settlements) placed in the 10th house in D1 with Sun (significator of fame); and is the 9th lord (of higher education) placed in the 9th house in D9 along with the 10th lord Moon and aspected by 11th lord Sun. However, because Mercury is the 3rd lord and the 12th lord, the native switched to another (even better) position in the Ketu *mahadasha*. Note that dispositor of Ketu in D1 is Saturn (7th lord of *pada praapti*) who is conjunct Rahu. In D9, the dispositor of Ketu is Mars who is the 7th lord of D9 and *yogakaaraka* in D1 and is also aspected by Saturn who is the 7th lord of D1, and a *yogakaaraka* in D9.

The native will not likely get a big chunk of the Rahu period in his life but will definitely have a 'blockbuster' Sun *mahadasha* in terms of power in career, global fame, and wealth – Sun (being 2nd lord in the 10th house) being in a *Pushkar navamsa* and also being the dispositor of Rahu. The native is also likely to have a very successful 'blockbuster' Venus *mahadasha* due to exalted Venus being the dispositor of Rahu in the D9 (the chart of fortune and destiny) and being the *nakshatra* dispositor of Rahu in D1. Venus, being *uccha vargottama*, is the 4th lord and 11th lord in D1 and aspected by 9th lord exalted Jupiter, in both the D1 and D9. In addition,

Venus and Jupiter are both influenced by *Pushkar navamsa* placed planets in D1. Thus, things Venus signifies will come in excess to the native during its period. Also note that Saturn (also a *vargottama* planet for the native and *yogakaaraka* in D9) being conjunct Rahu in *Pushkar navamsa* in D1 will also bring benefits to the native in its periods on matters of the 2nd ,7th, and 8th houses but only after 35 years of age due to the not so good placement of Saturn in its enemy *rashi*. We have seen this above for the native while discussing the impact of the Ketu *mahadasha*.

Example #3 (*Pushkar navamsa* Analysis)

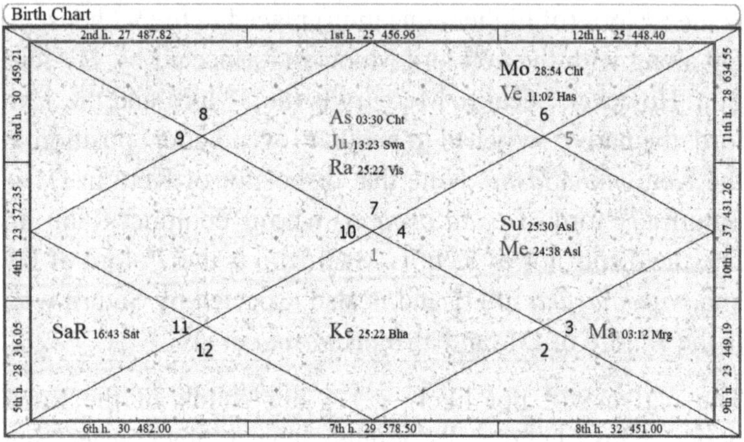

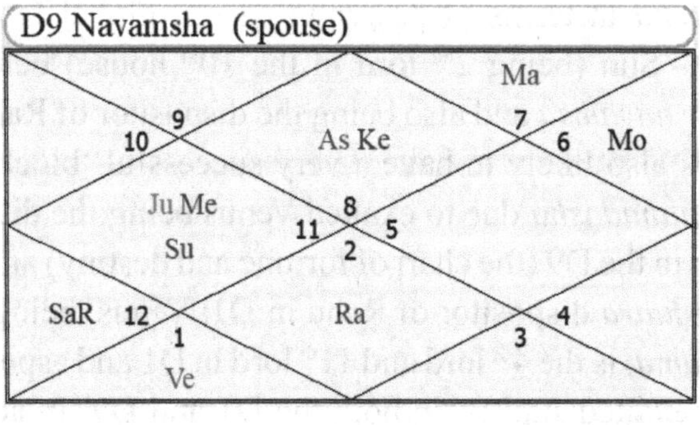

The native has Rahu (a natural malefic) in a *Pushkar navamsa* as it is in the 8th *navamsa* of Libra in D1. The native also has Saturn in a *Pushkar navamsa* as it is in the 6th *navamsa* of Aquarius in D1. Here, the dispositor of Rahu, i.e., Venus, is a natural benefic and also a functional benefic (being *lagna* lord). Rahu is with Jupiter who is the 3rd lord and 6th lord and acts as a naturally benefic and functional malefic (being lord of the 6th house).

Rahu is well placed (i.e., not in houses 6/8/12) in D1 and D9 and is conjunct Jupiter. Venus (who is the dispositor of Rahu) is not well placed in D1 (it's in the 12th house) and not well placed in D9 either (it is in the 6th house). Rahu is associated with the first house and its planets Jupiter in D1. In D9, Rahu's dispositor is Venus who mutually aspects Mars. Saturn is associated with the 5th house in D1 and the 5th house in D9 also and so quite well placed. In D1, Saturn aspects Ketu, and in D9 aspects Rahu and Moon. Therefore, Rahu and Saturn being in *Pushkar navamsas* associate with Jupiter, Venus, and Ketu in D1, and with Venus, Mars, and Moon in D9.

The native had an unfavorable Rahu *mahadasha* despite Rahu being in a *Pushkar navamsa* and being well placed in both the D1 and the D9. Why? This is because the dispositor of Rahu is ill placed (in 6/8/12 houses) in both the D1 and the D9. Another way to look at this (and we will cover this topic in Chapter 4 – hence the motivation to cite it now) is that in the *Rashi Tulya Navamsa* chart (wait till Chapter 4) Rahu goes to the 8th house or *nidhanamsa* – a bad placement for Rahu. The native has the *budhaditya yoga* in the D1 chart and is very smart, had a powerful placement of planets in the D1 chart but still the first 30 years of his life was not good – 20 of them was spent in the Rahu *mahadasha*.

On the other hand, the native is having an excellent Jupiter *mahadasha* with Jupiter being 3rd lord and 6th lord and associated with Rahu who being in *Pushkar navamsa* is not well placed in dispositorship in both D1 and D9. Again, the same question arises: *how and why?* This is because Jupiter is the 5th lord in D9, and in the *Rashi Tulya Navamsa* chart is placed in the 5th house along Saturn (who is in a *Pushkar navamsa*) with being placed in Lagna in D1. Hence, the positive placement of Jupiter in D1 and D9 and it being influenced by well-placed Saturn (surprisingly and logically not Rahu) in D1 and D9 is giving this huge success to the native in the Jupiter *mahadasha*.

This example is shown to appreciate the depths and difficulty of *jyotisha* analysis. Many things need to be seen microscopically and simultaneously to arrive at the right conclusion. Hence, in my opinion, Vedic astrology is the subject for the geniuses, not for the people of common intelligence, as our sages were the greatest geniuses that ever lived.

Example #4 (*Pushkar navamsa* Analysis)

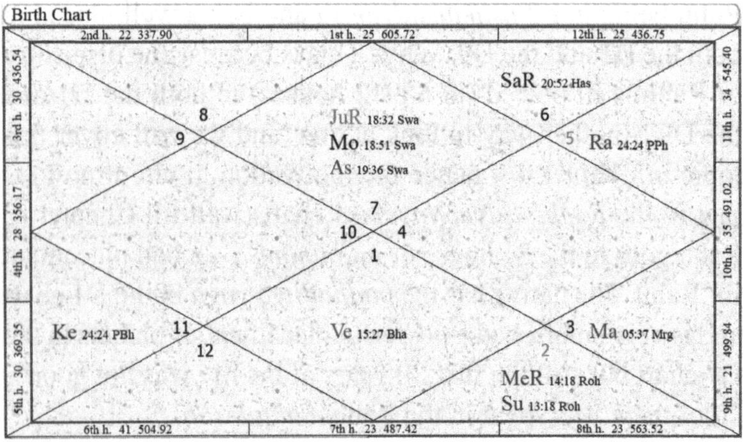

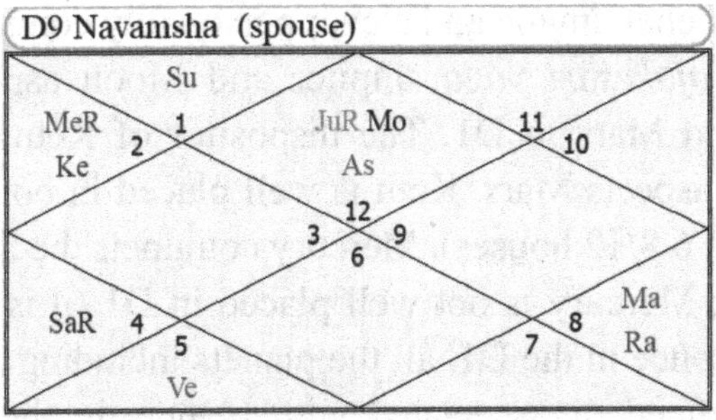

The native has the ascendant and four planets in the *Pushkar navamsas*. The ascendant is in the 6th *navamsa* of Libra (hence in a *Pushkar navamsa*). Jupiter is in the 6th *navamsa* of Libra (hence in a *Pushkar navamsa*). Moon is in the 6th *navamsa* of Libra (hence in a *Pushkar navamsa*). Mercury is in the 5th *navamsa* of Taurus (hence in a *Pushkar navamsa*). Finally, Ketu is in the 8th *navamsa* of Aquarius (hence in a *Pushkar navamsa*). Jupiter is a natural benefic, functional malefic, and powerful due to being retrograde. Moon is natural benefic and neutral for the native (as it is the benefic lord of the 10th house). Mercury is a natural benefic, and powerful due it being retrograde, furthermore it is *vargottama*, and the 9th lord in the D1 chart (and hence functionally benefic). The dispositor of Ketu is Saturn who is *yogakaaraka* for the native in D1, and hence functionally benefic. Sun is exalted in D9 for the native as the 11th lord. What a chart!!

The ascendant is very powerful as Jupiter and Moon are *bhavottama* (placed in the same house in the ascendant in both the D1 and the D9). This forms a very powerful *Gajakesari yoga* in both the D1 and the D9 and gave immense worldwide fame. Both Jupiter and Moon become well placed (not in 6/8/12 houses) both in the D1 and in the D9. In addition, all the planets including the ascendant are in Rahu's *nakshatra*, where dispositor of Rahu, i.e., Sun, is exalted. This gave an extremely charismatic and clever personality complemented by the *Gajakesari yoga*. Jupiter and Moon aspect Ketu, Venus, and Mars in D1. The dispositor of Ketu is Saturn mutually aspects Mars. Ketu is well placed in both D1 and D9 (not in 6/8/12 houses). Mercury conjuncts the Sun in D1. However, Mercury is not well placed in D1 (it is in the 8th house). Hence in the D1, all the planets including ascendant are influenced or associated with planets in the *Pushkar navamsas*. In the D9 chart; Jupiter aspects Saturn, Mercury associates with Ketu, Mars, and Rahu; and Ketu associates with Venus.

The native was a legend in film acting and also a legend in politics. It is not uncommon for an actor to become a politician in India - however, to be a legend in both acting and politics is a very rare combination. The legend of acting was made when the native was going through his Saturn and Mercury *mahadashas*. Note that Saturn is *yogakaaraka* in D1, mutually aspects Mars who is 7th lord of *pada praapti*, and made the native work very hard (Saturn retrograde in 12th house) even though the period gave him wealth, accolades and fame (dispositor of Saturn is in *Pushkar navamsa*, retrograde, and conjunct with exalted Sun). On the other hand, Mercury (9th lord), Venus, and Moon form a relationship (a combination for actors), with Moon and Mercury both in *Pushkar navamsas*. Rahu in the 11th house of gains and networking has its dispositor Sun (significator of fame), who is sitting with a retrograde (powerful) Mercury in the house of Venus who is aspected by Moon. Hence, an acting legend. In D9, Mercury is the 7th lord of *pada praapti* that is mutually aspecting the 9th lord own house Mars, and Saturn is the 11th lord, that aspects the 6th lord and exalted Sun.

The native became a political legend in the *mahadasha* of Venus who is mutually aspected by Jupiter and Moon (significator of politics, and masses, respectively), both in *Pushkar navamsas*, and forming a *Gajakesari yoga* in both the D1 and the D9 charts. On the other hand, Venus is the dispositor of fame *kaarak* and exalted Sun in D1. This Venus, the Lagna Lord of D1, moves to *trikonamsa* in D9 (any planet moving to 1, 5, 9 *amsas* in D9 is considered good – wait till Chapter 4 to cover this concept) and is well placed in sixth house in D9 (forming *Vipreet raj yoga*, 8th lord in the 6th house) and has good dignity and strength to fight enemies. Its dispositor from D1, Mars, is *bhav vargottam* in D9 and conjunct with Rahu in 9th house in D9 and aspected by Jupiter (forming *Hamsa yoga* in D9), by Moon (in D1 and D9) and by Mercury (in D9 from its own house of communication). Further, Venus's dispositor in D9 is Sun (Sun is exalted in D9 and makes a connection with Mars and Rahu by virtue of its dispositor, Mars). Saturn (*yogakaarak* in D1) also a planet of masses and governance is well placed in D9 in trine and aspected by Jupiter and Moon (Moon is also its dispositor and aspects its own house). So, we see that Venus, Saturn (planet of masses and governance), Sun (planet related to politics), Mars all make a connection with Jupiter and Moon – both in *Pushkar navamsas*, and planets related to politics. The above analysis makes it evident that the native became a legendary politician.

3.8 *Vish navamsa*

We will now discuss another central concept in relation to the *Navamsa* chart - a *Vish navamsa.* As the name suggests, such a *navamsa* brings poisonous effects from the planets placed in such a *navamsa*. However, one should be very careful to assess the negative connotation of the term *'vish'* (poison) and not see it as an 'end of the world' for the native if a planet is placed in such a *navamsa*. However, before we delve into what exactly is the "poison" that might affect a native, let us first lay down the conditions on when a planet is said to be in a *vish navamsa*. A planet (or ascendant) is in a *vish navamsa* when

1. It is placed in the first *navamsa* of Aries, Taurus, Virgo, or Sagittarius. Such *navamsas* are collectively called as the *Sarpa* (snake) *navamsas*.
2. It is placed in the fifth *navamsa* of Gemini, Leo, Libra, or Aquarius. Such *navamsas* are collectively called as the *Gridha* (vulture) *navamsas*.
3. It is placed in the ninth *navamsa* of Cancer, Scorpio, Capricorn, and Pisces. Such *navamsas* are collectively called as the *Shookar* (hell) *navamsas*.

   A planet placed in these *navamsas* signifies harm only to the *sthir karaaka* signified by the planet – **not in any other arena of life**. As an example, if Moon occupies such a *navamsa* then harm can come to the mother of the native. More specifically, a PAC (Placement, Aspect, Conjunction) analysis along with a yoga analysis needs to be done to assess the overall degree of harmful effects of the placement of planets in the Vish navamsa.

Example #1 (Vish navamsa)

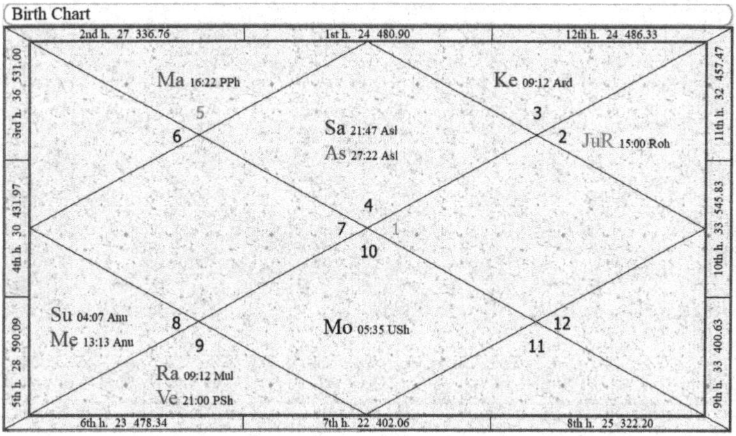

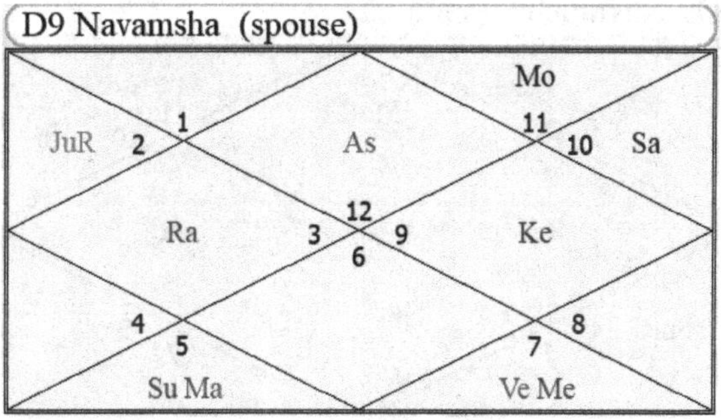

The native has Mars placed in a *Vish navamsa* (fifth *navamsa* of Leo). The native did not have siblings, as Mars signifies siblings of a native. A sibling that was there died very young. Due to a *Parivartan yoga* between Mars and Sun, the native was not bothered, and preferred being alone without siblings.

Example #2 (Vish navamsa)

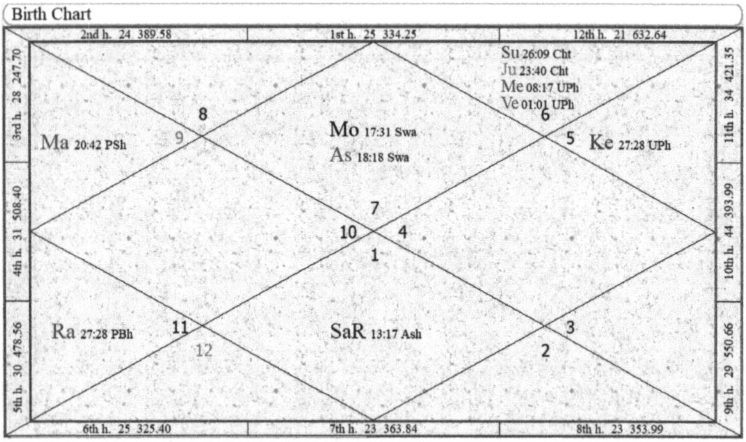

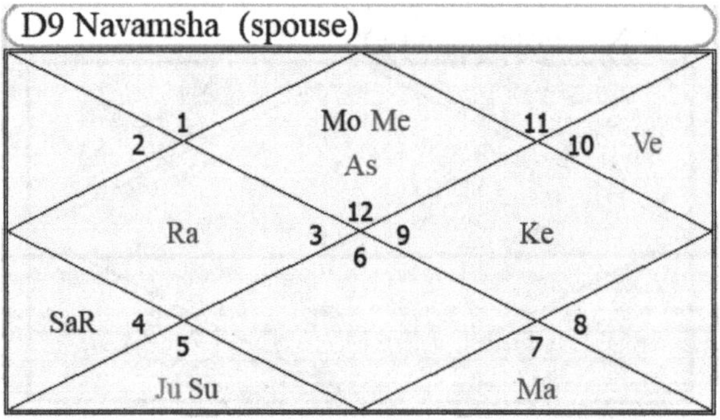

The native has Venus placed in a *Vish navamsa* (first *navamsa* of Virgo). The native married but got divorced, as Venus is the significator of spouse for this native. The *nakshatra* lord of Venus is Sun and is in the 12th house of losses in D1 and in 6th house in D9 (12th from house in D1); divorce was bitter.

Example #3 (Vish navamsa)

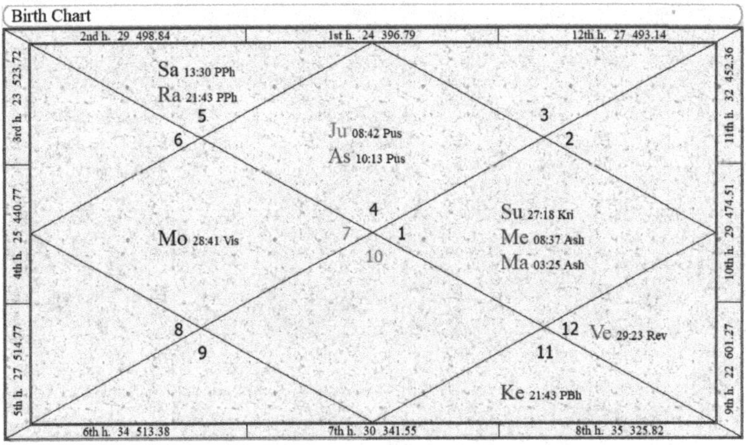

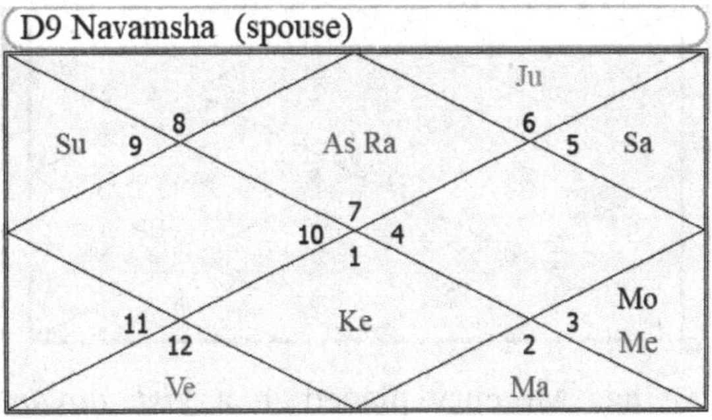

The native has exalted Venus placed in a *Vish navamsa* (ninth *navamsa* of Pisces). Unlike the previous native, this native is not divorced but has a peaceful detached relationship with partner. Note that Venus is aspected by the 6th lord and 9th lord Jupiter and is *vargottama* in 6th house of D9 and also aspected by 3rd lord and 6th lord Jupiter. Marriage suffers but not bitterly as exalted D1 Jupiter for the native takes some poison out of the relationship.

Example #4 (Vish navamsa)

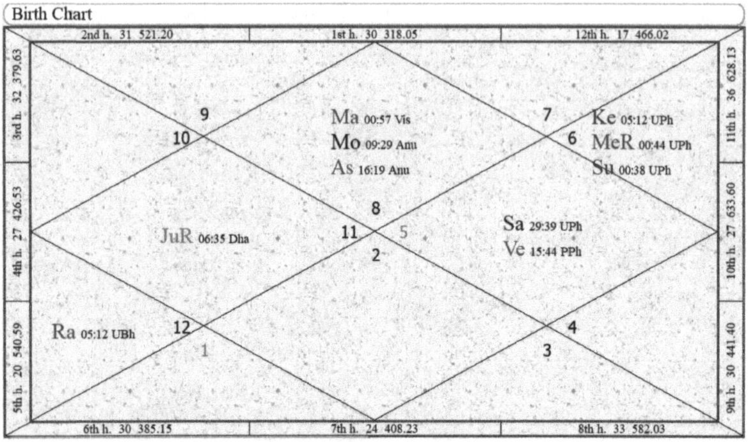

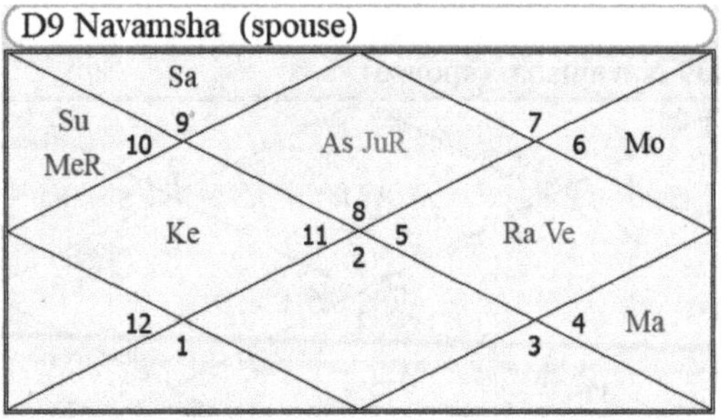

The native has Mercury placed in a *Vish navamsa* (first *navamsa* of Virgo). Mercury denotes maternal relations, and the native suffered in this area (there was not much presence of the maternal family in his life). The native also has Sun placed in a *Vish navamsa* (first *navamsa* of Virgo). Sun denotes father for a native, and the native suffered in this area also (the father could not give the native the best upbringing in relation to materialistic matters). The native also has Venus in a *Vish navamsa* (fifth *navamsa* of Leo). The native's relationship with his wife also suffered (the native was mostly detached with his wife). However, Mercury and Sun are well placed in the 11th house, and both are in the *nakshatra* of the *kendra* lord Sun. Venus is also in a *kendra* hosted by its own *nakshatra* (the native did not feel the absence of his wife in a detrimental fashion). In addition, the native has multiple *Raja yogas* and the *Amara yoga*, and hence the native overcomes all the challenges in life posed by significances contributed by the *Vish navamsas*.

A thing to note about *Vish navamsas* is one needs to check the strength (e.g., *shadbal*) of the planet (and ascendant) overall to judge degree of harm. The primary effects will be seen in the *dasha* periods.

CHAPTER 4

Nadi Amsas and *Rashi-Tulya Navamsa*

In the previous chapter, we discussed the houses of the D9 chart and the effect of planets in the *vargottama* and the *Pushkar navamsas*. We provided multiple chart examples to understand the use of these concepts to analyze relevant native affairs that can be viewed independently from the D9 chart (or using a combination of the D1 and the D9 charts).

In this chapter we will delve a bit deeper into how the planets in the D1 (birth) chart get positively or negatively positioned in the D9 chart (that is nothing but a microscopic view of the D1 chart). After all, the *vargottama* and the *Pushkar navamsas* will most likely not contain all the planets in the D1 – so apart from the planets in these key *navamsas*, how can we judge the placement of the other planets in the D9? In other words, how good is the overall D9 placement of planets in relation to the D1 (and vice versa)? The answer to these two questions answers the all-important and goal question in *jyotish*: *does the D9 chart realize (and to what degree) the promise of the planetary placements in the D1 chart?* We study the *bhava-soochak navamsa* as a first step to this goal.

4.1 *Bhava-soochak navamsa*

A central essence of analyzing the *Navamsa* (D9) chart in general (according to the *Deva Keralam*, i.e., a legendary treatise in *Nadi jyotish*) is to see in which *bhavas* (houses) of D1 are the planets in D9 chart placed. Why do we need to do this? We do this because we want to know relative to the birth ascendant where the microscopic placement of D9 planets is in the D1 chart. It is one of the most effective ways that we can know how the planets in the D1 (birth) chart get positively or negatively positioned in the D9 chart.

In the *Navamsa* chart, when a planet (and ascendant) moves to the following house from the birth *lagna* in D1 it is deemed to be in the corresponding *bhava-soochak navamsa (a Nadi amsa)*:

First House – *Lagnamsa*

Second House – *Vittamsa/Dhanamsa*

Third House – *Vikramsa/Dhairyamsa*

Fourth House – *Sukhamsa*

Fifth House – *Putramsa*

Sixth House – *Rogamsa/Ariamsa*

Seventh House – *Bharyamsa/Kalatramsa*

Eighth House – *Nidhanamsa*

Ninth House – *Bhagyamsa*

Tenth House – *Karmamsa*

Eleventh House – *Labhamsa*

Twelfth House - *Vyamsa*

Let us now illustrate the concept of the *bhava-soochak navamsa* with the following example.

Example (Bhava-soochak navamsas)

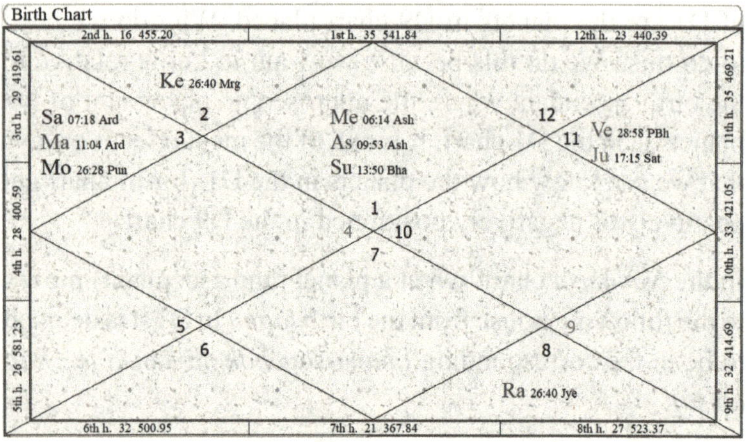

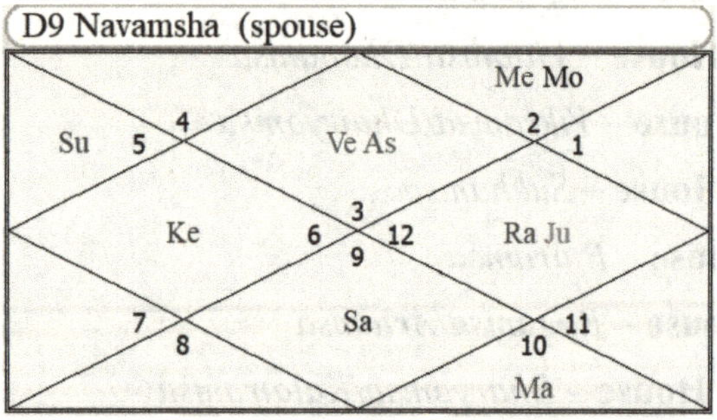

First House – *Lagnamsa* – no planet/ascendant

Second House – *Dhanamsa* – Mercury, Moon

Third House – *Vikramsa* – Venus, D9 ascendant

Fourth House – *Sukhamsa* – no planet/ascendant

Fifth House – *Putramsa* - Sun

Sixth House – *Rogamsa* - Ketu

Seventh House – *Bharyamsa* – no planet/ascendant

Eighth House – *Nidhanamsa* – no planet/ascendant

Ninth House – *Bhagyamsa* - Saturn

Tenth House – *Karmamsa* - Mars

Eleventh House – *Labhamsa* – no planet/ascendant

Twelfth House – *Vyamsa* – Rahu, Jupiter

Note that the first, fourth, seventh and tenth *bhava-soochak-navamsas* are known as the *kendramsas*, and the first, fifth, and ninth *bhava-soochak-navamsas* are known as *konamsas*. In addition, if any planet is exalted in a *bhava-soochak navamsa*, it is called its *ucchamsa* position. Similarly, if any planet is debilitated in a *bhava-soochak navamsa*, it is called its *neechamsa* position.

Though we will analyze in detail the role of the *bhava-soochak navamsa* very shortly when we discuss the *Rashi-Tulya Navamsa* chart, it makes sense to say a few sentences about the connection of planets placed in a certain *bhava-soochak navamsa*, and how one should interpret the placement.

In the example illustration, Moon is in *ucchamsa* for the native. Since Moon is the 4th lord in D1 and goes to the *Dhanamsa*, the native could earn wealth from home (or from a place of peace for the native). In addition, since Mercury, the 3rd lord and 6th lord of D1 is also placed in the *Dhanamsa*, the native is likely to work very hard and use her local contacts or communication skills (Mercury is the *karaka* of communication) to earn wealth while being at home or a place very near to home.

As a further illustration, Lagna Lord Mars of the native goes to the *karmamsa* and is placed in an *ucchamsa* position – indicating a constant action-oriented and very hardworking personality in profession. As Mars is also the 8th lord in D1, the native researches on headhunting talent, and insurance matters in her profession. In addition, the native has an action-oriented and very hardworking approach to learning the occult sciences.

4.2 The *Rashi-Tulya Navamsa Chart*

Having understood the concept of the *bhava-soochak navamsas*, we move on to understanding the idea behind the *Rashi-Tulya Navamsa* chart and its application. We educate the reader with the fact that the *Rashi-Tulya Navamsa* is a concept from *Nadi jyotish* as it is derived from the essence of the *bhava-soochak navamsas.* It works as an excellent complement with the Parashari system of *jyotish.*

Remember that a native's birth chart is the inherent potential of a native to achieve in various arenas of life, whereas the D9 chart denotes how much of that potential can be realized in the current life. Hence, fixing the birth ascendant in the D1, and placing in D1 the planets in the D9 chart in the same signs they occupy in D9 will give a relative assessment of how much of the D1 potential can be realized. **The chart formed thus by placing the planets via the above logic is the *Rashi-Tulya Navamsa* chart.**

To literally illustrate the construction of the *Rashi-Tulya Navamsa* chart, say, Mars is the 10th lord in the birth chart with Cancer ascendant, and it is exalted in the D1 (showing great professional potential and promise of the native), but Mars moves to its debilitated position in the D9. Then the *Rashi-Tulya Navamsa* chart will show 10th lord Mars in its debilitated position in Cancer with ascendant still being in Cancer and will evidently not showcase the same power of Mars as 10th lord in D1. The native will not be very brave, will be somewhat defensive in work personality, and/or will not be much action-driven in this life as promised in the D1. However, **since the 10th lord in D1 is exalted, the degree of strength of Mars in the *Rashi-Tulya Navamsa* will diminish but not disappear** – a very important concept to remember. **The *Rashi-Tulya Navamsa* chart should only be used to analyze the power of *dasha* periods and *yogas* in the birth chart (D1).**

One might think here: *is there any difference between a chart denoting the bhava-soochak navamsas, and the Rashi-Tulya navamsa chart?* One must be tempted to think that the answer is a 'no' and that both charts are the same. However, in reality the two charts are different in a very small but subtle manner. **The *Rashi-Tulya navamsa* chart is nothing but a superimposition of the *bhava-soochak navamsa* chart as the visible upper layer that contains below it, as a hidden layer, the D1 chart necessarily needed to make accurate predictions and assessments.** In my personal opinion, the *Rashi-Tulya Navamsa* is a must to study while making predictions and assessments.

Let us illustrate this idea literally using a small but very interesting example of a native the author knows personally. Say that a Virgo ascendant native has Mars (the 3rd lord) exalted in the D9 chart in Capricorn, and sitting alone and unaspected. Let there be Rahu placed in Capricorn in the D1 chart. Now, if we simply consider the *bhava-soochak navamsas*, one can say that the siblings/co-born of the native will be very successful as un-touched and unafflicted Mars goes into the 5th house or *Putramsa* and is also a *konamsa* (which is a very good placement). Correct? Let us see.

Well, in reality, the native went to an astrologer in a very long and struggling phase of his sibling's life and could find no reason why the astrologer said "things are great with your younger sibling as your Mars is well placed in the D9 chart" when clearly things were not going well. The astrologer possibly only looked at the *bhava-soochak navamsa* placement of Mars – he possibly did not check the *Rashi-Tulya Navamsa*, that had Rahu in the 10th house of Capricorn in the hidden layer capturing the D1. In reality, the sibling did quite well in life later – exactly as the astrologer predicted or assessed, but not without the long struggling period that Rahu gave to the native's younger sibling. The *Rashi-Tulya Navamsa* shows this very important information of Rahu hidden in Capricorn and together with visible Mars, and the *bhava-soochak navamsa* positions do not show this subtle information. Does the reader now get the difference? I believe they do now. A tip from the author here is *always see the Rashi-Tulya Navamsa chart that includes the hidden layer of D1*, else there is no difference between this chart and the chart with only the *bhava-soochak navamsas*.

The *Rashi-Tulya Navamsa* is an astro-engineering marvel that merges *Nadi jyotish* and Parashari *jyotish* together in the most beautiful manner, where both are needed to predict accurately. Unfortunately, not many teachers teach or mention this. My *jyotish Guru* was very impressed when I personally found this connection (that of the hidden layer) an told me one thing "you have understood the *Navamsa* chart" (and probably that is why I feel confident today of writing this book).

We will now illustrate the idea of the *Rashi-Tulya Navamsa* in detail using two example charts. We will touch upon some key houses and explain the significance of the *Rashi-Tulya Navamsa* planetary placements in the visible and the hidden layers. The reader is expected to apply a similar analysis to other houses to draw inferences.

Example #1 (Rashi-Tulya Navamsa)

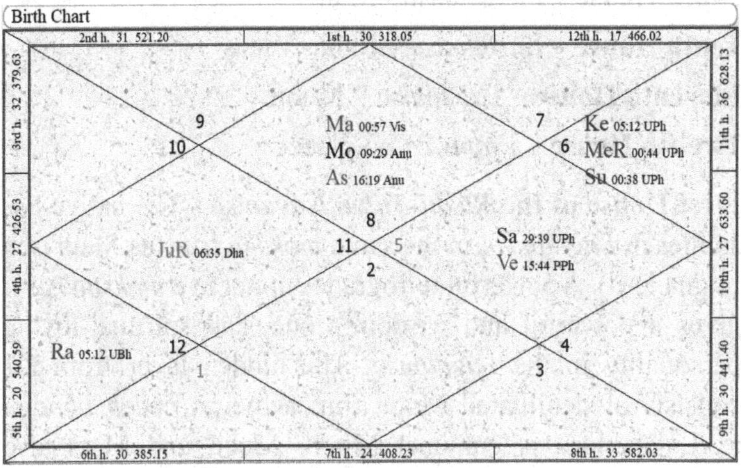

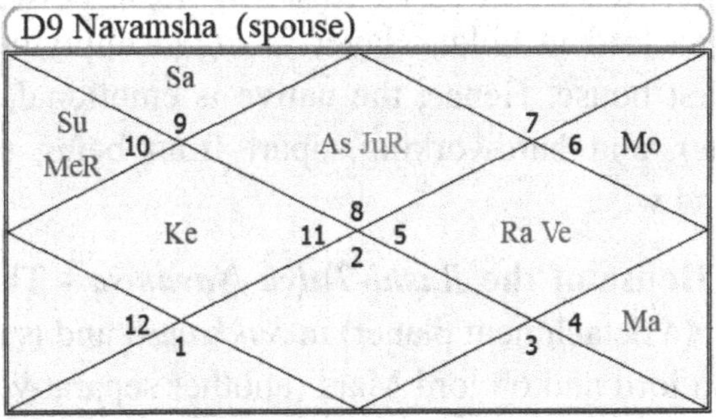

First House – *Lagnamsa* – Jupiter (R)

Second House – *Dhanamsa* – Saturn

Third House – *Vikramsa* – Sun, Mercury (R)

Fourth House – *Sukhamsa* – Ketu

Fifth House – *Putramsa* - Sun

Sixth House – *Rogamsa* – no planet

Seventh House – *Bharyamsa* – no planet

Eighth House – *Nidhanamsa* – no planet

Ninth House – *Bhagyamsa* - Mars

Tenth House – *Karmamsa* – Rahu, Venus

Eleventh House – *Labhamsa* – Moon

Twelfth House – *Vyamsa* – no planet

First House of the *Rashi-Tulya Navamsa* - The native has Jupiter in *Lagnamsa*, in the same *moksha* trine as Mars (the Lagna lord). A powerful retrograde Jupiter in a *moksha rashi* gives a powerful and wisdom-prone, and spiritual-loving personality in the *Lagnamsa*. The hidden layer from D1 consists of debilitated Moon (but achieves *neech bhanga* as Lagna lord is conjunct Moon, Moon and Mars also form a *kendra-trikona raja yoga*). The *lagna* is *vargottama* and Lagna lord in hidden layer in *lagna* implying a very strong first house. Hence, the native is emotional, martian (valorous), and hardworking, apart from being spiritual-loving and wise.

Fourth House of the *Rashi-Tulya Navamsa* - The native has Ketu (a detachment planet) in *Sukhamsa* and is aspected by Lagna lord and 6th lord Mars (another separative planet) from the 9th house via its 8th house aspect; and the 7th lord and 12th lord Venus from the 10th house. The native is devoid of home peace and comforts and frequently travels away from home and mother. Now when we check the hidden layer from D1, the 4th lord is a separative planet Saturn that aspects the 4th house from the 10th house. Jupiter is the 5th lord in the 4th

house but is 12th from his own house. Hence, this reinforces the fact that the native is devoid of home peace and comforts contributed by commitments to work life.

Tenth House of the *Rashi-Tulya Navamsa* - The native has Rahu and Venus in *Karmamsa,* where Venus is the 7th lord of *pada praapti*, and the 12th lord. The native is always hungry for work achievements and part of such achievements are obtained through the help of females, and also by the government (as Sun is the dispositor of Rahu). Now when we check the hidden layer from D1, the 4th lord (Saturn) and the 7th lord and female *karaka* (Venus) conjoin in the 10th house and aspected by the 5th lord Jupiter. There is a mutual relationship between the natural significators of *dharma* (Jupiter) and *karma* (Saturn) and pushed the native to work hard, and achieve big in the government, helped by females. Note that Venus is *vargottama*, The *Karmamsa* and the hidden layer from D1 promise a great career.

Eleventh House of the *Rashi-Tulya Navamsa* - The native has Moon in *Labhamsa,* where Moon is the 9th lord of *dharma* and *bhagya*, and is aspected by the 3rd lord, and 4th lord Saturn who is in a *Pushkar navamsa*. This is a very favorable combination of the native to get increase in gains and power through fortune combined with hard work and courage, and via the use of creative and inspirational impulses. Now when we check the hidden layer from D1, the 11th house has Sun (10th lord) and Mercury (retrograde and 11th lord and exalted) along with Ketu. The native will gain from the government as the significator goes to the 2nd house from its own house and will use his communication and calculative ability to a brilliant extent to achieve such gains. Note that this hidden layer from D1 in the *Rashi-Tulya Navamsa* chart says a lot of additional things about how and from where the gains of the native would be attained that was not possible to deduce from the *bhava-soochak navamsa* (i.e., the *Labhamsa*) in this case. Also note that for the native the 11th house in the hidden layer is on the Rahu/Ketu axis. Hence, the gains will come to the native but not without the native going through sudden events, challenges and litigations. This was also not evident from the *bhaav-soochak navamsa*.

Example #2 (Rashi-Tulya Navamsa)

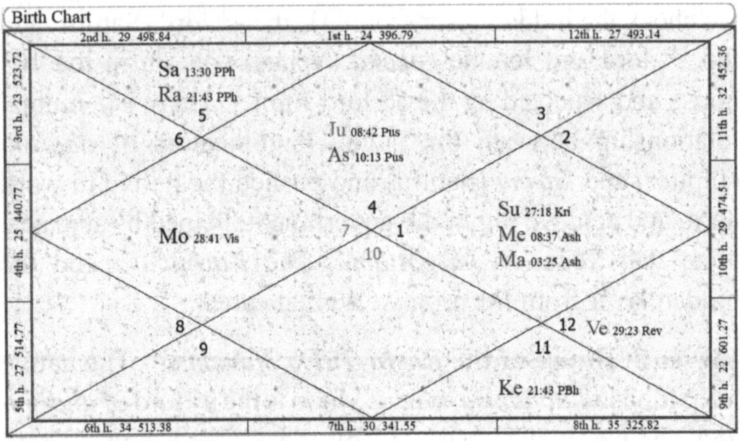

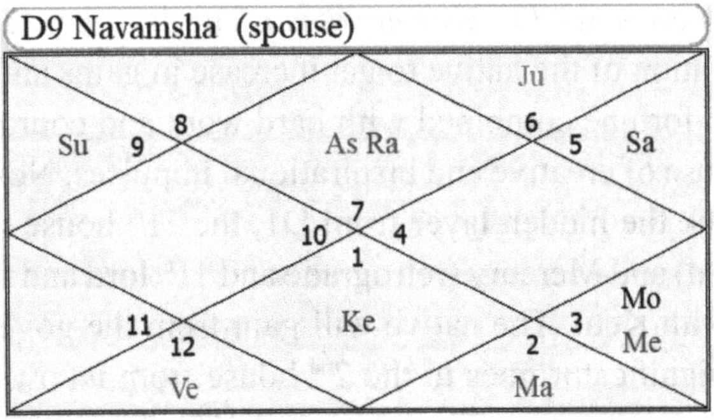

First House – *Lagnamsa* – no planet

Second House – *Dhanamsa* – Saturn

Third House – *Vikramsa* – Jupiter

Fourth House – *Sukhamsa* – Rahu, Ascendant

Fifth House – *Putramsa* – no planet

Sixth House – *Rogamsa* – Sun

Seventh House – *Bharyamsa* – no planet

Eighth House – *Nidhanamsa* – no planet

Ninth House – *Bhagyamsa* - Venus

Tenth House – *Karmamsa* – Ketu

Eleventh House – *Labhamsa* – Mars

Twelfth House – *Vyamsa* – Moon, Mercury

First House of the *Rashi-Tulya Navamsa* – The native has no planet in *Lagnamsa*, and its lord (Moon who is also the *karaka* of the mind, homeland, and mother) goes into the 12th house (*Vyamsa*). The native likes solitude, foreign lands, bed pleasures, introspection and detachment, and usually does not want to make feelings publicly open. The mind of this native likes to dream and also literally has dreams every night. However, being in the *rashi* of communicative Gemini and with Mercury, the native likes to communicate and is an expert in speaking his mind. The hidden layer from D1 consists of exalted Jupiter in the first house who contributes to multiple *mahapurusha yogas* in the native and is aspected by *yogakaaraka* Mars. The native has a magnanimous, jovial, martian, and magnetic personality on the outside that goes together with his deep liking for introspection, solitude, and emotional detachment from within – the *Rashi-Tulya Navamsa* shows both.

Second House of the *Rashi-Tulya Navamsa* – The native has Saturn in the *Dhanamsa*, and its lord Sun being in *Pushkara Navamsa* goes into the 6th house (*Rogamsa*). The native works very hard and carefully to gain wealth, gets it from powerful authorities and/or the government, and gets wealth relatively later in life. However, the wealth the native earns is sustainable (as Saturn makes one work hard to get something and makes sure that once it is there, the native respects and keeps it). Saturn is also *vargottama* for the native. However, Saturn being in enemy sign makes the native (at times) selfish, careless, and irresponsible to earn wealth. Saturn is mutually aspected by Mars who is in the *Labhamsa*. Hence, hard work and a fighting (not giving up) mentality brings in wealth and gains for the native. The hidden layer from D1 consists of Saturn and Rahu in the second house, whose dispositor Sun is exalted. Hence, the native has to amplify his hard work to gain wealth, and Rahu amplifies the properties of Saturn, along with making the native very strategic in earning wealth. Rahu also leads the native to take unnecessary risks in earning wealth at certain times. Since Sun is exalted, the native sustainably gains from authorities/government in plenty though not without delays and hard work.

Ninth House of the *Rashi-Tulya Navamsa* – The native has exalted and *vargottama* Venus in the *Bhagyamsa*, and its lord Jupiter goes into the 3rd house (*Vikramsa*) mutually aspecting each other. The native receives very good *bhagya* from good and educated women, and *bhagya* is gained from efforts as the 3rd house is an *upachaya* house. The native is very lucky to uphold *dharma* in his life with the Jupiter-Venus association. The hidden layer from D1 consists of exalted Venus in the 9th house, whose dispositor Jupiter is also exalted. Hence, the above effects in relation to the *Bhagyamsa* get multiplied – especially when Jupiter and Venus are part of multiple powerful *yogas* in the horoscope.

Tenth House of the *Rashi-Tulya Navamsa* – The native has Ketu in the *Karmamsa*, and its lord Mars goes into the 11th house (*Labhamsa*) where it is aspected by both Jupiter (6th lord and 9th lord) from *Vikramsa*, and Saturn (7th lord and 8th lord) from *Dhanamsa*. The native is into research and consulting activities in relation to engineering and defense related matters. The lord of the *karmamsa* (Mars) is aspected by Saturn (*karaka* of *karma*), and Jupiter (*karaka* of *dharma*). It also forms a *dharma-karma adhipati yoga* in the *Rashi-Tulya Navamsa*, Mars, the 10th lord is aspected by Jupiter the 9th lord. The native works hard and earns wealth through research and consulting in engineering and defense. Since Ketu is in the *Karmamsa*, the native has to face sudden challenges and events pertaining to his career. The hidden layer from D1 consists of exalted 2nd lord Sun, 3rd and 12th lord Mercury, and own house and *yogakaaraka* Mars in the 10th house. These three planets are aspected by the *lagna* lord Moon. In addition, to the points made above on planets placed in the *Karmamsa*, the native has a career in a foreign country (as 12th lord in conjunct the 10th lord in the 10th house in the hidden layer), that is helped and boosted by the government and authorities (Sun is exalted), and the career involves teaching and communication due to the influence of Mercury. The native is a research scientist and faculty member at a premier university in the USA who does research in cybersecurity and advises.

CHAPTER 5

Nidhanamsa and Ashtamamsa

In the previous chapter, we discussed the *Rashi-Tulya Navamsa*. We reserve here a separate and short chapter to discuss two important concepts in relation to the *Rashi-Tulya Navamsa* – (i) the placement of a planet in the *Rashi-Tulya Navamsa* in the 8th house of the D1 chart, and (ii) the placement of a planet in the D9 and the *Rashi-Tulya Navamsa* chart that is in the 8th house from its placement in the D1 chart. The first placement is the called the *Nidhanamsa* placement of a planet, and the second placement is called the *Ashtamamsa* placement of a planet. We will now discuss the meaning of these placements.

5.1 *Understanding Nidhanamsa*

According to the *Jataka Parijata*, when the lord of any house in the D1 chart is placed in a *Nidhanamsa* position in the 8th house in the *Rashi-Tulya Navamsa* chart, there will be a 'death' to the significance(s) of that house without much support received during death. If the lord of the ascendant were in the *Nidhanamsa*, the native would die with no relations by his/her side. Let us look at three examples.

Example #1 (Nidhanamsa)

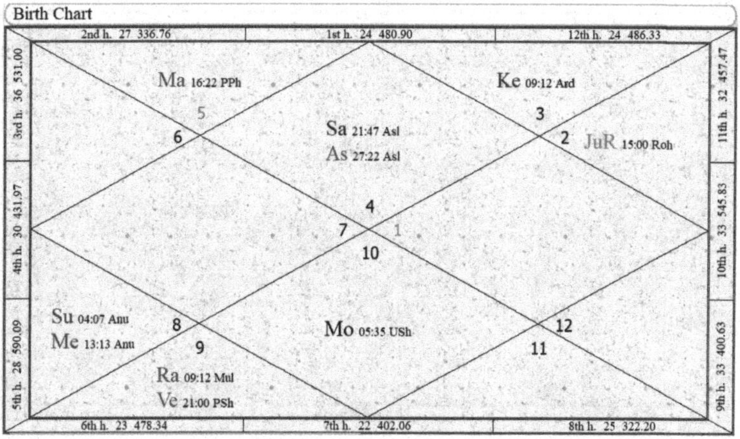

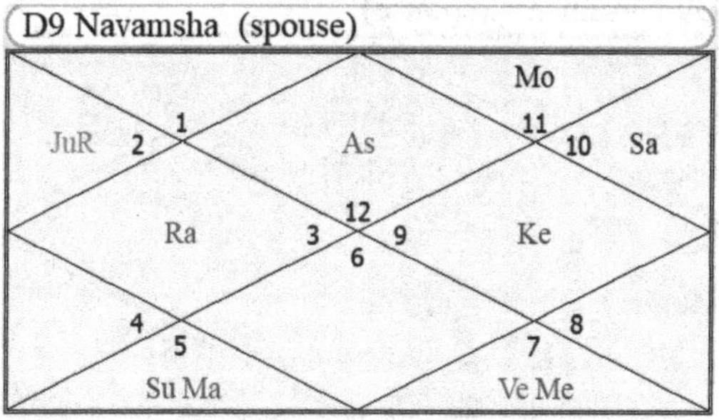

The ascendant lord of the D1 chart is Moon and it goes to the *Nidhanamsa* position in the *Rashi-Tulya Navamsa* chart. See that the Moon is placed in sign Aquarius in the D9 chart and Aquarius is the 8th house for natives born with *lagna* in the Cancer sign.

The native died with no blood relations by her side. The death was bloody as Mars aspected the *lagna* lord in D9 where the latter is placed in an enemy sign.

Example #2 (Nidhanamsa)

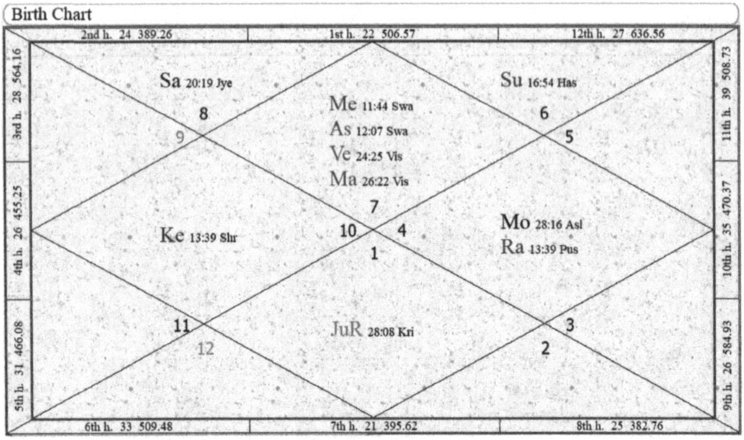

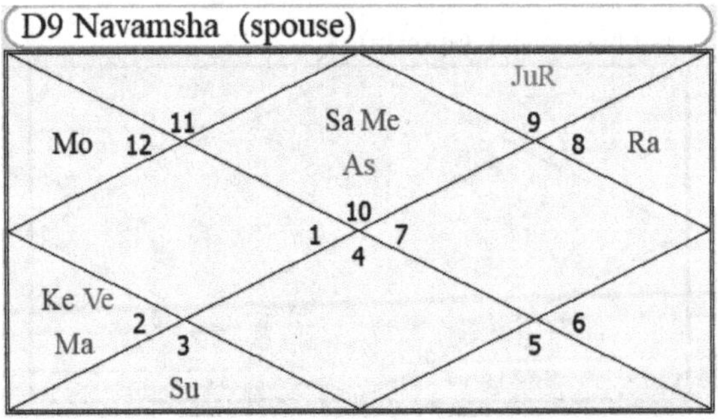

The ascendant lord of the D1 chart is Venus and it goes to the *Nidhanamsa* position in the *Rashi-Tulya Navamsa* chart. See that Venus is placed in sign Taurus in the D9 chart and Taurus is the 8th house for natives born with *lagna* in the Libra sign. The native died with no blood relations by his side. The death was bloody as Mars conjunct the *lagna* lord in D9 along with Ketu (hence double Mars) where Mars is placed in an enemy sign.

Example #3 (Nidhanamsa)

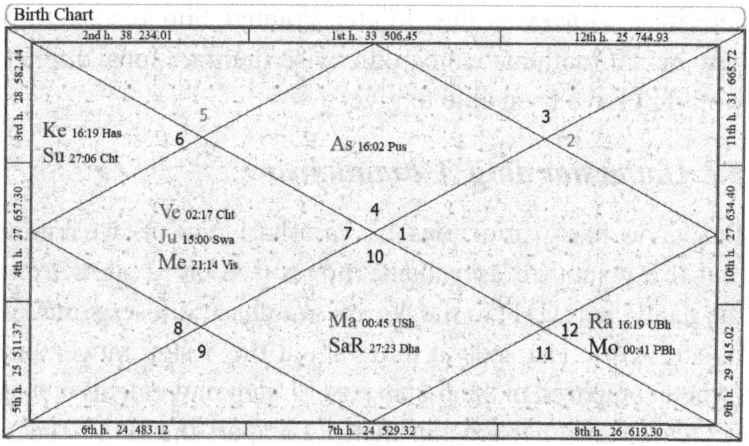

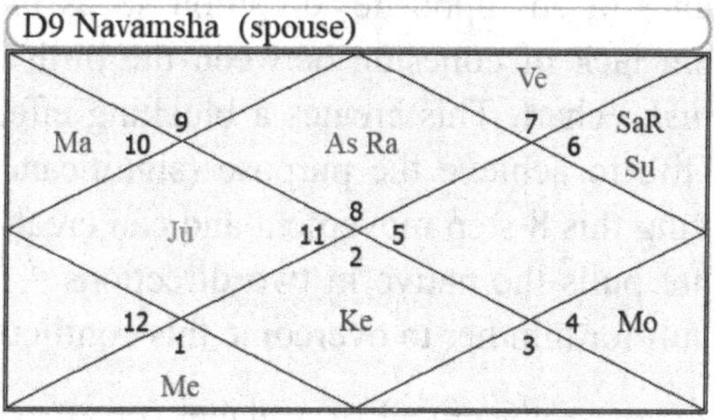

The 9th lord of the D1 chart is Jupiter and it goes to the *Nidhanamsa* position in the *Rashi-Tulya Navamsa* chart. See that Jupiter is placed in sign Aquarius in the D9 chart and Aquarius is the 8th house for natives born with *lagna* in the Cancer sign. The native and the organized religion around him was Christianity. However, he was called as the evil man in the society of Christians as he followed all sorts of non-Christian concepts in life that ranged from Hinduism to Egyptian philosophy. He had several marriages and affairs etc. and was into weird occult stuff such as planchet (calling spirits). It is evident that this is the 'death' of the significance of the 9th lord as a regular Jupiter would shy away from such activities. However, this Jupiter granted him discovering new occult methods which otherwise the traditional Jupiter wouldn't have been able to give.

5.2 *Understanding Ashtamamsa*

Based on basic principles of Parashari *jyotish*, we know that if a planet (or ascendant) moves 6, 8 or 12 signs from the natal chart (D1) to the *Navamsha* chart, it loses some of its strength. The special thing about the 8-sign movement (when compared to the 6-step and 12-step movement) is that it creates an inner tension that pulls apart the significance of the planet in an 'opposite' direction so as to generate a maximum lack of cohesion between the birth chart and the *Navamsha* chart. This creates a blocking effect for the native in life to achieve the purpose (significance) of the planet having this 8-step movement and can create an inner conflict that pulls the native in two directions – making it very difficult for him/her to overcome this conflict.

The *Ashtamamsa* placement of a planet (or ascendant) can only occur in 8 possible ways (out of 108), if one does astrological mathematics (check it out yourself as part of a *nakshatra* analysis and D9 element placement exercise). If a native has planets (or ascendant) in any of the following places on the birth chart, they go to an *Ashtamamsa* position in the D9 chart.

Aries (goes to Scorpio *navamsa*) and **placed between 23d20' and 26d40'** (*Bharani pada* 4)

Gemini (goes to Capricorn *navamsa*) and **placed between 10d00' and 13d20'** (*Ardra pada* 2)

Cancer (goes to Aquarius *navamsa*) and **placed between 23d20' and 26d40'** (*Ashlesha pada* 3)

Virgo (goes to Aries *navamsa*) and **placed between 10d00' and 13d20'** (*Hasta pada* 1)

Libra (goes to Taurus *navamsa*) **and placed between 23d20' and 26d40'** (*Vishakha pada* 2)

Sagittarius (goes to Cancer *navamsa*) and **placed between 10d00' and 13d20'** (*Mula pada* 4)

Capricorn (goes to Leo *navamsa*) and **placed between 23d20' and 26d40'** (*Dhanishta pada* 1)

Pisces (goes to Libra *navamsa*) and **placed between 10d00' and 13d20'** (*Uttarabhadrapada pada* 2)

As examples (not exhaustive) of what are the implications of planets (or ascendant) going into an *Ashtamamsa* position (see the mapping above), consider (a) Venus in Taurus *navamsa* (own house and earthy and *arth* sign) – may give the native a picture of heavenly materialistic bliss, but does not give it and generates lot of frustration in the native, (b) Jupiter in Cancer *navamsa* (and exalted) – despite exaltation, might give problems to a native via the loss of *Guru* or husband (for females) or children and push the native to the spiritual world, and (c) Venus in Libra *navamsa* (own house and *kaam* sign) – the native might deal with relationship struggles a embrace and will then embrace spirituality. The author hopes that readers got the main logic here to interpret planets/ascendant going to *Ashtamamsa*. Now let us look at two chart examples.

Example #1 (Ashtamamsa)

Birth Chart

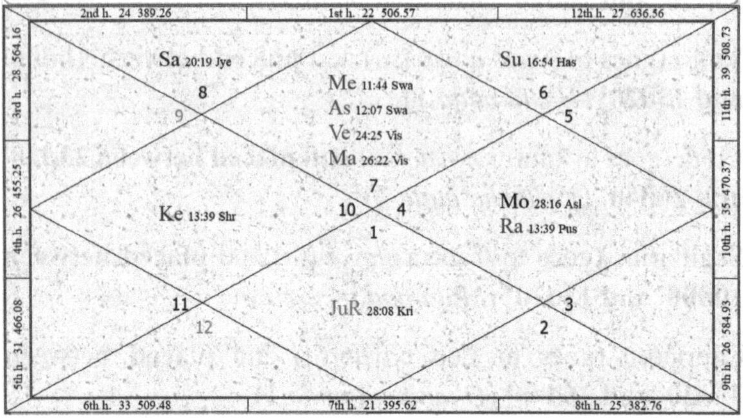

D9 Navamsha (spouse)

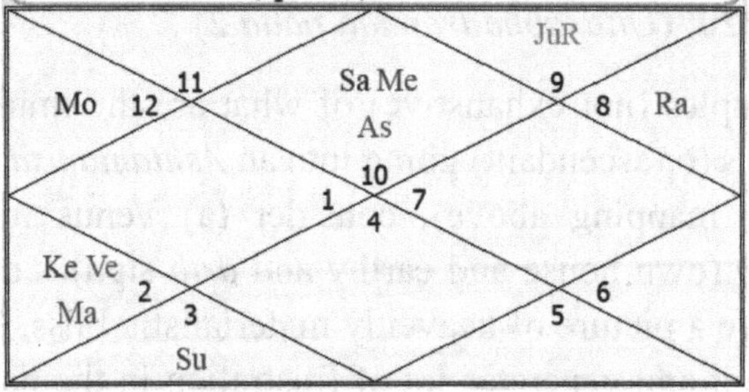

The native has his ascendant lord Venus of D1 in its own sign Taurus in the *Navamsa* chart, and hence the ascendant lord is in *Ashtamamsa* and also in the *Nidhanamsa* at the same time. While we have seen earlier what the *Nidhanamsa* placement of ascendant lord can do to the native, the *Ashtamamsa* placement of the native made the native non-materialistic in relation to luxury goods and a sex maniac (Mars conjunct Venus) turned into a celibate. The native would probably remain frustrated for sex and material pleasures for life if not for Venus conjunct spiritual/detached Ketu acting as savior from the frustrations related to materialistic Venus.

Example #2 (Ashtamamsa)

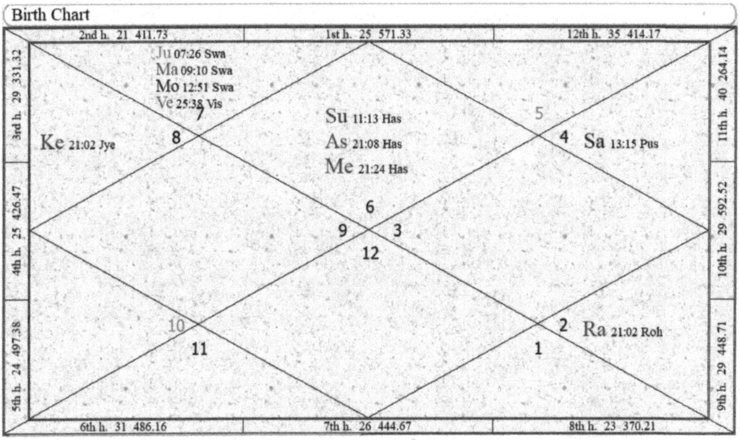

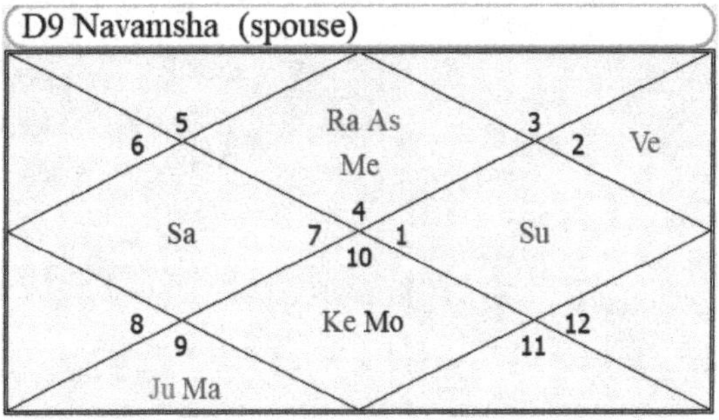

The native has her 9th house lord Venus (also 2nd house lord) placed in Libra of D1 go to its own sign Taurus in the *Navamsa* chart, and hence the 9th lord (and 2nd lord) is in *Ashtamamsa*. In addition, Sun (12th lord) for the native is in Virgo in D1 and goes to Aries in the *Navamsa* chart. Hence Sun is also in *Ashtamamsa*. Both Sun and the 9th lord are common significators of father, and the native lost her father when she was very young, due to both being in *Ashtamamsa* (common significator). Note here that in the D9, Sun is also the 2nd lord and acts as a *maraaka* on 9th house matters (i.e., *bhagya*/*dharma*).

Part 2

The Art of Prediction

(with Examples)

CHAPTER 6

The Steps to Analyze D9

In Part 1 of this book, we discussed the basic fundamental concepts of the D9 chart. Part 2 of this book is about how one can use these fundamental concepts to predict and time nature and events in relation to a native. *The first milestone towards this goal is to lay down in a structured and logical fashion the steps to analyze the D9 along with the D1 in close correspondence.*

However, before we delve into the art of prediction using the *Navamsa*, it is important to remember the following timely invariant truth about making predictions: No astrologer can have a statistical prediction success rate of close to a 100% accuracy over time. Only *trikaal darshis* (the cosmically conscious soul to whom time (*kaal*) unfolds) have that capability, and they are not astrologers. Astrologers have cosmic vision limitations – even the greatest ones those who are godly natured and live very austere lives. No matter what tools and tricks they use, they can at most get 80% of statistical accuracy in their predictions over time. Even for the serious student who aims to become a very good astrologer, there is only a certain level to which education can take him/her. The rest is divine intervention and blessing without which that "magic" will never be bestowed on him/her. This was onc of the first lessons my *Guru* Richa Shukla told me. Hence, one should consciously stay away from astrologers who advertise their high prediction accuracies. It is a signal of a less confident and insecure astrologer.

6.1 Is the D9 Operative Around 35+ Years?

The basic 101 of prediction using the *Navamsa* chart begins with answering a basic and controversial question we get in many forums on the Internet and also in multiple astrology classes. *Is the D9 chart operative on/after 35 years of age for a native?* The answer to this question is both a 'yes' and a 'no'. We are not trying to be politically correct here. There are sound logical reasons for the answer to be both an 'yes' and a 'no'.

Let us first understand as to why the answer is a 'no'. There is no mention in any astrological classics that the D9 should be seen after 35 years of age or after mid-life. When the sages and masters have not mentioned this, there is no rule as to why the D9 chart should be seen if the native is beyond 35 years of age. I mean look at it this way – *if the D9 is a magnified view of the D1, how is it possible that D9 is operative after 35 years of age and the D1 is active from birth?* Not logical, correct? Moreover, how does one justify that a child is born, and we do not look at the D9? or someone has an early death in infancy or childhood, and we do not look at his/her D9? or even more strikingly a sportsman whose career is usually over by around 35 years of age, and we do not look at his/her D9?

Now, let us understand as to why the answer is an 'yes'. One should note here that every planet has a maturity age in Vedic astrology. Out of all the non-shadow planets, Saturn has the maximum age of maturity – i.e., it matures around

35+ years in a native's life. Other planets mature earlier. Let us remember this in mind for now. At the same time, also remember from earlier chapters that the *Navamsa* chart is a microscopic view of the D1 chart. The D9 chart is the fruits pertaining to the seed that is the D1 chart. So, would it not make sense for the D9 chart to showcase all the fruits clearly (and their impact on the native) when all the planets have matured for the native (which is around 35+ years of age +/- 5 years)? One would logically believe this argument to be true, and hence many astrologers (including my *Guru* Richa Shukla) are of the opinion (based on their experience) that the D9 chart is more important after 35+ years of age. However, they never imply that the D9 chart does not operate before 35+ years of age. It very well does.

However, there is a catch again. What about people who live only till 10 or 20 years of age? Or sportsmen whose career starts in their teens and finish by mid-age? Should D1 primarily dictate these natives? The answer is a 'no'. Both D1 and D9 are very important for such natives. Note that different planets have different maturity ages, and for a sportsperson, the planet Mars is an important planet. Once it has matured (in the 20s), it will show its effects fully for a native in every divisional chart, not just the D9. Hence, the career for the person should be seen both from the D1 and the D9 chart with the assumption that some planets would be giving their full effects while the sportsman is still active, and some will give their full effects post-retirement for the native.

On the same catch as mentioned above, what about people who live a small span of life, i.e., a life span of less than 30 years or around. The same logic holds here that some planets that mature earlier than 30 years of age (e.g., Mars, Venus) will showcase their full effects in the D9 chart (and also in the D1). Hence it is sufficient to see D1 for these natives and giving it relatively much more importance than the D9. In addition, except for rare cases, how much can a native achieve before 30 in the different areas of life? Not much one would guess.

6.2 The Steps to Analyze a D9 Chart (Basic)

We come to the main part of this chapter which showcases the steps that are important and necessary to analyze the D9 chart along with the D1 chart.

We start by stating the **necessary elements** that need to be judged for any predictions in relation to the D9. These elements are (in no order of importance):

(i) Lagna lord of the D9.

(ii) Lagna lord of the D1 chart.

(iii) *Karaka* of the D9, i.e., Venus.

(iv) Lagna of D1.

(v) Lagna of D9.

(vi) Trine houses and their lords in D9.

(vii) Moon and its lord (dispositor) in D9/D1.

(viii) Sun and its dispositor in D9/D1.

Note that the Sun, Moon, and Lagna are the representative (significators) of the soul, mind, and body, respectively and they together have a role to play in every action of a native. After all, it is only through the sync of the mind, body, and soul that *karma* (and its quality) is performed.

The **situational elements** to be checked in the D9 (along with in the D1) pertain to the query at hand. As an example, say we need to study/analyze the condition of the 10th house in D1. Then one needs to primarily check/judge in the D9 chart the strength of (in no order of importance)

(i) the 10th lord of D1,
(ii) the planets placed in the 10th house of D1,
(iii) the *karaka* of the 10th house,
(iv) the 10th house (i.e., lord and planets) from the *karaka* of the 10th house, and
(v) the 10th house from the *mahadasha* lord.

For each of the **necessary** and the **situational** elements (planets and ascendant), check their placements in (no order of importance)

(i) the *Rashi-Tulya Navamsa* chart (which *bhava-soochak navamsa*),
(ii) the relative number of houses these elements move to in D9 from D1,
(iii) the house in the D9 chart in which these elements are placed,
(iv) lordship in D9 of these elements, and
(v) the placement of the lord of the house (in the D9 chart) in the D9 and the D1 charts.

The **simple rules of analysis** are:

(i) The **necessary elements** must be placed in good houses of the D9 chart. The bad houses are 3, 6, 8, and 12. One must note here that several good/ powerful *yogas* might be forming in relation to the bad houses (e.g., the *Vipareeta Raja yoga*) in the

D9 chart. In such a case the native will eventually (conditioned on getting the relevant *dasha* periods) get good results but after a lot of struggles and hard work.

(ii) The **situational elements** must be placed in good houses of the D9 chart. If such elements are well placed in the D1 chart but poorly placed in the D9 chart, the native can eventually (conditioned on getting the relevant *dasha* periods) get good results as promised in the D1 chart but after a lot of struggles and hard work.

(iii) Any element (**necessary** or **situational**) placed in the 2nd house in D9/D1 gives good results in relation to wealth but not so good results in family relations as the planet(s) is 8th from the 7th house.

(iv) *Digbali* planets (i.e., those acquiring directional strength) become auspicious for the native in the D9 chart in relation to the house it becomes *Digbali*. Note that Mercury and Jupiter have full directional strength in the first house; Moon and Venus have full directional strength in the fourth house. Saturn has full directional strength in the seventh house. Sun and Mars have full directional strength in the tenth house. A point of caution here is – if any planet (e.g., Venus) is in his house of zero directional strength, one needs to check the age of the individual to check whether the planet will give adverse results. A native with Venus in the 10th house but getting the Venus MD after 50 years of age will likely enjoy life without much focus on career, as he/she need not - after lot of hard work he/she might have put in between the ages of 25 and 50.

(v) Natural and/or functional malefics in the *upachaya* (growth) houses of the D9 chart make the native grow and progress in life by defeating challenges (in relation to the houses signified by the necessary and situational elements). Richa Shukla (the author's *Guru*) often says that in the *Kaliyuga*, it is needed for a native to have planets in the *upachaya* houses to gain sufficient materialistic desires.

(vi) Planets posited in the good houses of the D9 chart, irrespective of they being weak, natural malefic, or functional malefic will give good results to a native in matters related to the significances of the houses and planetary lordship (and also give some bad results, as it is their nature). Similarly, benefic and/or strong planets in bad houses of the D9, or if debilitated, combust, or conjunct enemy planets in D9, will not give desired benefic results.

(vii) The dispositors of planets and ascendant placed in the D9 should be checked for in the D1 chart – especially those for which their hosted planets (or ascendant) are not well placed in the D9 chart. These dispositors should not be badly placed, or have poor strength (i.e., debilitated, combust) in the D1 chart that will make the D9 placement of their hosted planet much worse. A good dispositor placement and/or strength in the D1 is a blessing.

(viii) Karaka of D9 - Venus in *lagna bhava* of the D9 is not so good for spouse but could be good for other matters. For spousal matters only, a weak Venus in *lagna bhava* is better than strong Venus in the same. However, if Venus is a birth *yogi* planet (see later in the book), or in its *nakshatra* in D1 then bad effects of Venus in 1st house of D9 should not be predicted.

One must note here that while applying these simple rules one must apply the traditional ***(P)****lacement,* ***(A)****spect,* ***(C)****onjunction),* ***(E)****xchange* logic to analyze the strength of any house. We also emphasize that there are many other rules of analysis for the D9 – however, the basic rules are easy to remember and sufficient to obtain the correct analysis of a house when combining a D1 and D9 analysis. A tip for students is to avoid using complex rules directly (as a shortcut) as there are many to remember, and complex rule application can go faulty. We now illustrate these discussed concepts through **two** example charts.

Example #1 **(Steps in D9 Analysis)**

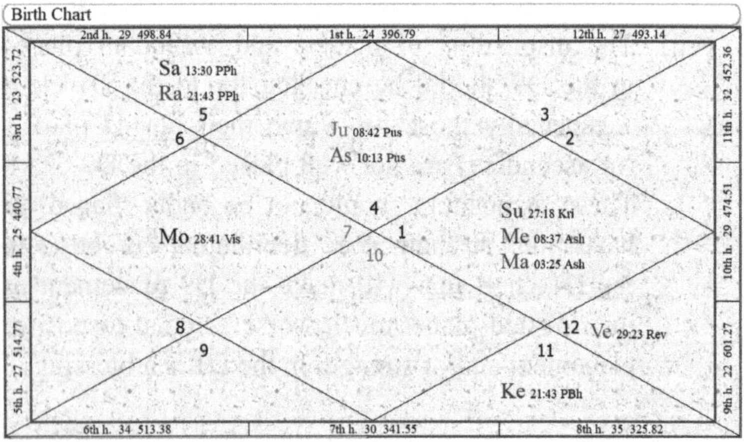

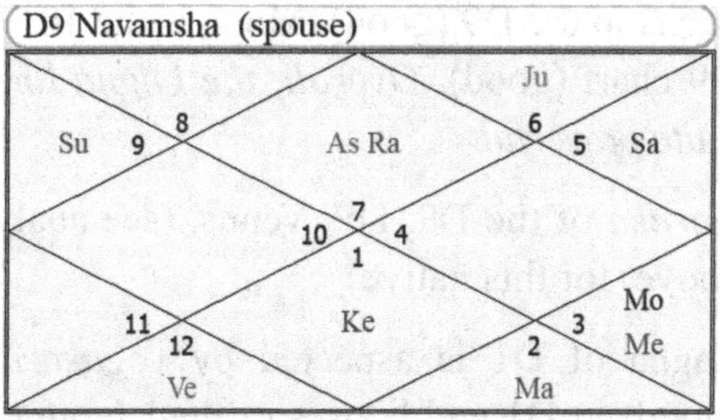

A placement analysis for the native of his **necessary elements** in D1 and D9 is as follows.

(i) Lagna lord of the D9 (Venus) is placed in the *Bhagyamsa* (good); it is exalted and *vargottama* (good); it is placed in the 6th house of the D9 (not good); the 6th lord of the D9 chart is placed in the 12th house in the D9 chart (forming a *vipareeta Raja yoga* in the D9 chart) and is exalted in the first house of the D1 (good) and aspected by *yogakaarak* Mars (good). Venus also forms the powerful *Amala* and the *Bheri yogas* in the D9. *Overall, the Lagna lord of D9 is quite powerful.*

(ii) Lagna lord of the D1 chart (Moon) is placed in the *vyamsa* (not good but dispositor of *vyamsa* is in *kendra* in D1); goes to nine houses forward in D9 relative its position in the D1 (good); it is placed in the 9th house of the D9 (good); the 9th lord of the D9 chart is placed in its own house in the D9 and forms multiple powerful *yogas* in the D9 (good); this 9th lord of D9 is placed in the 10th house of the D1 conjunct *yogakaarak* Mars, and exalted Sun (good). Moon forms the *Gajakesari*, *Chamaara*, *Dharma-Karma Adhipati*, and *Raja Sambandhi yogas* in the D9 (good). Moon is the 10th lord of the D9 chart (good). *Overall, the Lagna lord of D1 is quite powerful.*

(iii) *Karaka* of the D9, i.e., Venus. (see analysis for (i) above, for this native)

(iv) Lagna of D1 is aspected by *yogakaraaka* Mars (good) in D1 and houses exalted Jupiter who is 6th lord, and 9th lord (good) and in the *nakshatra* of Saturn who is *vargottama* (mixed as Saturn is 7th lord and 8th lord in D1, but *yogakaaraka* in the D9). *Overall, the Lagna of D1 is quite powerful for the native.*

(v) Lagna of D9 is on the Rahu-Ketu axis (not good) but is in a *kendra* position relative to the D1 placement of the Lagna (good). The dispositor of the Lagna in D9 is Venus and is powerfully placed in D1 and D9. *Overall, the Lagna of D9 is of medium to good strength for the native.*

(vi) Trine houses and their lords in D9 are of utmost importance in the D9. Lord of the first house of the D9 is Venus (see (i) above for analysis). The lord of the 5th house of the D9 chart is Saturn who is *yogakaaraka* in D9 (good), forms a *Raja yoga* with Mars (2nd lord and 7th lord in D9) in the D9 (good), is placed in the *Arthamsa* (good), is the 7th and 8th lord in D1 (not so good), is placed in the 11th house of D9 (good) in an enemy house (not good) with dispositor exalted (good). The lord of the 9th house is Mercury who is placed in his own house with Moon and forms multiple powerful *yogas* in the D9 (good) that include the *Budha-Aditya Yoga*, the *Chamaara Yoga*, the *Bheri Yoga*, the *Dharma-Karma Adhipati Yoga*, and the *Brahma Yoga*. *Overall, the trine houses in D9 of the native are powerful.*

(vii) Moon and its lord (dispositor) in D9/D1 (see (ii) and (vi) above for an analysis).

(viii) Sun and its dispositor in D9/D1. Sun is placed in *Ariamsha* in the D9 (good as malefic in *upachaya* house). It is in a *Pushkar navamsa* (good). It is placed in the 3rd house of the D9 (good as malefic in *upachaya* house) and moves 9 places in D9 relative to its position in the D1 (good). It is the 11th lord of the D9 chart (good). The dispositor of Sun in the D9 is Jupiter placed in the 12th house of D9 but forms a *vipareeta Raja yoga*, the *Gajakesari Yoga*, the *Bheri Yoga*, and the *Brahma Yoga* in the D9 (good), and multiple powerful *yogas* in the D1 chart (good). *Overall, the Sun in the D9 chart of the native is quite powerful.*

Moreover, the native has the *Daamini yoga* in the D9 chart (7 planets in 6 signs). **In simple terms, the necessary elements of the native's horoscope are quite powerful for him to achieve great things in most areas of life and face challenges**, conditioned on proper planetary *dashas* running in the life of the native (see Chapter 7 for more details).

We now analyze the **career** of the native as an example of a **situational element** that needs to be judged. The 6th house and the 10th house of a native are primarily related to his career. According to the *bhavat bhavam* principles, the 7th house is also important as it is the 10th from the 10th house (and the house of *pada praapti*), and so is the 11th house as it is 6th from the 6th house. The *karaka* of profession (multiple *karakas* including Saturn, Sun, and Mercury) also needs to be analyzed.

The 10th lord of the D1 chart is Mars that is *yogakaarak* in the D1 chart (good) and conjunct with exalted 2nd lord Sun who is in *Pushkar navamsa* (good) and 3rd lord and 12th lord Mercury (medium strength but gives foreign settlement in job); is placed in the *Labhamsa* in the *Rashi-Tulya Navamsa* chart (good); moves two houses in the D9 chart relative to its placement in the D1 chart (good); is the lord of the 2nd house and the 7th house in D9 (good for career) being aspected by Jupiter (3rd lord and 6th lord and exalted in D1) from the 12th house (good, but needs lot of effort and hard work); and forms a powerful *Raja yoga* with Saturn who is *vargottama* (good but with hard work and delay).

The 10th lord of D1 is Mars and placed in an *artha rashi* of Venus in the D9 and aspected by Jupiter also from an *artha rashi* (and Saturn from a *dharma rashi*) – **the native is an engineer and educator in the field of cybersecurity and its management** *(artha rashi* and *fixed sign* significance) developing creative solutions (Mars is 5th lord in D1, and in Venetian sign in D9 in Moon's exalted sign) as a researcher (Ketu in *Karmamsa* of the *Rashi-Tulya Navamsa* chart).

The planets Mercury and Sun placed in the 10th house of D1 have been analyzed above as part of being the necessary elements of the native's chart. Sun and Mercury are also *karakas* of the 10th house. *Vargottama* Saturn is also a *karaka* of the 10th house and is the 7th lord of *pada praapti* in D1 of the native. Saturn who is *yogakaaraka* in D9 (good), forms a *Raja yoga* with Mars (2nd lord and 7th lord in D9) in the

D9 (good), forms a powerful Raja yoga in the D9 with Mars (good); is placed in the 11th house of D9 (good) in an enemy house (not good) with dispositor exalted (good), is placed in the *Arthamsa* (good), and is the 7th and 8th lord in D1 (not so good). **The native will achieve sustainable power, fame, and gain of very high quality in career matters (in foreign countries) but with lots of hard work and delay.** The lord of the 11th house in (6th from 6th) in D1 is Venus and is analyzed as part of being the necessary elements of the native's chart. Note that Venus is also the 10th lord from Saturn in the D1. In D9, the 10th house from Saturn has Mars and the lord is Venus, both of which have been analyzed as part of necessary and situational elements.

***Example #2* (Steps in D9 Analysis)**

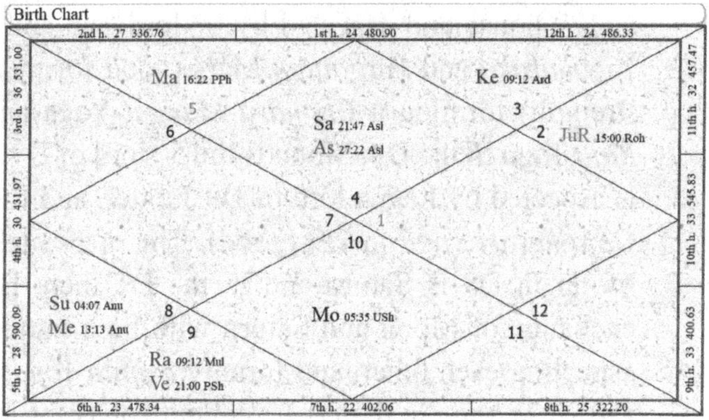

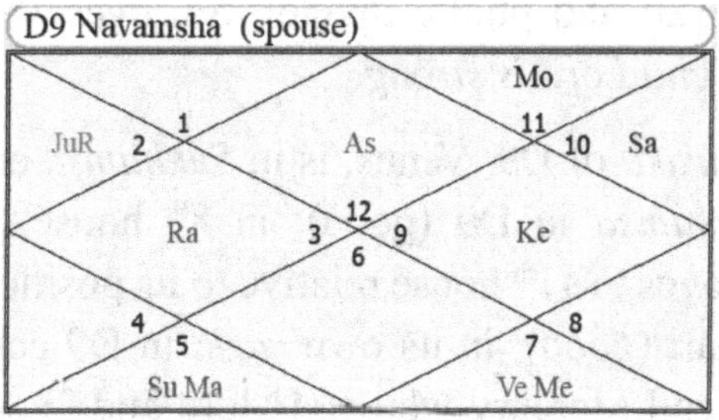

A placement analysis for the native of her **necessary elements** in D1 and D9 is as follows.

i) Lagna Lord of D9, Jupiter (R), is *Vargottam* (good), is the 10th lord (good), and placed in *Labhamsa* (good) in the third house of D9 (not good). Its dispositor, Venus (in a *Pushkar navamsa*), is placed in 6th house and is on Rahu/Ketu axis in D1, is the 11th lord of D1, and also has exchange with 6th lord and 9th lord Jupiter in D1 providing strength to both but indicates gains by sustaining (with luck) extreme challenges from foes. So, *overall, the strength of Lagna lord of D9 is very good.*

ii) Lagna lord of D1, Moon, is placed in *nidhanamsa* (not good) and moves two places in D9 and is placed in 12th house and aspected by 6th lord Sun and D1 *Yogakaraka* and *Vargottam* Mars (good for mental strength) forming a *Chandra-Mangal* Yoga and a *Raja Yoga* in the D9. Moon is the 5th lord of D9 and is aspected by Lagna lord of D9 Jupiter, and forms *Gaja-kesari yoga* in D9 (good). The dispositor of Moon in D9 is Saturn and in the D1 there is an exchange of Moon and Saturn with both mutually aspecting each other, and forms *Parijata Yoga and Pushkala Yoga* in the D1 (excellent *yogas* for mass appeal and public image). *So, overall strength of Lagna Lord is strong.*

iii) *Karaka* of D9, Venus, is in *Sukhamsa* and *Pushkar navamsa* in D9 (good); in 8th house (not good); moves to 11th house relative to its position in the D1 chart (good); in its own *rashi* in D9 conjunct with friend Mercury who is 4th lord and 7th lord (good);

is the 3rd lord and 8th lord in D9 (not good); and aspected by Saturn who is 11th lord and 12th lord of D9 (medium). Venus's dispositor in D9 is on Rahu/Ketu axis in D1 and in a good house exchange in with Jupiter in D1 (medium strength because of a good exchange but on the Rahu/Ketu axis). *Hence, the karaka is of medium strength for the native.*

iv) Lagna of D1 is in a *Vish navamsa* (not good) and is aspected by the Lagna lord, Moon itself in D1 (good). The Lagna goes to the *Bhagyamsa* in the D9 (good) and is aspected by Saturn who is the 11th lord and 12th lord of D9 (medium) and by *vargottama* 2nd lord and the 9th lord Mars in D9 (good). *So, overall, the strength of the Lagna is quite strong.*

v) The Lagna of D9 is the trine (9th house) house relative to D1 placement of the Lagna (good) and *lagna* lord, Jupiter, has overall good strength as we have seen above in (i). Lagna is aspected by Saturn and Mars (*yogakaraka* of D1) and hence gives a governing, fiery, and Martian personality. *Hence, the Lagna of D9 is quite strong.*

vi) Trine houses of D9 - We discussed the Lagna lord, Jupiter, earlier in (i). The lord of the 5th house of D9 is Moon who is the Lagna lord of D1 and we have discussed this above in (ii). The 5th house is aspected by a well-placed *Swarashi* Saturn in the D9 chart, but the aspect is on its non-friendly house (not good). Moon's dispositor is Saturn that is positioned in the Lagna in D1 but goes to its non-friendly sign and mutually aspected by Moon (not good). The third trine is lorded by *yogakaraka* of D1, Mars, who is *vargottam* and placed in 6th house in *Arthamsa* with Sun. This is a good placement for Mars and Sun (malefics in *upachaya* houses). The 9th house is aspected by *Vargottam lagna* lord, Jupiter, and Mars itself making this trine house very powerful.

vii) Moon is the Lagna Lord of D1 - please refer to earlier analysis on Lagna lord in (ii).

viii) Sun is placed in the *Arthamsa* in the *Rashi-Tulya Navamsa* (good); moved 10 places relative to its position in the D1 chart (good); is placed on the 6th house of the D9 (good, as a malefic is placed in an *upachaya* house) which is its own house (good) and and is conjunct friend Mars who is the 9th lord (good). The dispositor Sun of its own house is well placed in the 5th house of D1 with friend Mercury forming a *Budh-Aditya Yoga*, aspected by 9th lord Jupiter, and *yogakaarak* Mars. *Hence, Sun is very powerful in the chart of the native.*

It can be inferred that the native has powerful necessary elements in her chart for achieving very good heights in many areas of life while facing challenging situations in all areas of life.

We now analyze the **marriage** of the native as an example of a **situational element** that needs to be judged. We will consider the 7th house and lords in D1 and the D9, *lagna* and its lord in D9, 8th house of D1 and D9, and 2nd house of D9 (sustenance of marriage); and Venus (*karaka* of marriage) in D1 and the D9.

We start with the 7th lord of D1, Saturn. Saturn is placed in *lagna* and in mutual exchange with its lord (Moon). This can be a challenging position where both native and the spouse try to overpower, impose and influence each other which can be detrimental to happy married life. Saturn (7th lord of D1) moves 7 places in D9 and is placed in *Kalatraamsa* in D9 in its own *rashi* in 11th house (good) - so the native did have gains from the marriage. This Saturn (7th lord of D1) is placed in *Swarashi* and is *Digbali* by its placement in 7th house in the *Rashi-Tulya Navamsa* chart (good for marriage stability). However, Saturn is also a separative planet, and its presence in the 7th house indicates problems in marriage/ married life. Saturn, being 8th lord too is placed 6th from its own house in D1 and forms a *vipareet raja yoga*. The 7th house of D1 and D9 and Lagna lord of D1 receive positive aspect of powerful/*vargottama* Jupiter (R) which is the 9th lord of D1 and Lagna lord of D9 (good) - blessing the native with marriage and its stability. The 7th lord of D9, Mercury (who is also the 4th lord and placed in *Sukhamsa*), is placed in 8th house with a very strong 8th lord, Venus (*swarashi* and in *pushkar navamsa*) and aspected by separative Saturn. Overall, marriage has stability with lots of hard work and compromises being put into it.

Lagna of D9 receives the aspect of Saturn (the 11th lord and 12th lord of D9) and *yogakaraka* of D1, Mars but the 2nd lord and 7th lord (acting as a *maraka* in the D9) in the D9, and aspects the *lagna* of D9 from the 6th house of challenges. Hence, marriage personality is one of challenges and war-room struggles. But the *lagna* in D9 is nine places from the *lagna* in D1, and is a fortunate sign for marriage stability also.

The 8th house of D1 (*mangalya* house for women) is aspected by a strong *vargottam* and *yogakaraka* Mars. Further, the 8th lord of D1, Saturn, is placed 6th in the first house in D1 indicating sudden transformative events in marriage but could lead to beneficial outcomes as it forms a *vipareeta raja yoga*. So, the 8th house of D1 does not provide good indications about the longevity of the marriage – even though other factors need to be accounted for.

The second house of D9 is lorded by Mars (2nd lord and 9th lord) who is placed in 6th house in fire sign conjunct with fiery and separative planet Sun (who is 6th lord of D9). The second house does receive aspects of Venus (3rd lord and 8th lord) and Mars from the 8th house (not good for marriage sustenance). The benefic aspects of (a) Mars (*yogakaraka* for the native) who is conjunct *swarashi* Sun and (b) Venus being conjunct 4th and 7th lord Mercury and in *Sukhamsa*, and *Pushkar navamsa* probably saved the marriage of the native in spite of differences and war-room scenario between the native and spouse from early in the marriage.

Venus who is the *karaka* of D9 and marriage is on Rahu/Ketu axis in 6th house in D1 signifying amiss in marital bliss. However, it is in the *Sukhamsa* in the D9 chart (good), moves 11 places in the D9 relative to its position in the D1 (good), but is in the 8th house of D9 (not good), and is the 3rd lord and 8th lord (not good for romance and marital juice). Venus does not give emotional warmth and marital romance.

6.3 The Steps to Analyze a D9 Chart (Advanced)

We will now discuss a very interesting, extremely accurate, and brilliant D9 analysis method (for finer analysis and predictions) that is hardly ever publicly mentioned. The author got to know this mathematical (*nakshatra*-flavored) method many years ago via reading scholars in Eastern Indian and Southern India. Later he was also pushed by his *Guru* to get to the depths of D9 analysis using advanced parts of the *Brihat Parashara Hora Shastra* (BPHS) that has the root of the methodology we will study in this section. However, **before we describe the methodology, we need to cover some new basics.**

6.3.1 - The (Mathematical) *Sripati* House System

The *Sripati* system (mentioned in the *Surya Siddhanta* and the BPHS) is an unequal house/*bhava* system (recommended by our sages). Usually, hardly anyone uses it in practice (because calculation by hand is tedious for modern enthusiasts). In the *Sripati system*, the ascendant degree in the birth chart will be at the exact center of the 1st house. However, the width of the houses can be exactly 30 degrees, lesser, or even more than 30 degrees in extent. Interesting isn't it! As you go away farther from the equator some of the houses will be greatly lengthened and some greatly shortened. Interpreting such houses in a birth chart requires a lot of practice as two or more signs can make up a house and very importantly two or more planets can act as part rulers of the house. Note that all the houses/ *bhavas* in a native's birth chart will be exactly 30 degrees in width only if the birth was on a day when the day and night duration was exactly 12 hours at the birthplace. In all other cases, the houses will always be greater or lesser than 30 degrees in width and one will have varying widths for various houses in the birth chart. However, **in very simple terms**, the following two points need to be remembered for the readers:

- If the birth location is geographically within the Tropics of Cancer and Capricorn on the world map, the reader is advised to use the *Equal Houses* system with the *Bhav-Chalit* (BC) chart. Here each of the 12 houses will be 30 degrees in width with the birth ascendant degree being the midpoint of the first house.
- If the birthplace of a native is beyond the Tropics of Cancer and Capricorn, then readers should apply the *Sripati House* system in toto. However, to avoid tedious mathematical calculations, the *Bhav-Chalit* (BC) chart can be used as a very good approximation to the *Sripati* system.

Let us illustrate the *Bhav-Chalit* idea.

Example #1 (BC Chart as *Sripati* Approximation)

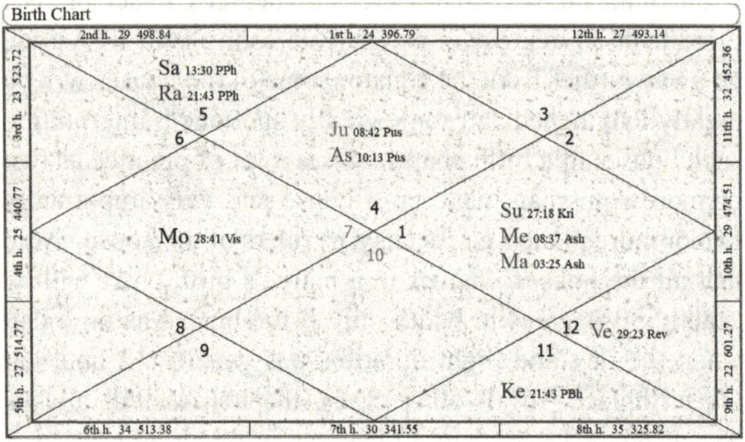

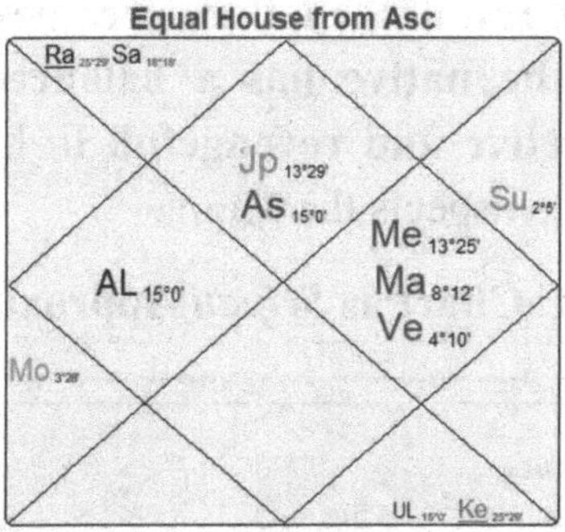

In this example, the ascendant degree of the native in the birth chart is made the midpoint of the first house of the BC chart. Since the house is 30 degrees, the ascendant is placed at 15 degrees, and planet Jupiter is shifted by the same distance between Jupiter and birth ascendant in the D1 chart.

Hence a birth ascendant of 10d13' in D1 in Cancer is placed in 15d of the first house in the BC chart of the native, and Jupiter placed at 8d42' in D1 in Cancer is placed at 13d29' in the BC chart. The difference between birth ascendant and Jupiter is 1d31' in both the D1 and BC charts, and this shows that the calculation is correct. **However, note that while the first house of the D1 chart is entirely the sign Cancer, the first house of the BC chart is partly Cancer and partly Gemini.** This also explains, in part, why the native is communicative as a personality (first house is a mix of Cancer and Gemini signs). One must note here that the *nakshatra* placement are those of that in the D1 chart, and planets are fixed placed on *nakshatras*.

Now let us check Moon that is placed in the fourth house in Libra in the D1 chart but goes in the fifth house in the BC chart due to midpoint calculations. Hence, Moon (*karaka* of mind) has influence of Scorpio on the native to a certain extent, while the rest of the influence comes from the Libra Moon. **Hence the native has a balanced mind but is somewhat secretive and revengeful.** In both D1 and the BC chart, the Sun aspects the Moon.

***Example #2* (BC Chart as *Sripati* Approximation)**

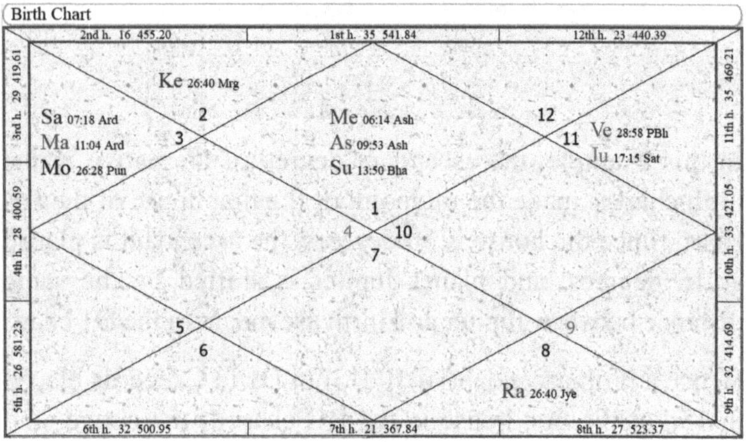

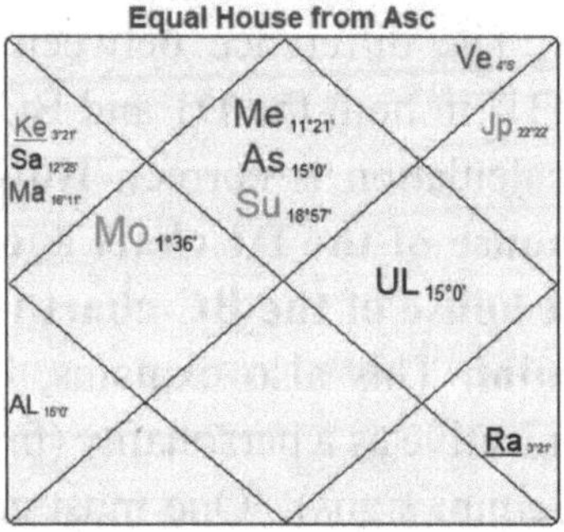

In this example, the ascendant degree of the native in the birth chart is made the midpoint of the first house of the BC chart. Since the house is 30 degrees, the ascendant is placed at 15 degrees, and planet Mercury and Sun are shifted by the same distance between Mercury/Sun and ascendant in the D1 chart.

Hence a birth ascendant of 9d53' in D1 in Aries is placed in 15d of the first house in the BC chart of the native, and Mercury placed at 6d14' in D1 in Aries is placed at 11d21' in the BC chart. The difference between birth ascendant and Mercury is 3d39' in both the D1 and BC charts, and this shows that the calculation is correct. The same calculation is applied for position of the Sun. **However, note that while the first house of the D1 chart is entirely the sign Aries, the first house of the BC chart is partly Aries and partly Pisces.** This also explains, in part, why the native is empathetic, caring, intuitive and wise besides the Arian qualities (first house is a mix of Aries and Pisces signs). One must note here that the *nakshatra* placement are those of that in the D1 chart, and planets are fixed placed on *nakshatras*.

Now let us check Moon that is placed in the third house in Gemini in the D1 chart but goes in the fourth house in the BC chart due to midpoint calculations. Hence, Moon (*karaka* of mind) has influence of Cancer on the native to a certain extent, while the rest of the influence comes from the Gemini Moon. **Hence, the native exhibits a mix of Gemini and Cancer mental traits. She is emotional, deeply loyal, loves to spend time at home, and moody at times besides exhibiting socializing Gemini traits.**

6.3.2 - The *Dagdha Rashis*

Certain signs (*rashis*) become *dagdha* (burnt) on certain *tithis* (lunar days) and are called *dagdha rashis*. Hence, the propensity of these *rashis* to impart their goodness is diminished on these *tithis*. For every *tithi*, in both Krishna and Shukla *pakshas*, two signs become *dagdha* – exceptions being *Chaturdashi* where four signs (*rashis*) get *dagdha*, and *Poornima* (full Moon) and *Amavasya* (new Moon) *tithis* when no *rashi* gets *dagdha*. Note here that the nature of *dagdha* varies from *rashi* to *rashi*. A watery *rashi* will feel a different sense (i.e., less) of burn than an airy, fiery, or earthy *rashis* that amplify fiery propagation. One needs to take these fine physical properties into account while drawing inferences and predictions. We list below the *tithis* and map them with the *rashis* that gets *dagdha* in both the Krishna and Shukla *pakshas*.

Prathama – Libra and Capricorn

Dwiteeya – Sagittarius and Pisces

Triteeya – Leo and Capricorn

Chaturthi – Taurus and Aquarius

Panchami – Gemini and Virgo

Shashthi – Aries and Leo

Saptami – Cancer and Sagittarius

Ashtami – Gemini and Virgo

Navami – Leo and Scorpio

Dashami – Leo and Scorpio

Ekadashi – Sagittarius and Scorpio

Dwadashi – Libra and Capricorn

Trayodoshi – Taurus and Leo

Chaturdashi – Pisces, Gemini, Virgo, and Sagittarius

Poornima and Amavasya – No *rashi* is *dagdha*

Example #1 (*Dagdha Rashis*)

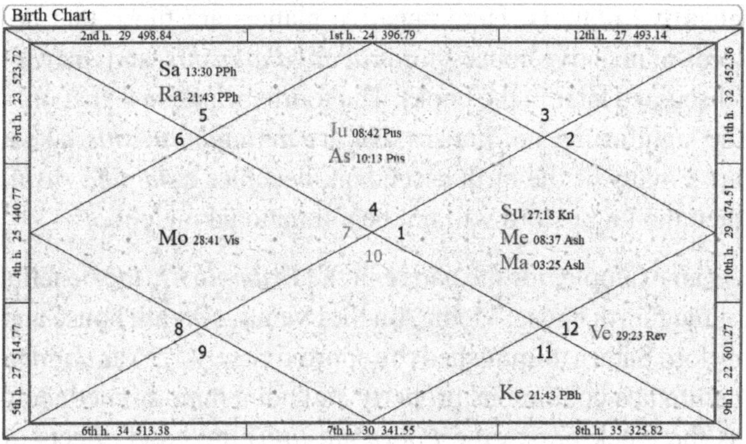

This native was born in the *tithi* of Krishna *paksha Prathama*. Hence, Libra and Capricorn become the *dagdha rashis* for this native. However, note that the native had just passed the *Poornima tithi* slightly, i.e., only around 12% of the *Prathama tithi* had passed. Hence, on the birth chart it looks that the native was born on a *Poornima*, when he was born slightly after the *Poornima tithi* had ended and the *Prathama tithi* had started. While a *Poornima tithi* birth would have given the native a birth with zero *dagdha rashis*, a slight difference of few hours in the time of birth gave the native a birth with two *dagdha rashis*. Hence, for precise predictions the exact *tithi* becomes very important.

Application Principles - A principle of *dagdha rashis* is that, if they fall in houses 3, 6, 8, 12, it is expected to give good results. The second principle of a *dagdha rashi* is that if falls in a good house, it spoils some results of that house. The third principle of dagdha *rashis* is that the lord of the *dagdha rashi* and the planets placed in that *rashi* carry the same blemish, **unless they are placed in negative houses**

(3,6,8,12), or negative *nakshatras*, i.e., *nakshatras* of negative planets. Here negative planets are those that are lords of negative houses, lords of *dagdha rashis*, and *Avayogi* (discussed later in the book). The fourth principle is that only the significances of houses that are in *dagdha rashis* take a hit. Finally, if the birth ascendant, becomes a *dagdha rashi*, then the Lagna lord will not be a functional malefic.

As an example, for the native in the *Example #1*, the benefits of the fourth house, Moon, 4th lord Venus, seventh house and its lord Saturn, diminished (by approximately 12% as *dagdha* nature is a continuous property and not a jump immediately as the clock passes the *Poornima tithi*) the good effects of the fourth house (home/homeland/motherly peace), seventh house (marriage and partnerships), Moon significance (all benefits related to mother, mind, emotions), and Venus (relationships, romance, arts). However, note that the Moon in 4th house is in the *nakshatra* of Jupiter (who is the 6th lord) – hence this will result in lessening the diminishing effect of Moon power. The native will be less emotional due to Moon (Lagna lord) being in *dagdha rashi* but some of it is restored by it being in Jupiter's *nakshatra*. He will mostly be away from home. Exalted Venus is in the *nakshatra* of Mercury (3rd lord and 12th lord) – hence this will result in lessening the diminishing effect of (exalted) Venusian power. Overall, Venus is good but will take some sheen of romantic life and home peace. Saturn (8th lord) in 2nd house is in the *nakshatra* of Venus who is *dagdha rashi* lord – hence this will result in lessening the negative effect of Saturn (as negative planet in negative *nakshatra*) on 7th house matters.

Example #2 (Dagdha Rashis)

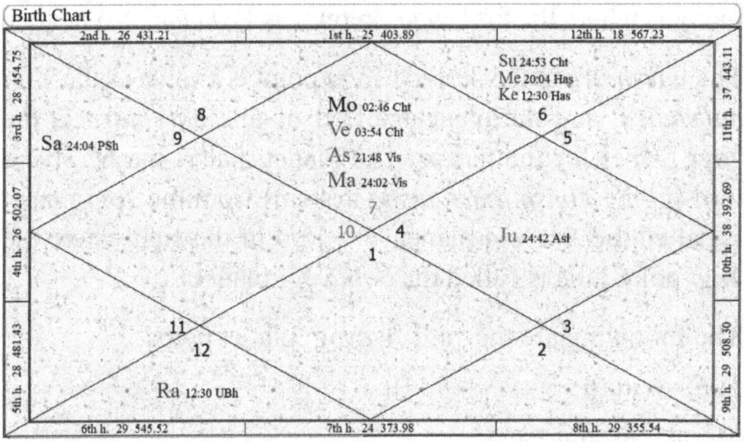

The native was born on the *Shukla paksha Pratipada*. Hence Libra (first house) and Capricorn (4th house) become the *dagdha rashis* for the native. Moon (*karaka* of emotions) and Venus (*karaka* of romance and marriage for the native) are burnt. Mars, the 7th lord is also in a *dagdha rashi*. Venus and Moon are in *nakshatra* of positive planet (so does not help). The native was not inclined towards romance in his life and did not get married. Since the 4th house is a *dagdha rashi*, the native did not enjoy peace of home and spent much of his life away from home.

6.3.3 – *Yogi, Avayogi*, and their Calculations

A *Yogi* planet promotes a native's material prosperity and fortune. An *Avayogi* planet indicates the opposite and is an obstructer to material prosperity.

To know the *Yogi* planet for a native, we first need to know the *Yoga* point for the native. The *Yoga* point is obtained by adding the longitudes of the Sun and the Moon and adding a fixed constant of 93d20' to the sum of the longitudes. 93d20' is the start location of the *Pushya nakshatra* (signifying mother) where the first *yoga* (known as *Vishkumbha*) begins.

The *nakshatra* at the derived *Yoga* point is known as the *Yogi nakshatra*, and the planetary lord of this *nakshatra* is the *Yogi* planet for the native. The planet that is the 6th *dasha* lord (in the *Vimshottari dasha* system) from the *Yogi* planet is called the *Avayogi* planet. The lord of the sign where the *Yogi* point falls is called the *Sahayogi* planet.

The following are the *Yogi-Avayogi* planet pairs.

Sun – Saturn

Moon – Mercury

Mars – Ketu

Mercury – Mars

Jupiter – Sun

Venus – Jupiter

Saturn – Moon

Rahu – Venus

Ketu – Rahu

Application Principles - A *Yogi* planet or *Avayogi* planet is considered well placed if they are in quadrant or trine houses. **Here, a house is based on the *Sripati* house system, and we assume the BC chart in this book as an approximation to the *Sripati* house system.** Note here, that the *Yoga* point calculation is not necessarily only about the Sripati house system – as it simply a calculation on longitudes. However, for prediction purposes ahead in this chapter using advanced concepts, we will work with the *Sripati* House system and its approximation, i.e., the Equal House *bhava chalit* chart. The *Yogi* and *Avayogi* planets for a native are considered not-so-well placed if they are placed in houses 3, 6, 8, and 12. They are considered neutrally placed if they are placed in houses 2 and 11. Similarly, houses 3, 6, 8, 12 here give better predictions according to the *Sripati* House system (or its approximation) – though it is not entirely faulty to use it on the birth chart house system, i.e., D1.

Yogi and *Avayogi* planets are strong if they are in their own sign, exalted, in their own *nakshatra*, and/or retrograde. They are also strong if they are in a positive *rashi*, *house*, or *nakshatra*. They are weak if they are debilitated (without getting *neechbhanga*) or combust. In order to gain on a material plane, the *Yogi* planet should be strong for a native, and the *Avayogi* planet should be weak (in negative house, *rashi*, or *nakshatra*). Conversely, to gain on a non-materialistic (spiritual) plane, the *Yogi* planet should be weak for a native, and the *Avayogi* planet should be strong. Note that if a *Yogi* planet is placed in a *dagdha rashi*, it will not lose its *yogi* character. However, if an *Avayogi* planet is placed in a *dagdha rashi*, then it will lose its power to cause obstruction to material prosperity.

In the *Yogi* friendship space, (Ketu, Moon, and Jupiter) are mutual friends, so are (Venus, Mars, Saturn), and so is (Sun, Rahu, Mercury). In any of these triplets, if any one planet becomes a *Yogi*, then the other two planets will take on a *Yogi* character.

Example #1 (Yogi-Avayogi)

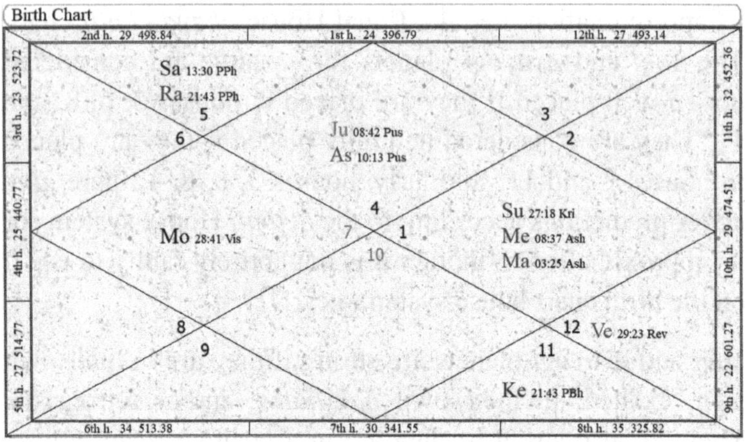

Equal House from Asc

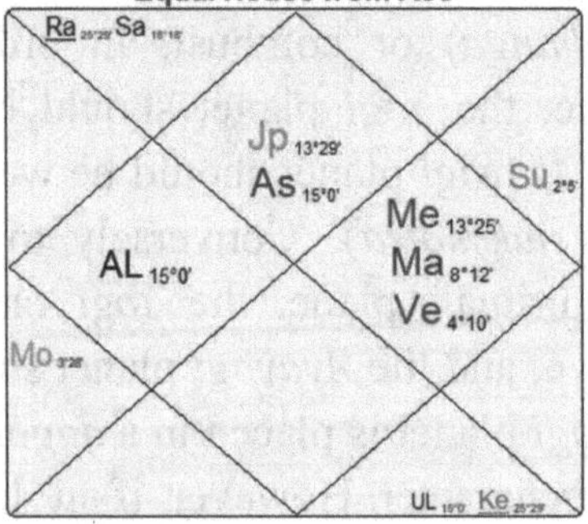

The *Yogi* planet for the native is **Jupiter**, as the Sun longitude is 27d18', the Moon longitude is 208d41', the constant additive factor is 93d20, adding all three gives 329d20'. This longitudinal point lies in Aquarius and in the *nakshatra* of Jupiter. Jupiter is placed in a positive *Yogi*-promoting *nakshatra*. The *Avayogi* planet for the native is **Sun** (6th *Vimshottari dasha* lord from Jupiter). Sun is placed in a negative *nakshatra* but is exalted in a positive house. Hence, the *Avayogi* power of Sun will be medium. The *Sahayogi* planet for the native is **Saturn**, as the *Yoga* point lies in Aquarius. Saturn (lord of a *dagdha rashi*) is in a negative *nakshatra*, positive house, and a non-negative *rashi*. Saturn *Yogi* power is medium.

The *Yogi* planet lies exalted in the first house (very good for native to quench materialistic desires). Surprisingly, since Jupiter, Ketu, and Moon form a triplet, Ketu also supports the native to achieve his materialistic desires (though in principle Ketu is considered a non-materialistic planet). In the ongoing Ketu *mahadasha* (MD), the native is indeed blessed with achieving on the materialistic front relatively more than what Ketu usually signifies. In addition, Ketu is in the *nakshatra* of Jupiter, that is a well-placed *Yogi* planet. The *Avayogi* planet is also exalted in the 11th house and is strong, hence it is very good for the native to boost the spiritual life of the native in its MD later in life that will be catalyzed by materialistic lifestyle outcomes. The *Sahayogi* planet is neutrally placed and of moderate *Yogi* strength.

6.3.4 – Advanced Concepts in *Navamsa* Analysis

We use concepts mentioned in Sections 6.3.1 to 6.3.3 to analyze areas of a native's life using the D9.

Example #1 **(Advanced *Navamsa* Analysis)**

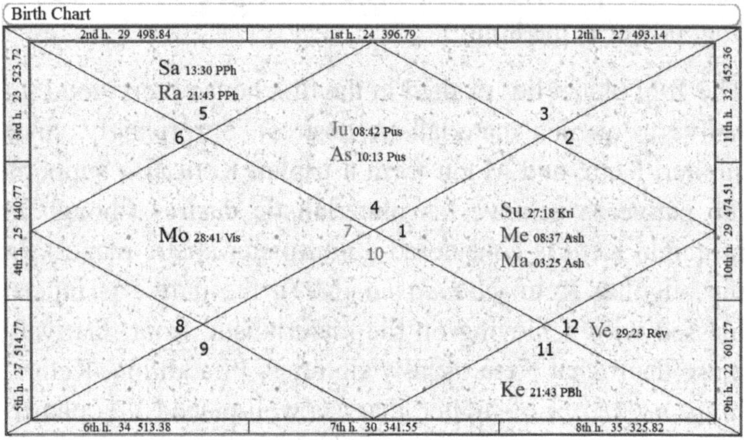

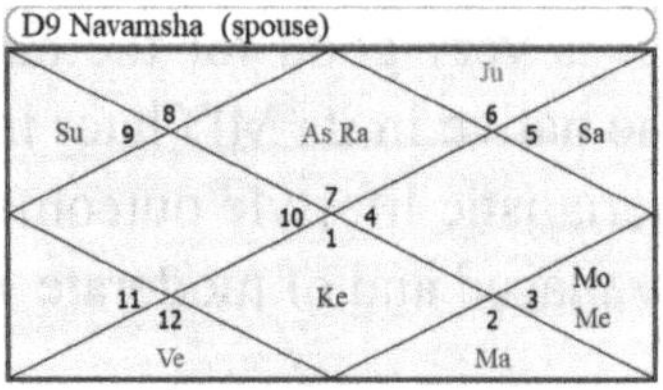

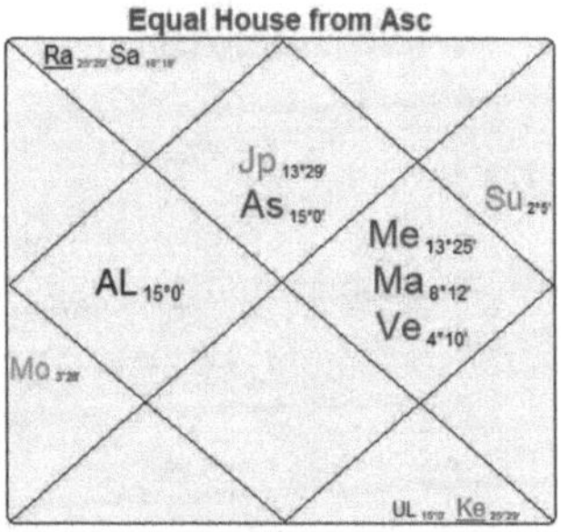

Let us analyze **wealth aspects** for this native using some advanced concepts discussed in Section 6.3. The *Yogi* planet is Jupiter who is the significator of wealth. Its placement in *Sahayogi's nakshatra* gives great *Yogi* power. The *Avayogi* planet is Sun who is the lord of the wealth house for the native. Jupiter is exalted in House 1 (of the BC) for the native and promotes wealth accumulation, on the other hand Sun that is also exalted and in the 11th house (of the BC) promotes the non-accumulation of wealth on one hand but is also in negative *nakshatra* promoting wealth accumulation to some extent. Sun also aspects Moon (mind significator). Since the *shadbal* of Sun is greater than Jupiter, there will be more non-accumulation mindset compared to accumulation. Saturn is the *Sahayogi* planet and placed in the 2nd house of the BC chart but is the lord of a *dagdha rashi* for the native – however, it is also placed in a negative *nakshatra* (good). Rahu with Saturn takes up Yogi power. In addition, 11th lord Venus is exalted but also a lord of the *dagdha rashi* – though 11th house significance is not affected. From D1/BC, it can be inferred that **the native has mixed interests in monetary wealth but is very interested in gains.**

In D9, the 2nd lord Sun of D1 goes to 9th from its own position (good), is in the *Ariamsa* (good), and is the 11th lord of D9. However, the Sun is an *Avayogi* planet for the native and its good placement implies more obstruction to accumulating wealth. It is also placed in the *nakshatra* of the *Avayogi* planet (good for wealth). The *bhava madhya* of the 2nd house (of BC chart) is at 8d53' in Leo that falls in the Gemini *navamsa*. The second lord from the Gemini *navamsa* is Sun that is an *Avayogi* planet for the native and well placed with strength in the D1 and the D9 (not good for wealth) – but in a negative (*Avayogi's*) *nakshatra* (good for wealth). Hence, mixed effects with bias to a non-accumulative monetary mindset.

Jupiter, the *Yogi* planet goes to the 12th house of D9 (not good), and in the *Vikramsa* (not good). Saturn the *Sahayogi* planet is *Vargottama*, in the *Labhamsa* (good) but in the *navamsa* of a *Avayogi* planet (not good for wealth accumulation). In D1, Saturn (lord of *dagdha rashi*) is in the *nakshatra* of exalted Venus who is *Vargottama* and the 11th lord (good) but is also the lord of a *dagdha rashi* (good as negative planet placed in negative *nakshatra*). Venus is in *nakshatra* of negative planet Mercury (good) who is conjunct *Yogi* promoter Moon (good). Venus is also the lord of the *navamsa* (Taurus) of the *bhava madhya* point (7d34') of the 11th house (in the BC chart). The 11th lord from Taurus is Mercury who is conjunct with the *Avayogi* planet in D1 (not good) and is aspected by *Avayogi* planet in the D9 chart (not good). Note here that only placement of a negative planet in a negative house, *rashi* or *nakshatra* is considered positive. Conjunction (aspect) of negative planet with (on) negative planet does not make the situation positive. In addition, the native does not have major *dhana yogas* in the D1 or the D9 charts; however, has multiple *raja yogas* and *mahapurusha yogas* in D1 and the D9 charts.

It is evident **from (counting the #good vs #not goods)** the D1 and D9 analysis that the **native is much more interested in fame, authority, and prestige when compared to accumulating money.** The native has a decent amount of monetary wealth that is below excess but enough to make native enjoy his life. He strives for gains towards fame/ authority.

Example #2 (Advanced *Navamsa* Analysis)

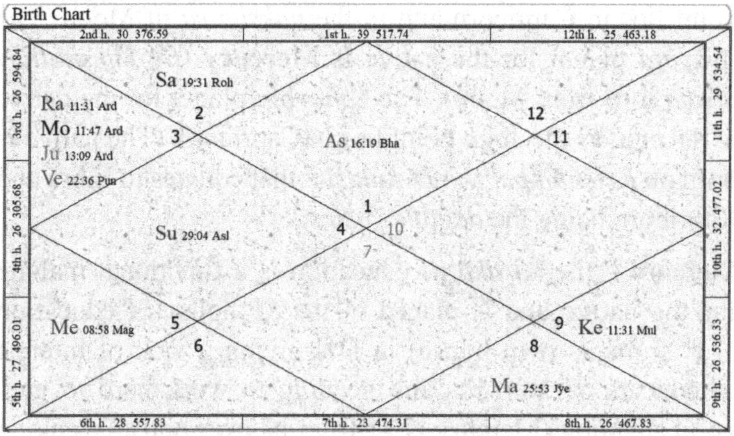

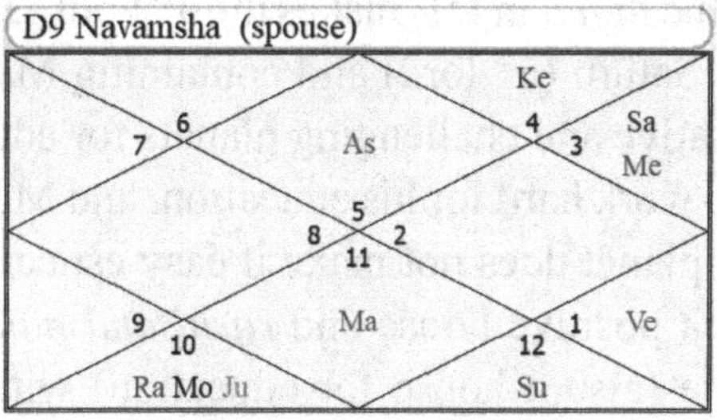

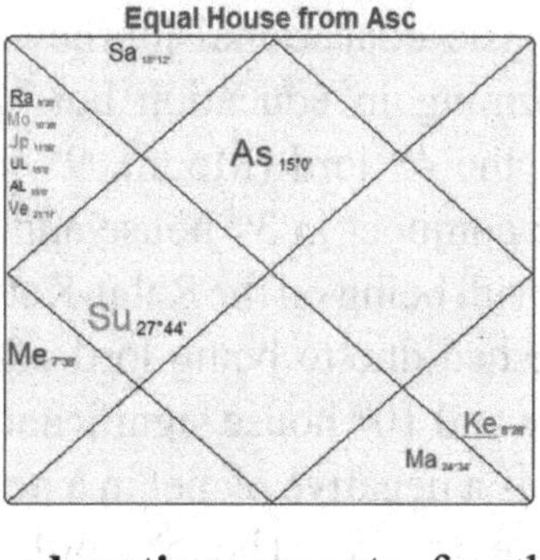

Let us analyze **education aspects** for this native using advanced concepts discussed in Section 6.3.

The *Yogi* planet for the native is **Moon**. This longitudinal point lies in Capricorn and in the *nakshatra* of Moon. The *Avayogi* planet for the native is **Mercury** (6th *Vimshottari dasha* lord from Moon). The *Sahayogi* planet for the native is **Saturn**, as the *Yoga* point lies in Capricorn. The native is born on *Krishna paksha Dwadashi*, that equates to Libra and Capricorn being the *dagdha rashis*.

Mercury – the *karaka* of education is a functional malefic for the native and is placed in the 5th house of education (12th from its own house) in D1, giving a lack of interest in educational pursuits and needing to work hard to gain good standing (Mercury is 3rd from its own house). Making Mercury as the *lagna* in D1, makes the 4th house from it being aspected by Saturn (6th lord) and containing Mars (9th lord) – both separative and challenging planets for education. The native has to work hard for his education, and Mercury being the *Avayogi* planet does not make it easy especially when it is placed in a positive house and *rashi and nakshatra*. The second house (also a house for education) with Saturn (in *Yogi's nakshatra*) and aspected by Mars from the 8th house does not make basic educational journey easy – will give hurdles in performing in education but will sail through. Also, in the D1, the 4th lord (Moon), 9th lord (Jupiter), 2nd lord (Venus), are conjunct in 3rd house and in a *paapkartari* formation along with being on the Rahu-Ketu axis. Venus and Saturn are blemished due to being lord of *dagdha rashis* – but only 7th house and 10th house significances suffer, not the 2nd house. Venus is a negative planet in a negative nakshatra, in negative house (good). The 5th lord of college level education and creativity in general (needed in education) is in the *Ashlesha nakshatra* whose lord Mercury is an *Avayogi* planet for the native, and a functional malefic. A basic review of D1 says that **the native has had lot of hurdles in primary and middle school education to perform but sailed through.**

In D9, the 2nd lord of D1 (Venus) (lord of a *dagdha rashi* that takes some sheen off Venus's 7th house prowess) goes in *Lagnamsa* (good), moves 11 positions relative to its position in D1 (good), is in the 9th house of D9 (good), and is the 10th lord of D9 (neutral, being a natural benefic) and also the 3rd lord of D9 (not good). In D9, the 4th lord of D1 (Moon) is a *Yogi* planet (good) that goes to *Karmamsa* (good), is with Jupiter (5th lord of D9) who supports *Yogi* power (good) that is boosted by Rahu and Moon but is the 12th lord (not good). Moon is not placed in positive *nakshatra* or house in D1. The *karaka* of education, Mercury (the *Avayogi* planet) is in the *Vikramsa* (not good) is with a *Yogi* supporter Ketu and *Sahayogi* Saturn (good) – with Saturn being lord of a *dagdha rashi* and placed in positive *nakshatra* and negative house in BC (mixed), is on the node axis (not good), Mercury (*karaka*) moving 11 places in D9 relative to its position in D1 (good) and is in the 11th house and 11th lord (good).

The 4th house *bhava madhya* is at 97d11' in Cancer and falls in the Virgo *navamsa* that is lorded by *Avayogi* planet Mercury. The 4th lord from Virgo *navamsa* is lorded by Jupiter that promotes *Yogi* power but is debilitated (getting no *neechbhanga* in D9) and is in negative house. The 4th house from Virgo is aspected by *Avayogi* planet Mercury, is on the Rahu/Ketu axis, but supported by *Sahayogi* Saturn's aspect who is with *Yogi* promoter Ketu for the native. A microscopic look into the D9 chart confirms that **the native has had lot of hurdles in primary and middle school education to perform, but because of a mixed strength**

of educational parameters, cleared school exams though without pomp, and with hard work.

6.3.5 – Finer Assessment using D9 Dispositors

One must note that the sign in which planets and the ascendant lie in the D9 chart are nothing but *rashis* whose lords are lords of the *nakshatra padas* where the corresponding planet is placed in the D1 chart. Hence, the placement (and association) strengths of these lords primarily in the D1 (and to some extent in the D9) are of paramount importance in judging the effects of planets placed in a *nakshatra pada*. Realize that the *nakshatra pada* lord contributes to the most fine-grained predictions in D1 and D9.

Consider a planet (and/or ascendant) placed in any sign in the D9 chart. The strength of the lord (dispositor) of that particular sign in the D1 chart contributes to the quality of the planet's lordship in the D1 chart and the subsequent quality of the results contributed by the lordship. As an example, if the ascendant lord in D9 is Venus, then the placement strength of Venus in the D1 chart adds corresponding strength and influence on the ascendant matter (personality) of the native. In general, **if the quality of the ruler of a house in D1 is to be judged**, then the following principles should be applied in relation to the D9 lord of the ruler of that house.

(i) If the D9 lord is in *kendra* or *trikon* from D1 ascendant, very good results could be expected of the house matters in D1.

(ii) If the D9 lord is in *exaltation*, *mooltrikon*, own house, or in the house of a friend in the D1 chart, then good results can be expected of the house matters in D1.

(iii) If the D9 lord is in 6, 8, 12 houses in the D1 chart, or in debilitation, enemy signs, or aspected by natural malefics, then unfavourable results might be expected of the house matters in D1 (one would need to check for *neechbhanga/vipareeta raja yogas* for mitigation of negative effects).

(iv) If the D9 lord of 2, 5, 11 lords in D1 are exalted/ *mooltrikon*/friendly house state in D1 and is in PAC with 9th house or its lord, native would be a scholar, famous, arts lover, creative, and attractive.

Please note that the dispositor strength of a D9 house in the D1 also influences the matters of the corresponding house(s) in the D9 chart of which the dispositor is the lord. Also note that the overall fine-grained quality of results of any house in the D1/D9 chart is also dependent on PAC relationships alongside the dispositor strengths mentioned above. Let us work out a few examples.

Example #1

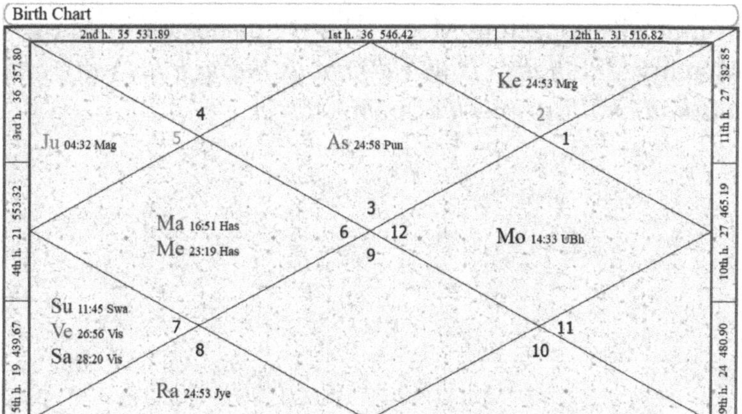

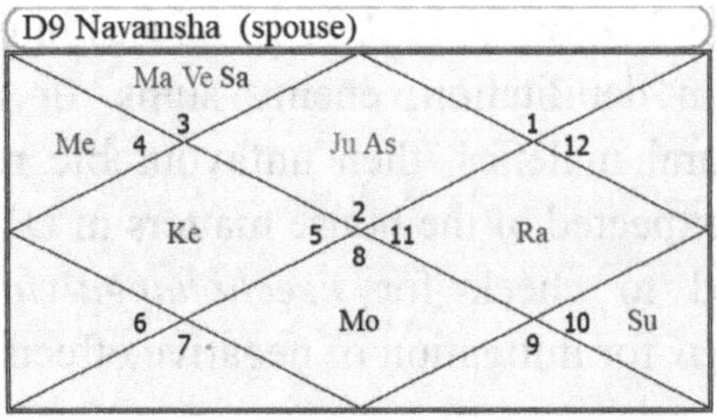

Consider the career of this native. The 10th lord in D1 is Jupiter that is placed in the Taurus *navamsa* (ruled by Venus) and is in the *lagna* of D9. Venus is in his own and *mooltrikon* house in the D1 chart; is in a D1 *trikon*; and with friend Saturn who is exalted, and with enemy Sun who is debilitated. Saturn is placed in the Gemini *navamsa* and lord (dispositor) Mercury (a karaka of career) is in *kendra*, own, and *mooltrikon* house in D1. It is conjunct with Mars whose D9 dispositor is Mercury. If we consider Saturn also as a *karaka* of career of a native (10th house has multi-*karakas*), Saturn is placed in a *trikon* and its exalted sign in D1. The D9 dispositor of Saturn is Mercury that is exalted in D1 and in a *kendra* house. Mercury is conjunct with the D9 dispositor of mutually aspecting Moon. The D9 dispositor of Mars is Mercury. *The native is world-famous through his work and has had an illustrious leadership career.*

Example #2

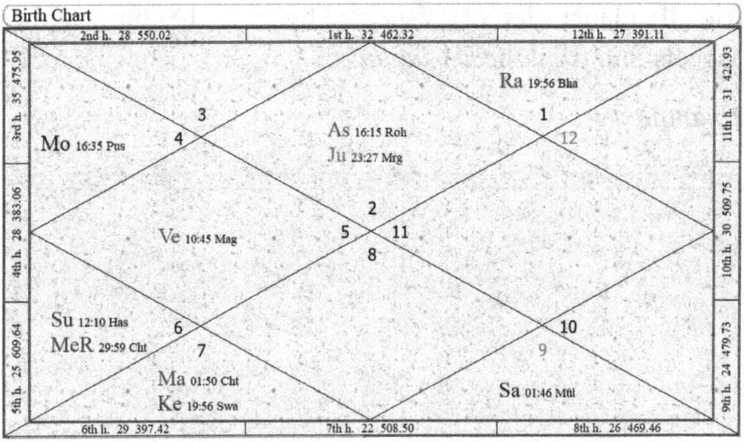

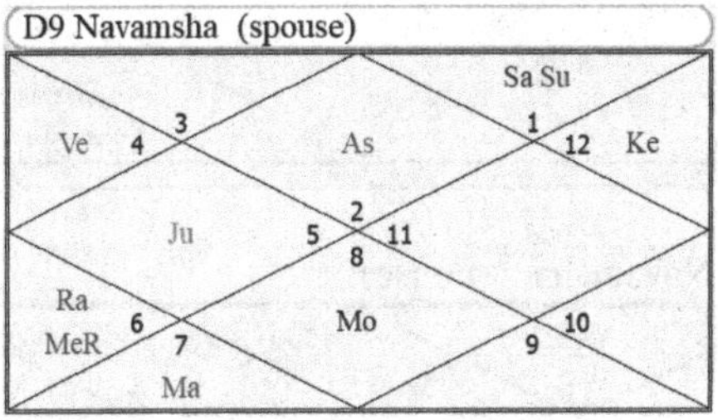

Consider the speech of this native. The 2nd lord in D1 is Mercury (also *karaka* of speech) that is placed *vargottama* in the Virgo *navamsa* (ruled by Mercury). Mercury (2nd lord and the 5th lord in D1) is placed in a *trikon* in the D9, in its own *mooltrikon* (and exalted) sign, is aspected by 9th and 10th lord (and friend) Saturn and is conjunct 4th lord (and friend) Sun. *The native had one of the finest voices and used it very creatively and intelligently to mesmerize audiences worldwide.* Jupiter being the 11th lord in D1 aspects the 5th house and the 2nd lord Mercury. Jupiter is also placed in the *lagna* giving a persona that wants to widely reach out to the world in the lifetime. The D9 dispositor of Jupiter is Sun who is placed in a *trikon* house in D1 conjunct exalted and friendly planet Mercury, aspected by 9th lord Saturn. Jupiter aspects Sun from the D1 *lagna*.

Example #3

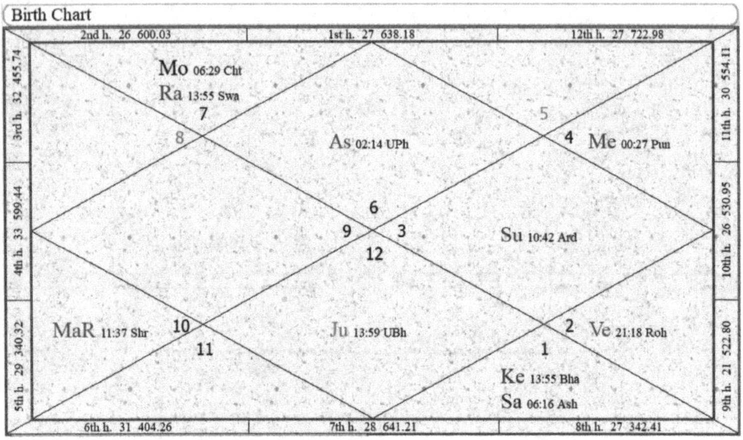

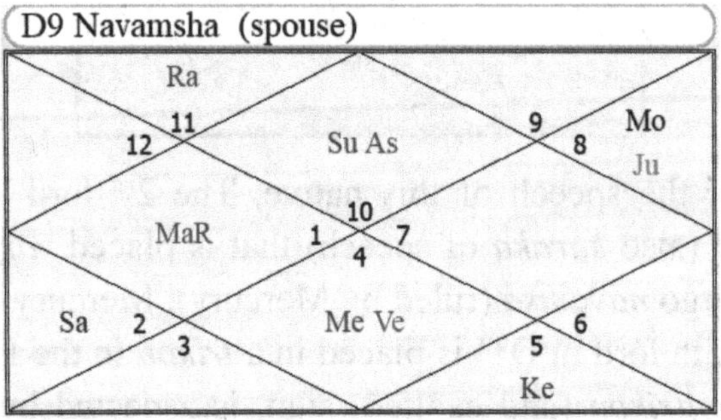

Consider the creative personality of this native. Mercury is the *lagna* lord in D1, it is in the 11th house and aspects the 5th house of creativity. Mercury is in Moon's *navamsa* who is ill-placed with Rahu in D1 in the 2nd house. It is however aspected by 5th lord Saturn. The native was a playback singer but did not get recognition as a singer. The 11th lord's *navamsa* is owned by Mars that is placed in its exaltation sign in D1 and is aspected by *lagna* lord Mercury. Mars is also placed in the 5th house of creativity in D1, and Mercury is the 9th lord from the Moon. Saturn acting as 5th lord is in *Parivartan yoga* with the 8th and 3rd lord Mars (placed in the 5th house) in D1. The native though a non-famous singer, was one of the best, creative music composers India has ever produced.

Example #4

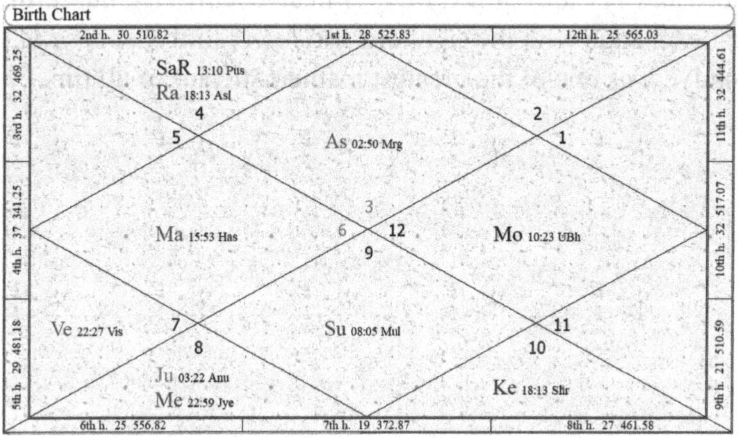

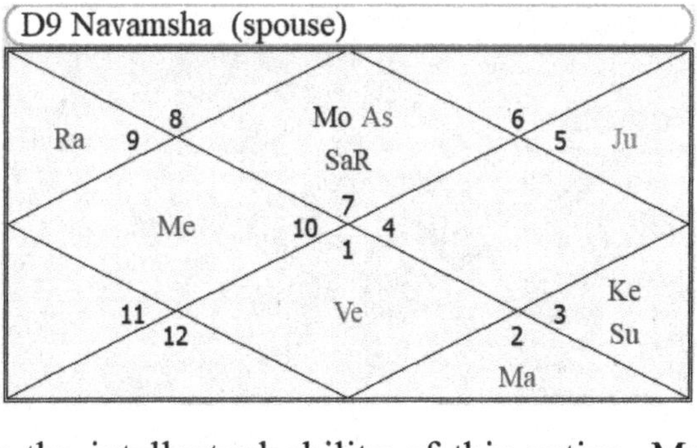

Consider the intellectual ability of this native. Mercury is the *lagna* lord in D1 (and also the karaka of intellectual ability) and forms a *Parivartan yoga* with 11th lord Mars.

The 5th lord Venus (also the *karaka* of creativity) is in its own house (*trikon*) in D1 and unafflicted. Venus is in the *navamsa* of Mars, i.e., D9 dispositor of Venus in Mars. Mars in D1 is placed in a *kendra* house in D1 and is mutually aspected by the 2nd lord Moon from the 10th house and is aspected by 9th lord Saturn from the 2nd house. This Mars and Saturn combination gave discipline driven prolific working ability to the native. Venus is the D9 dispositor of the 2nd lord and 11th lord of D1. Mars is in an enemy sign but forms an exchange with the sign lord and *lagna* lord Mercury. The native was one of the greatest mathematicians of all time.

CHAPTER 7

Timing of Events Using D9 and *Vimshottari Dashas*

In the previous chapter, we discussed, via examples, the steps to judge a D9 chart. This analysis gives us precise inference about the static elements of a birth horoscope such as personality, health, wealth, career etc. In this chapter, we go a step deeper to judge the dynamic elements of a birth horoscope, i.e., the **timing of events**, as promised by the D1 and the D9.

The timing of events judgement usually consists of **two main parts**: the primary part which is the *Vimshottari dasha* analysis, and the secondary part which is the transit analysis. The *Vimshottari dasha* analysis showcases in which *dasha* periods an event in the life of a native is most likely to happen. As the *jyotish* legend, Shri K. N. Rao states – *dasha disha dikhati hai,* no life event can be predicted without a detailed analysis of its promise shown via a *dasha* analysis. The transit analysis further narrows down the event fructification period. In this chapter, we only discuss *dasha* promise of events in the D1 and the D9 and leave a transits analysis to Chapter 8.

An important point to remember here is that *dasha* promise always dictates what the transit periods can deliver. **If the *dasha* period is not favorable, transits will not help in fructification of an event.** From the author's experience, students often fashionably speak about transits in general as if they are the ones fructifying the event. This is incorrect. Transits only deliver results that *dasha* periods promise. So, predicting timing of events based upon transits, without judging the *dasha* and *antardasha* periods a native is a wrong thought process.

7.1 – The Factors Required for *Dasha* Analysis

There are five primary requirements to judge in both the D1 and the D9 charts:

(i) The houses governing the event should astrologically associate with the MD and AD lords.

(ii) The *bhavat bhavam* (BB) of the houses governing the event should associate with the MD and AD lords (the BB of a particular house is the storeroom of effects pertaining to that given house).

(iii) The Lagna lord (LL) and/or the first house should associate with the houses governing the event (after all the body and personality has an integral role to play in everything we do in life).

(iv) The natural *karaka* **of the event should associate with the MD and AD lords, and**

(v) The mutual house distance between the MD and AD lords, their mutual relationships, and their relationship with the LL should be favourable to ensure smoothness in the event fructification process.

7.2 – The Decision Logic of Timing with Examples

The more the number of requirements that are satisfied, greater the chances of event fructification (in a smooth manner) within the MD/AD period. **The relative importance between the D1 and the D9 charts of satisfying these requirements is roughly in the ratio of 60:40 (as per K. N. Rao).** The principle to remember here is that things are additive towards better event fructification possibility. Out of the five requirements, at least three should be satisfied in both the D1 and the D9 to give fair confidence to the success of an event occurrence.

We also emphasize here that LL usually pertains to the first house of the D1 chart, **unless** LL is an enemy of both the dispositors of the Sun and the Moon. In this case, using the *Sudarshan Paddhati* **mentioned in the classic** Parashari *dasha* **system treatise (applied along with** *Laghu Parashari* principles*)*, the first house should be considered from the Moon if not from both (preferred) the Sun and the Moon. We leave principles on the *Laghu Parashari* to the reader (and assume its knowledge), and do not cover it in this book. We now cover a few example applications.

Example #1 (*Dasha* Analysis on Childbirth)

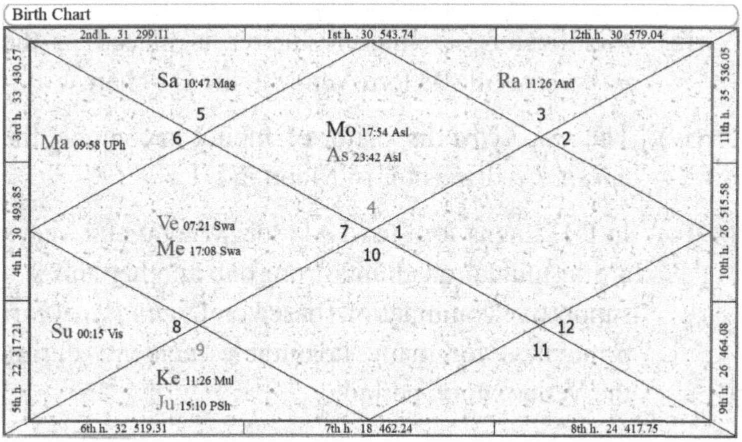

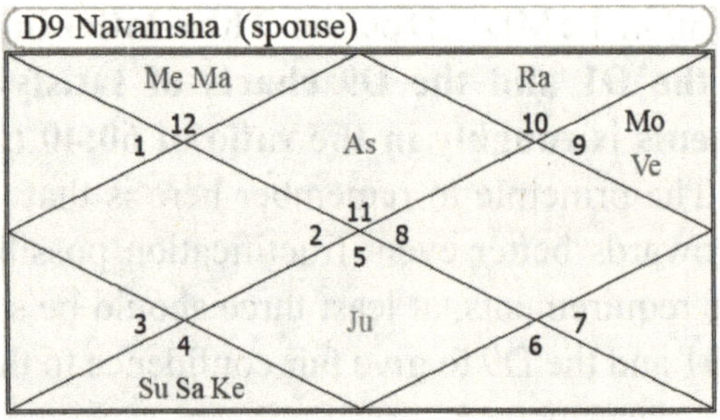

In this example, we analyze the event of the native giving birth to a child in the Venus/Moon **period**, i.e., in the Venus MD and Moon AD. The houses under consideration are the first house, the 5th house, and the 9th house (i.e., the BB of the 5th house). Let us list down how the MD and the AD lords connect with these houses.

(i) In D1, Lagna lord (and AD lord) Moon is placed in the *nakshatra* of Mercury who is conjunct MD lord Venus.

(ii) In D1, the *nakshatra* lord of MD lord Venus is aspected by Jupiter – the significator of children, and who is also the 9th lord.

(iii) Significator of children Jupiter is placed in the *nakshatra* of MD lord Venus in the D1 chart.

(iv) The *nakshatra* dispositor of Jupiter is conjunct the *nakshatra* dispositor of Moon in D1.

(v) In D1, Lagna lord (and AD lord) Moon and Venus are in mutual quadrants from one another and is a supportive combination (based on *Laghu Parashari* principles) for many favourable incidents during the Venus/Moon period.

(vi) In D1, the fifth house from Jupiter is aspected by Venus (MD lord).

(vii) In the D9, both Moon (AD lord) and Venus (MD lord) are placed in the sign of Jupiter – the significator of children, and Moon and Venus are also aspected by Jupiter.

(viii) In the D9, Jupiter is placed in 9th house from both Moon and Venus (if we make the MD and AD lords as *lagna*).

(ix) In the D9, the 5th lord from the MD and AD lords is Mars that is placed in the sign of Jupiter (significator of child).

(x) The *Rashi-Tulya Navamsa* has Mars (as 5th lord of D1) in the *Bhagyamsa*, and Jupiter in the *Arthamsa*.

(xi) The *Yogi* planet for the native is Moon and the *Sahayogi* planet is Venus. Hence, Jupiter also enjoys *Yogi* power due to the triplet rule. In addition, Mars (as 5th lord in D1) is friends with Venus in triplet rule for the *Yogi* concept.

Overall, the Venus/Moon period is conducive to childbirth for the native (even though the chart of the partner needs to be analyzed also). It is very important to note that certain factors will not support childbirth – **however, it is always about how many factors support versus how many do not.** Hence, significant number of factors supporting a life event will boost the chances of occurrence of that event. Moreover, the placement of planets in *shubh/ashubh panchak*, *yogas* determines quality of fructification of events, **i.e., whether there will be struggles or smoothness in the fructification of events.**

Example #2 (*Dasha* Analysis on Higher Education)

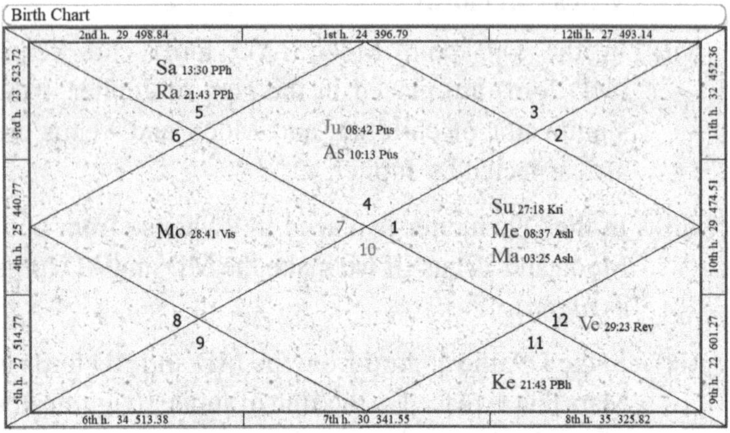

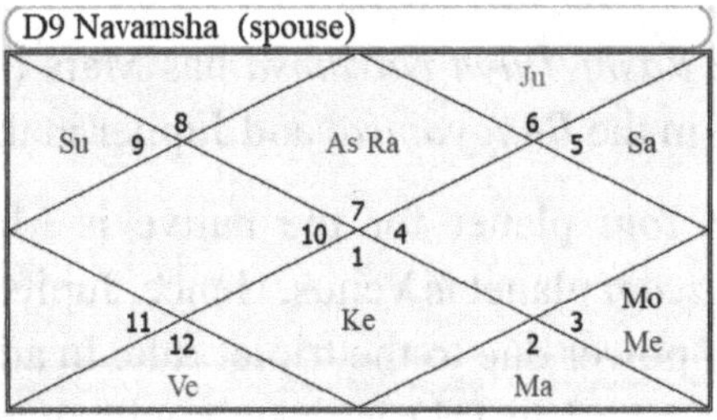

In this example, we analyze the event of the native getting his PhD degree in the Mercury/Rahu **period**, i.e., in the Mercury MD and Rahu AD.

The primary houses under consideration are the first house, the 8th house (for research as the degree concerned is the PhD), the third house (being the BB of the 8th house), the 9th house, and the 5th house (being the BB of the 9th house). Let us list down how the MD and the AD lords connect with these houses.

(i) In D1, Lagna lord Moon is mutually aspecting MD lord Mercury (3rd lord in the D1 chart).

(ii) Jupiter placed in the first house is in a *vidya bal* (i.e., strength of learning ability) combination with Mercury in the D1, i.e., Mercury is placed 8 houses from its *Mooltrikon* position in D1, and the 8th house from the placement of Mercury is aspected by Jupiter (his 5th house aspect) – providing immense intelligence in academics. Mercury is MD lord.

(iii) In D1, the *nakshatra* lord of MD lord is ruled by Ketu (who is the significator of research and co-lord of the 8th house of the *kaalpurush kundali*) and is conjunct the 5th lord Mars who is *yogakaraka*.

(iv) The dispositor of Rahu (AD lord) is exalted and placed in conjunction with Mercury (3rd lord) and Mars (5th lord). Rahu is also conjunct Saturn who is the *nakshatra* lord of the birth *lagna*, and influences *lagna* lord Moon as Saturn aspects Moon in D1.

(v) Significator of higher education Jupiter forms *vidya bal* with Mercury (MD lord) in the D1 chart and is placed in the *nakshatra* of the 8th lord Saturn who influences the 10th house (where Mercury is placed) as dispositor of Saturn is placed in the 10th house. Jupiter is also the 9th lord of the native in D1, is exalted and associated with Mercury. Saturn is also the 7th lord of *pada praapti* for the native (earning a PhD is an example of *pada praapti* in higher education)

(vi) In the D1 chart, if we make Mercury (MD lord) as the Lagna, then the 5th lord Sun is conjunct Mercury; LL and 8th lord Mars is Mercury is conjunct Mercury; 9th lord Jupiter is influencing Mercury.

(vii) In the D1 chart, if we make AD lord Rahu as the Lagna, then it is conjunct the 7th lord (Saturn) of *pada prapti*, with LL exalted in the 9th house. The 8th lord (exalted) Jupiter aspects the 8th house that has exalted 3rd lord Venus. The 9th house has the 9th lord Mars, 11th lord (of gains) Mercury, and LL Sun placed in it.

(viii) In the D9 chart, Jupiter (significator of higher education) and the 3rd lord aspects the Lagna lord (Venus).

(ix) In the D9 chart, the MD lord is the 9th lord and is placed in his own sign in the 9th house, and is aspected by the 11th lord Sun. There is a *vidya bal* combination between Jupiter and Mercury (MD lord) in the D9 chart.

(x) In the D9 chart, if we make the house containing Mercury (MD lord) as the first house, we observe the 3rd lord (Sun) aspecting the first house and its lord.

(xi) In the D9 chart, if we make the house containing Rahu (AD lord) as the first house, the dispositor (who is the 8th lord) is aspected by Jupiter (who is significator of higher learning) who is the 3rd house lord, and aspects his own house, and also aspects Mars who is the 7th lord of *pada praapti.*

(xii) In the D1, MD lord, Mercury, forms *Saraswati yoga* and *Brahma yoga* (both excellent for scholarly pursuits) with exalted Jupiter, (significator of higher education and placed in *lagna*) and exalted Venus (placed in 9th house of higher learning).

Mercury also forms the *Nipuna yoga* with exalted Sun in 10th house, *Chaamara yoga* with Venus which is again excellent for higher learning. There are several yogas in D9 as well like *Nipuna yoga, Chaamara yoga, Brahma yoga* and *vipareet raja yoga* supporting scholarly pursuits besides other events.

(xiii) In the *Rashi-Tulya Navamsa* chart, the Lagna lord Moon is placed in the *Vyamsa* (good for doing PhD studies in a foreign country, but with success struggles) and conjunct MD lord Mercury in his own house (very good), the *lagna* moves to the *Sukhamsa* (good) and is with Rahu (AD lord); Rahu is in trine with MD lord and allows the native to be successful in solving difficult intellectual challenges characteristic of PhD studies; Ketu (significator of research) goes to the *Karmamsa* (good) and is on the MD lord axis; the 9th lord goes into the *Vikramsa* (good for scholarly pursuits) and aspects dispositor of AD lord Rahu. The 8th lord Saturn who is placed in *Labhamsa* aspects AD lord Rahu.

(xiv) The native has Mercury and Rahu in the same *Yogi* triplet as Sun who is a *Avayogi* planet but placed in the *nakshatra* of the *Avayogi* planet (good). Moreover, Rahu (AD lord and a natural malefic) is placed in the *nakshatra* of a negative planet (Venus – lord of a *dagdha rashi*) provides boost to materialistic outcome fortunes. Mercury (MD lord who is 3rd lord and 12th lord) is in the *nakshatra* of Ketu (a natural malefic, but a *Yogi* power planet). Hence, Mercury will promote materialistic outcomes in his MD.

Overall, the Mercury/Rahu period (and favorable *yogas*) has been instrumental for the native getting his PhD degree during this period.

Example #3 (*Dasha* Analysis on Career)

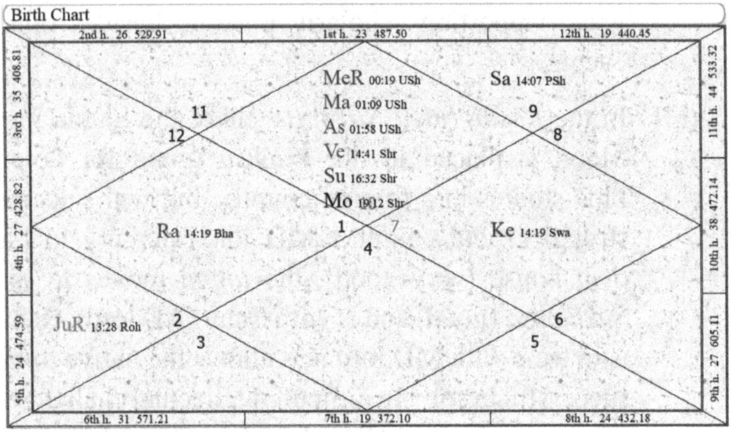

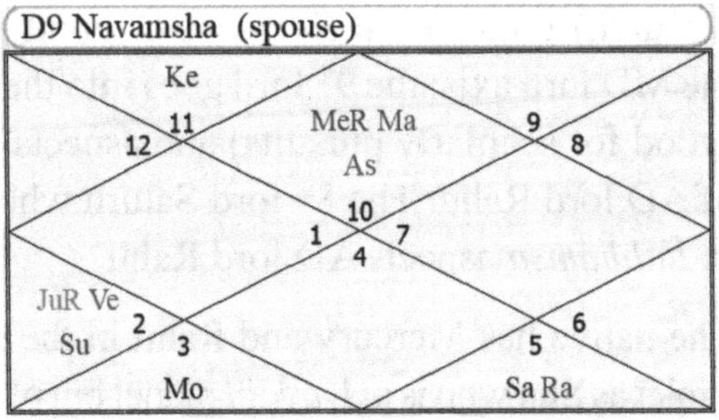

In this example, we analyze the event of the native starting to rise in his career in it in the Rahu/Moon period and excelled in the Jupiter MD **period** respectively, i.e., in the Rahu MD and Moon AD periods followed by the Jupiter MD.

The primary houses under consideration are the first house, the 6th house (for research as the degree concerned is the PhD), the 10th house, and the 7th house (the BB of the 10th house and the house of *pada praapti*). Let us list down how the MD and the AD lords connect with these houses.

(i) In the D1, the 10th house lord, Venus is in the first house. Venus (10L) is conjunct with Mercury (9L) forming *dharam-karamadhipati yoga*. The 7th lord is also in the first house. The dispositor of MD lord Mars (forming *ruchaka yoga*) is conjunct with the 10th lord, the 7th lord, and the 6th lord/9th lord in the first house.

(ii) In the D1, the AD lord Moon is in the first house and conjunct the 10th lord, the 7th lord, and the 6th lord.

(iii) In the D1, making the house where Rahu is placed as the first house, we get dispositor in 10th house, with 4th lord who is conjunct 7th lord and 5th lord, and aspected by 9th lord Jupiter.

(iv) In the D9, the 10th lord, Venus is in a trine house, in its own house, moves 5 houses relative to its position in D1, and aspected by Saturn who is conjunct MD lord Rahu. Moon is placed in the 6th house and is also the 7th lord.

(v) In the D9, making the house where Rahu is placed as the first house, we get the dispositor placed in the 10th house with the 10th lord. Rahu is conjunct the 6th lord and the 7th lord. Moon (AD lord) is placed in 11th from Rahu. Jupiter who is conjunct the 10th lord goes to *Putramsa* (good) aspects 11th house and the first house giving a very good career and gains overall during the Jupiter MD.

(vi) In D1, Jupiter is in the *nakshatra* of the 7th lord who is placed in the first house and conjunct the 10th lord, 7th lord, and the 6th lord.

(vii) In the D1, making the house where Jupiter is placed as the first house, we get Jupiter aspecting the 9th house, the 6th lord, the 7th lord, and is the 11th lord.

(viii) In the D9, Jupiter is conjunct 10th lord, aspects the first house, the 9th lord and the 11th lord. Jupiter is *vargottama*, and so is the 10th lord and so is the 9th lord and the 11th lord.

(ix) In the D9, making the house where Jupiter is placed as the first house, we get Jupiter conjunct the 6th lord (Venus) aspecting the 9th house, the 5th lord, and the 7th lord.

(x) In the *Rashi-Tulya Navamsa* chart, Rahu goes to *Nidhanamsa* (not good) and Moon goes into the *Ariamsa* (not good). Hence native struggled during the Rahu MD period (breaks and sudden changes) towards a good career as Saturn who is conjunct Rahu (good for the native) aspects 10th house.

(xi) In D1, several noteworthy *yogas* form, like *Ruchaka yoga, Vosi, Kaahala, Trilochana, Nipuna, Chandra-mangala, Dharam-Karamadhipati yoga, Vipreet raj yoga* which support the native in his career and shape native's stellar personality. Several *yogas* like *Ruchaka, Brahma, Kalanidhi, Chaamara, vipreet raja yoga* form in D9 as well, further supporting the native in his career goals.

Overall, the Rahu/Moon and Jupiter periods (and favorable *yogas*) have been instrumental for the native getting a boost and stability in his career.

We finally conclude this chapter with a case study on marriage (an integral aspect of D9 analysis). *Our detailed analysis in this section will act as a blueprint of analyzing charts in Chapter 9 where we will provide practice case studies for students.*

Example #4 (*Dasha* Analysis on Marriage)

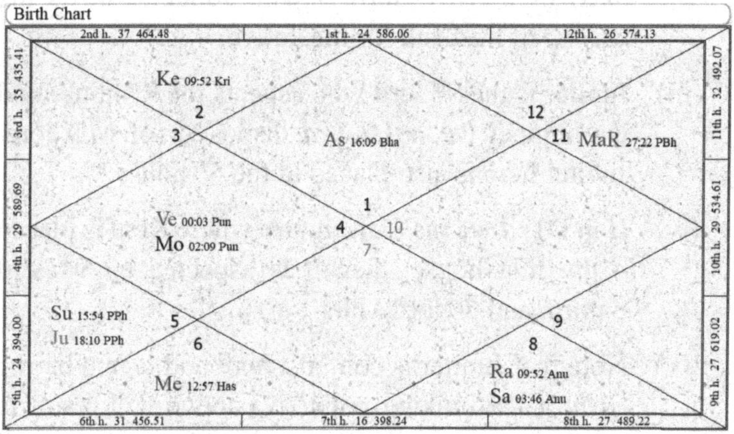

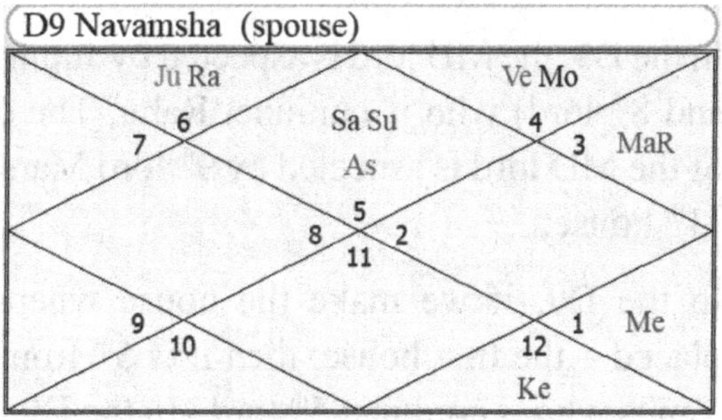

In this example, we analyze the event of the native marrying in the Ketu/Venus period, i.e., in the Ketu MD and Venus AD periods.

The primary houses under consideration are the first house, the 7th house, the 9th house, and the 5th house (the BB of the 9th house). Let us list down how the MD and the AD lords connect with these houses.

(i) In the D1, the MD lord's dispositor is Venus (*karaka* of marriage) who is conjunct Moon. Venus is also the 7th lord.

(ii) In the D1, the *nakshatra* lord (Sun who is the 5th lord) of the MD lord is with Jupiter who is the *karaka* of husband for the native.

(iii) Jupiter is the 9th lord who aspects the 9th house and is conjunct the *nakshatra* dispositor of MD lord. Jupiter here is also placed in the 5th house.

(iv) If in D1, if we make the house where Ketu is placed – the first house, then it is aspected by 9th lord Saturn, and 7th lord Mars.

(v) Note that Jupiter is combust here and is in a barren *rashi* and so taking point (iv) above will result in delayed marriage. Jupiter is weak for this native.

(vi) In the D9, the MD lord is aspected by Jupiter (5th lord and 8th lord) who is conjunct Rahu. The dispositor of the MD lord is aspected by 9th lord Mars from the 11th house.

(vii) In the D9, if we make the house where Ketu is placed – the first house, then it is 5th from AD lord Venus who is conjunct 5th lord. In the D9, Jupiter is placed in 7th house from MD lord.

(viii) In *Rashi-tulya navamsa* chart, the MD lord, Ketu moves 11 places (good) and is placed in 12th house (good place for Ketu but not from marriage perspective) in *Vyamsa* and is aspected by Jupiter (good). Venus, the 7th lord, AD lord and dispositor of MD lord is *rashi* and *bhav vargottam* and placed in fourth house in *sukhamsa* and conjunct with Moon. Both Moon and Venus, have *digbal* (good). Venus conjunct with Moon is not good for marriage. Saturn aspects the 7th house in *rashi tulya* leading to delay in marriage.

In addition, as special but important angles of analysis related to marriage - one needs to look at feasibility aspects from the 8th house (and its lord) and the 12th house (and its lord) when it comes to the timing of marriage. 12th house is related to bed pleasures and the 8th house is related to marriage *mangalya*. For this native, the 8th house has two malefics Saturn and Rahu and that is not good for normal timing of marriage. The 8th Lord Mars retrograde in 11th house in exchange with Saturn who is the 11th lord, and this is also not a good combination for normal timing of marriage. Moreover, the 12th house is aspected by Mercury (a natural benefic) that is good, but the 12th lord Jupiter is aspected by Mars and Saturn that is not good. Jupiter and Venus are both weak, as Venus and Moon conjunction is not good for marriage. Similarly, in D9, the 8th lord, Jupiter is on Rahu/Ketu axis and conjunct with Rahu and its dispositor, Mercury, is placed 8th from Jupiter in an enemy sign. Jupiter does get aspect from 9th lord Mars, who is retro and placed in 11th house of fulfillment of desires. Jupiter aspects its own house, 8th house of *mangalya*. The 12th lord, Moon is placed in 12th house itself conjunct with Venus. Even though Moon and Venus conjunction is not good for marriage, but its two benefic planets placed in 12th house, and a good placement for Venus with respect to *kaal purush kundli*. The native married but it was a delayed marriage.

CHAPTER 8

Transit Analysis using the *Navamsa* Chart

In the previous chapter, we discussed how the *Vimshottari dasha* system helps the astrologer in figuring out the broader time period (duration) during which an event is likely to fructify in the life of a native. In this chapter, we discuss how transits over the *navamsas* and the *Navamsa* chart narrow down for the astrologer the period of fructification of an event – whose promise is shown via a *dasha* analysis in relation to the event.

8.1 – *Dasha* Analysis as a Prerequisite

In *Parashari jyotish*, unless a *dasha* shows promise in **both the D1 and the D9 charts**, no event can fructify irrespective of the transit planetary combinations. It is but obvious that there will be multiple transit placements that can signal the fructification of an event – only the ones supported by the *Vimshottari dasha* system are timeline of interest. One must note here that transits must be observed from both the D1 and the D9 charts. One can have **four possible logical combinations** of *dasha/transit* promise, and their output in this regard.

(i) Strong *dasha* promise, weak/mild transit promise – event might not happen in transit.

(ii) Mild/weak *dasha* promise, weak/mild transit

promise – event will likely not happen in transit.

(iii) Strong *dasha* promise, strong transit promise – event is very likely to happen in transit.

(iv) Mild *dasha* promise, mild transit promise – event is not likely to happen in transit.

The moral of the story here is that it is much important to see the *dasha* period of a native (in both the D1 and the D9 charts) and then follow it up with a transit analysis (in both the D1 and the D9 charts) to arrive at providing insights into the fructification of an event. One could leave out transit analysis and do an MD/AD/PD analysis to arrive at fructification possibilities, where PD stands for *pratyantari dasha*. However, it is much easier to stick to an MD/AD analysis followed by a transit analysis. Some *jyotishis* make very fast predictions using certain transits alone – that could be because they are using some special *Nadi* principles. In this book, we do not focus on *Nadi jyotish* (apart from a few popular results) and propose combining *Nadi jyotish* with *Parashari jyotish* for best results.

8.2 – The *Navtara* and the *Taramsa* Concepts

The most important fundamental concept to understand transits accurately is the *taramsa*, in addition to the natal degree of the Moon and birth ascendant in the birth chart (D1). We would emphasize further to say that knowing the connections of these two in relation to planetary transits are sufficient to predict accurately (conditioned on *dasha* promise).

But before we do all that one must understand that the Moon *lagna* is the prime *lagna* for understanding the mental impact of a transit on affairs of a native's life. More than whether an event will materialize (fructify), it is about how will the materialization (or otherwise) will impact the mind negatively or positively during the fructification process (as per Mantreswara). Good things can also fructify with pain/ sadness at times (e.g., getting a much better career promise after losing or resigning from a job). It is also the case that the *Vimshottari dasha* system and its planetary sequence (for a native, i.e., the *dasha* periods) is sourced from the placement of the Moon in a birth chart, and rules events in a native's life. Biologically, Moon is the water essence, i.e., prana, that sustains life in a body as more than 70% of our body is water. Hence, Moon reigns supreme.

Now back to the concept the *taramsa*. The *taramsa* (*amsa* of a *tara/nakshatra*) concept is derived from the *navtara chakra* concept, that has its root in the *nakshatra* where the natal Moon is placed. There are three pivotal points from the *nakshatra/star/tara* where the Moon is placed: the *janma tara* (star) which is the star where the Moon is placed in the natal chart; the 10th star (also known as the *karma nakshatra* of the native) from the *janma tara* in *nakshatra* order (in the 27 *nakshatra* scheme); and the 19th star (also known as the *adhana nakshatra* of the native) from the *janma tara* in *nakshatra* order.

One would observe that the *nakshatra lords* of all these three stars for a native is ruled by the same planet. Hence 27 *nakshatras* divided into 9 groups (hence the name *navtara*) of 3 *nakshatras* each with each group of *nakshatras* having the same *nakshatra* lord. Let us take an example. Someone born having *janma nakshatra* as *Vishaka*, has the *karma nakshatra* as *Purva Bhadrapada*, and the *adhana nakshatra* as *Punarvasu* – all these three *nakshatras* are ruled by Jupiter. Each of these 9 groups are either generically good for the native, or otherwise.

The following *nakshatra* triplets (in the 27-*nakshatra* system) are generically positive for natives.

(1, 10, 19) – *janma tara* family

(2, 11, 20) - *sampat tara* family

(4, 13, 22) – *kshem tara* family

(6, 15, 24) – *sadhak tara* family

(8, 17, 26) – *mitra tara* family

(9, 18, 27) – *atimitra tara* family

In other words, if any planet in transit goes over *nakshatras* in these triplets the relative mental impact is more positive than negative for a native. Alternatively, even if bad lordship (e.g., 6, 8, 12) planets transit over *nakshatras* in these *tara* families they bring a relative calm when compared to adverse mental impact on the significance/*karakatwas* pertaining to the lordships (note that there could and will be negative impact during the transit due to planets having bad lordships). If the planetary lordships of transiting planets are good (e.g., 5, 9 lordships), then the transit has a calm and positive impact on the mind of the native in relation to the significance/*karakatwas* pertaining to the lordships. It is important to note here that we have only discussed a graded binary perspective (good/not good) of a planet transiting over a *tara* – without a proper *dasha* analysis and the relation of the *dasha* lord planets with the transiting planets over a *tara*, it is not possible to say to what degree of positive/negative the mind is subject to or whether an event will fructify for the native during the transit.

Similarly, the following *nakshatra* triplets (in the 27-*nakshatra* system) are generically negative for natives.

(3, 12, 21) – *vipat tara* family

(5, 14, 23) - *pratyari tara* family

(7, 16, 25) – *nidhan tara* family

In other words, if any planet in transit goes over *nakshatras* in these triplets the relative mental impact is more negative than positive for a native. Alternatively, even if good lordship (e.g., 5, 9) planets transit over *nakshatras* in these *tara* families they bring a relative adverse mental impact when compared to positive impact on the significance or *karakatwas* pertaining to the lordships (note that there could and will be positive impact during the transit due to planets having good lordships). If the planetary lordships of transiting planets are bad (e.g., 6, 8, 12 lordships), then the transit could have a rough impact on the mind of the native in relation to the significance/*karakatwas* pertaining to the lordships. Transits over *taras* are visible from the D1 chart. Now the important question left to be answered is: *what is the precise timing when such mental ups and downs will be felt by the native?* We need to understand the concept of *taramsa* for this.

A *taramsa* is an *amsa* of a *tara (nakshatra)*. Each *amsa* is 3d20', and there are four *amsas* in a *tara.* Each *amsa* is ruled by a different planet and is reflected as a house in the D9 ruled by the same planet. **One of the main points in the D1 chart is the degree and consequent *taramsa* in which the**

Moon ascendant lies – i.e., the *janma taramsa*. Note this is not to be confused with the *janma tara* that spans the entire 13d20'.

To assess the most (mentally) impactful positive or negative transit, one needs to observe and analyse transits over the same (as the *amsa* of the *janma tara*) *amsas* (and their lords) for the 27 *nakshatras* (in the 27-*nakshatra* system) in the *navtara chakra* system of the native. These transits are equivalent to planetary transits over the different houses of the D9 chart, and their analysis gives **high accuracy on the timing of the most mental impact (positive or negative) when planets transit over these *amsas*.**

Let us now consider an example to explain how *taramsas* should be analyzed. Consider a native born with Moon in 12d13' of the Libra *rashi*. The *janma tara* for this native is *Swati*, however the *janma taramsa* is the 2nd *amsa* of *Swati*. The corresponding *taramsa* grouping for this native is as follows:

(Swati, Satabhisha, Ardra) 2nd *amsa*

janma taramsa **(Lord – Saturn)**

(*Vishaka, Purva Bhadrapada, Punarvasu*) 2nd *amsa sampat taramsa* **(Lord – Venus)**

(*Anuradha, Uttara Bhadrapada, Pushya*) 2nd *amsa*

vipat taramsa **(Lord – Mercury)**

(*Jyestha, Revati, Ashlesha*) 2nd *amsa*

kshem taramsa **(Lord – Saturn)**

(*Moola, Ashwini, Magha*) 2nd *amsa*

pratyari taramsa **(Lord – Venus)**

(*Purvashada, Bharani, Purva Phalguni*) 2nd *amsa*

sadhak taramsa **(Lord – Mercury)**

(*Uttara Shada, Krittika, Uttara phalguni*) 2nd *amsa nidhan taramsa* **(Lord – Saturn)**

(*Sravana, Rohini, Hasta*) 2nd *amsa*

mitra taramsa **(Lord – Venus)**

(*Dhanishta, Mrigashira, Chitra*) 2nd *amsa*

atimitra taramsa **(Lord – Mercury)**

Transits of planets should be observed over these *taramsas* for this native (and their lords). As precision steps, one should (i) first see the lordship of transiting planets, then (ii) observe the type of *tara* (positive/negative) over which they are transiting, then (iii) observe the timing when these transiting planets will transit over the relevant *taramsa*, and finally (iv) during this same time analyze the influence of transiting planets (and their lordship nature) over the *taramsa* lord to assess the extent of mental/impact of the transit. **Note that without a proper *dasha* analysis in the D1, D9, one cannot and should not predict the outcome of events.**

Finer Points – According to the *Phaladeepika* (by Mantreswara), the Sun transiting in a *Vedha* star *amsa* to the *janma tara amsa* is not good. It entails injuries to life (degree conditioned by the operating *dasha* periods). Sun in *Vedha* to 10th *taramsa* from the *janma taramsa* or to the 19th *taramsa* from the *janma taramsa* is also not a good transit that influences loss of wealth and fear respectively (the degrees conditioned by the operating *dasha* periods). In general, natural malefics in *Vedhas* to these three *taramsas* causes trouble whereas natural benefics in *Vedhas* to these three *taramsas* is considered good. As a concept *Vedhas* are relationships between *nakshatras* that can indicate potential challenges or obstacles related to multiple affairs of a native.

Example # 1

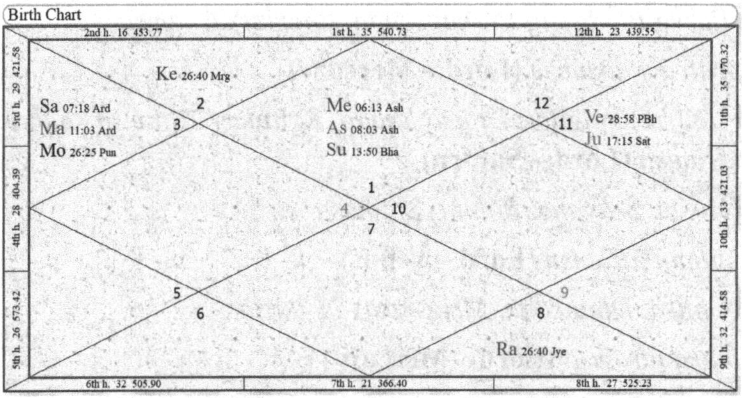

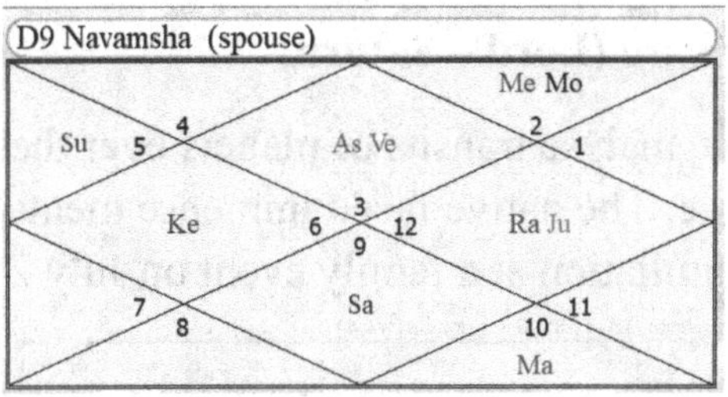

In this example for this person born with Moon in 26d25' of the Gemini *rashi*. The *janma tara* for this native is *Punarvasu*, however the *janma taramsa* is the 2nd *amsa* of *Punarvasu*. The corresponding *taramsa* grouping for this native is as follows:

(Punarvasu, Vishaka, Purva Bhadrapada) 2nd *amsa janma taramsa* **(Lord – Venus)**

(*Pushya, Anuradha, Uttara Bhadrapada*) 2nd *amsa sampat taramsa* **(Lord – Mercury)**

(*Ashlesha, Jyestha, Revati*) 2nd *amsa*

vipat taramsa **(Lord – Saturn)**

(*Magha, Moola, Ashwini*) 2nd *amsa*

kshem taramsa **(Lord – Venus)**

(*Purva Phalguni, Purvaashada, Bharini*) 2nd *amsa*

pratyari taramsa **(Lord – Mercury)**

(*Uttara phalguni, Uttara Shada, Krittika*) 2nd *amsa sadhak taramsa* **(Lord – Saturn)**

(*Hasta, Sravana, Rohini*) 2nd *amsa*

nidhan taramsa **(Lord – Venus)**

(*Chitra, Dhanishta, Mrigshira*) 2nd *amsa*

mitra taramsa **(Lord – Mercury)**

(*Swati, Satabhisha, Ardra*) 2nd *amsa*

atimitra taramsa **(Lord – Saturn)**

We will now analyse transits of planets over these *taramsas* for this native. The native faced immense mental agony due to public humiliation at a family event on July 24, 1996.

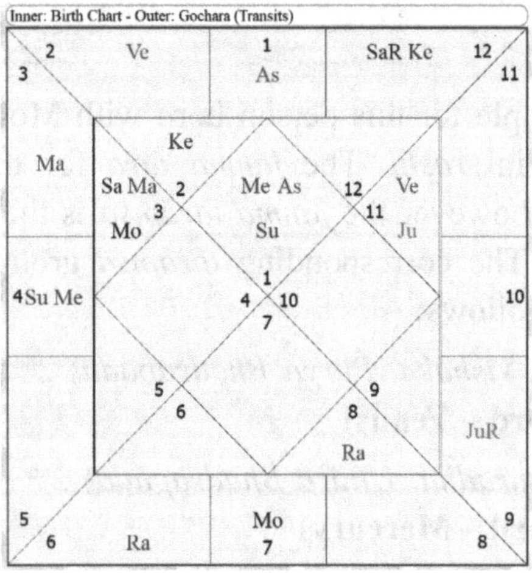

Gochara (Transits)

As	10:11:15		Ari	Ashwini	Lah	4,Ke/Sa/
Su	07:21:04		Can	Pushya	Hay	2,Sa/Ke/
Mo	07:41:37		Lib	Swati	Roo	1,Ra/Ra/
Ma	04:50:19		Gem	Mrigashi	Kee	4,Ma/Ve/
Me	20:41:33	c	Can	Ashlesha	Doo	2,Me/Ve/
Ju	16:34:49	R	Sag	P.Shad.	Bho	1,Ve/Mo/
Ve	25:27:01		Tau	Mrigashi	Vay	1,Ma/Ra/
Sa	13:34:11	R	Pis	U.Bhadra.	Jya	4,Sa/Ra/
Ra	16:48:46		Vir	Hasta	Nuh	3,Mo/Sa/
Ke	16:48:46		Pis	Revati	Day	1,Me/Me

We see that Rahu who is a natural malefic was transiting in Virgo *rashi* in *Hasta (nidhan taramsa).* Rahu behaves like Saturn (Saturn is *badhak* for this chart but also the 10th and 11th lord) and gave the native mental agony, fear and hardship but Saturn being the 11th lord did give gains in terms of fructification of marriage event for the native. We also note that Jupiter (9th and 12th lord for the chart) was in retrograde and transiting through Sagittarius *rashi* over *pratyari taramasa* in *Purvaashada* so showed effects of being the 12th lord (obstacles and possible losses for the native) but eventually effect of 9th lordship prevailed and the native got married.

8.3 – The Double Transit Concept

We now introduce a very important concept in relation to timing the fructification of events for a native – **the double transit rule.**

It is mentioned in the *Phaladeepika* that whenever any event of importance is to take place in a person's life, Saturn (the *karmadhipati*), in transit, must influence (PAC) the house and/or its lord that signifies the event; and then Jupiter (the *dharmadhipati*), must also transit and influence (PAC) that very same house and/or lord cleared by Saturn is blessed by him. This clearing of the house/lord by Saturn and the blessing of the house/lord by Jupiter, permitting it to yield results is the much-celebrated **double transit** of Saturn and Jupiter. This double transit rule should be applied from the Moon ascendant also and is to be accorded equal importance with the birth ascendant. The double transit rule has a modified version introduced by Pal and Shukla that is *the* **functional double transit** rule of the 9L and 10L of a chart (instead of only the Saturn and Jupiter double transit) should apply to the houses/lords primarily associated with the event taking both the birth ascendant and the Moon ascendant. We will showcase the double transit rule via **an example**.

Example #1

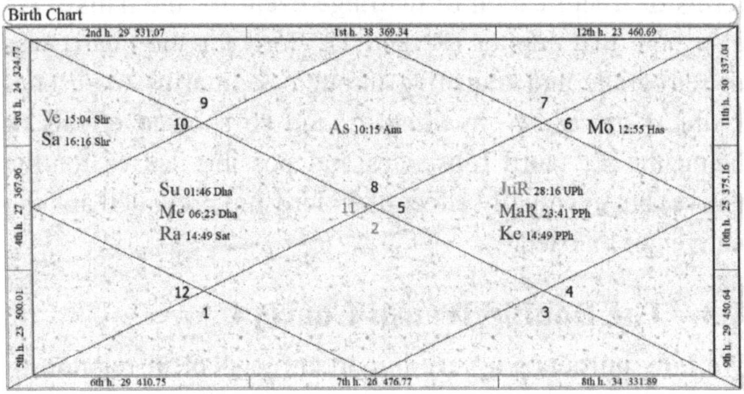

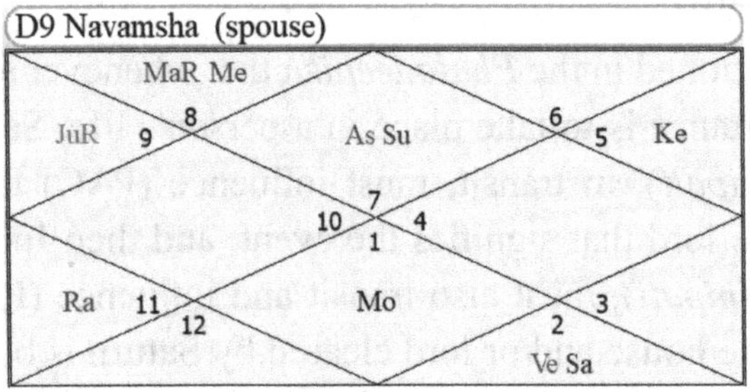

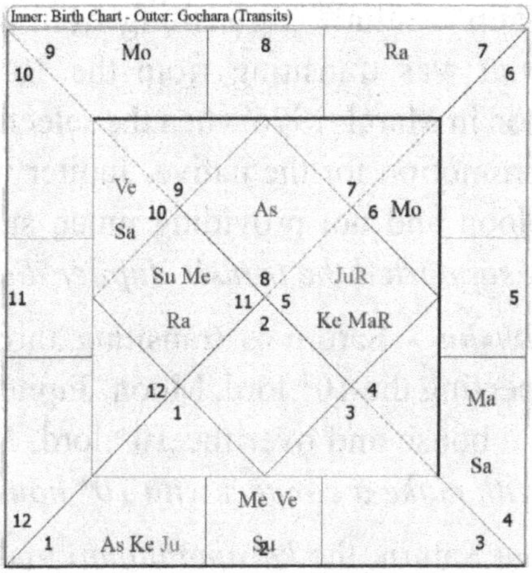

In the above chart, lets apply the double transit and analyse a career promotion event for the native on June 14, 1976, when Saturn was transiting Cancer sign and Jupiter was transiting in Aries. Saturn was conjunct with Mars (Lagna lord) in 9th house in transit during this time. Saturn was in retrograde motion till March 27th, 1976.

We will analyse Jupiter-Saturn double transit from viewpoints of i) birth ascendant in D1, ii) Moon ascendant in D1, and iii) repeat (i) and (ii) in the D9. We omit the feasibility analysis of the event via a *dasha* analysis (topic of Chapter 7) and let the readers know that the native was undergoing Jup/Sun period during the transit and the *dasha* analysis indicated career promotion feasibility.

From Ascendant - Saturn is transiting through the 9th house and aspects the transiting Jupiter and 11th, 3rd and 6th houses. Jupiter is transiting through the 6th house and aspects the 10th, 12th and 2nd houses (*Saturn and Jupiter, both make a connect with 10th house and 6th house)*.

From the Moon - Saturn is transiting from the 11th house from Moon but was transiting from the 10th house with respect to Moon in March 1976 when the selection board met and cleared promotion for the native. Jupiter was transiting eight from Moon and not providing much support for the event *(Saturn supported the transit, Jupiter did not).*

In the *Navamsha* - Saturn is transiting through the 10th house and aspecting the 10th lord, Moon. Jupiter is transiting through the 7th house and over the 10th lord, Moon *(Saturn and Jupiter both make a connect with 10th house/lord.*

So, we see that Saturn, the *karamadhipati* makes a connect with 10th / 6th house/lords in all three viewpoints whereas Jupiter, the *dharmadhipati misses* in one viewpoint – hence the fructification of the career promotion event during the transit has a very high probability with the *dasha* period supporting the event.

8.4 – Principles of Transits from *Nadi Jyotish*

In relation to the **accurate timing of the fructification** of events (conditioned on *dasha* period promoting), the certain principles must be kept in mind (borrowed from *Nadi Jyotish* propounded in the *Chandra Kala Nadi*). These principles specific to Saturn and Jupiter transits of slow-moving planets MUST be applied complementing transits analysis from *Parashari Jyotish* to obtain best results. *Nadi* transits are extremely effective in fine-timing events. Rahu and Ketu are also slow-moving planets, and their transits also signify event fructification (conditioned on *dasha* feasibility).

Through the following sutras (only related to Jupiter and Saturn transits), we showcase **only a few principles** from *Nadi Jyotish* to give an essence to the reader on how *Nadi* astrology operates in fructifying events. Note that *dashas* still predominate in controlling the timing and impact of events – where *dasha* analyses could either be derived from a *Parashari* viewpoint, or via *Nadi* "*dashas*" (progressions). **We suggest the reader to go through a course in *Nadi jyotish* before applying these results in complement to insights obtained from *Parashari* transits.** The following (non-exhaustive) sutras showcase the role of the transits of Saturn and Jupiter (we omit Rahu/Ketu transits) (*sthaan, kaal, vaatavaran* needs to be adjudged for best essence). **Feasibility of *dasha* is assumed**.

(i) When Saturn in transit coincides in degree with the natal position of any planet, or the trine position of the planet (**trines mutually influence each other in *Nadi jyotish***), the *Nadi* karakas associated (see any classical text of *Nadi jyotish* for a reference) with the planet will be ill influenced. As an example, if Saturn is in transit coincides with the degree of the Sun (or its trine positions), the native's father's health will suffer, or the native will suffer from the illness of some elderly male relative in the family. Similarly, when Saturn in transit coincides with the degree of the Moon (or its trine position), the native's mother's health will suffer, or the native will suffer from the illness of some elderly female relative in the family. Moreover, when Saturn in transit coincides with the degree of Mars (or is trine position), the native's brother/sister health will suffer, or the native will suffer from illness of some cousin relative in the family. The degree of suffering depends on the *dasha* analysis of the native and the relation of the *dasha* lords with *Nadi karaakas*.

(ii) Saturn in transit over the *navamsa* occupied by the lord of the 8th house from any given *bhava*, or its transit over a trine *amsa* to the said *navamsa* will adversely impact the good effects of the *bhava*.

(iii) Saturn in transit over a sign in the D9 where the lord of the D1 *lagna* is placed, or its transit over any of the trine signs results in adversely impacting the native's maternal uncle and/or grandmother.

(iv) Saturn in transit over a sign in the D9 where the lord of the 2nd house of D1 is placed, or its transit over any of the trine signs results in adversely impacting the native's wife.

(v) Saturn in transit over a sign in the D9 where the lord of the 12th house of D1 is placed, or its transit over any of the trine signs results in adversely impacting the native's progeny.

(vi) Saturn in transit over a sign in the D9 where the lord of the 11th house of D1 is placed, or its transit over any of the trine signs results in adversely impacting the native's mother.

(vii) Saturn in transit over a sign in the D9 where the lord of the 4th house of D1 is placed, or its transit over any of the trine signs results in adversely impacting the native's father.

(viii) Saturn in transit over a sign in the D9 where the lord of the 6th house of D1 is placed, or its transit over any of the trine signs results in adversely impacting the native's father through the latter's friends and co-borns. It will also result in mental anguish for the native at workplace, and to his co-borns.

(ix) Saturn in transit over a sign in the D9 where the lord of the 5th house of D1 is placed, or its transit over any of the trine signs results in adversely impacting the progeny of one's brother.

(x) Saturn in transit over a sign in the D9 where the lord of the 4th or the 5th house of D1 is placed, or its transit over any of the trine signs results in adversely impacting one of the sons of the native's relative.

(xi) Saturn in transit over a sign in the D9 where the lord of the 7th house of D1 is placed, or its transit over any of the trine signs results in adversely impacting the native's maternal grandmother.

(xii) Saturn in transit over a sign in the D9 where the lord of the 9th house of D1 is placed, or its transit over any of the trine signs results in adversely impacting the native's mother's sister's progeny.

(xiii) Saturn in transit over a sign in the D9 where the lord of the 11th house of D1 is placed, or its transit over any of the trine signs results in adversely impacting the native's mother's paternal family.

(xiv) Saturn in transit over a sign in the D9 where Venus is placed, or its transit over any of the trine signs results in adversely impacting the native's female relatives.

(xv) Saturn in transit over a sign in the D9 where Mercury is placed, or its transit over any of the trine signs results in adversely impacting the native's friends.

(xvi) Saturn in transit over a sign in the D9 where Rahu is placed, or its transit over any of the trine signs results in adversely impacting the native's co-borns if the 5th lord *dasha* is in operation.

(xvii) Saturn in transit over a sign in the D9 where Ketu is placed, or its transit over any of the trine signs results in adversely impacting the native's health, conditioned on relevant *dasha* in operation.

(xviii) Jupiter in transit over a sign in the D9 where the lord of the D1 *lagna* is placed, or its transit over any of the trine signs results in the birth of native's co-borns.

(xix) Jupiter in transit over a sign in the D9 where the 11th lord or the 9th lord is placed, or its transit over any of the trine signs results in the native experiencing happiness, employment boost, and wealth boost.

(xx) Jupiter in transit over a sign in the D9 where the 11th lord or the 2nd lord is placed, or its transit over any of the trine signs results in the native experiencing wealth boost.

(xxi) Jupiter in transit over a sign in the D9 where the 5th lord is placed, or its transit over any of the trine signs, or a transit over itself (significator of *putra*), results in the native experiencing childbirth.

Finer Points on Timing of Events – To get virtually the exact timing of when transits (in *Nadi/Parashari jyotish*) give results, note that Sun and Mars gives results (conditioned on *dasha* and transit being favorable) slightly before they arrive at a natal position of interest (e.g., planet degrees, *lagna* degree, Moon ascendant degree); Venus and Jupiter gives results at the time of crossing a natal point of interest; Saturn and Moon gives results after crossing a natal point of interest; and Mercury gives results during all the above three positions.

8.5 – Analysis Examples to Time Events

In this section, we rigorously analyze (via two examples) in a detailed fashion the fructification of events using *Parashari Vimshottari dasha* and transits. This section is purely from an expository viewpoint to help students of Vedic astrology get a simple and step wise methodology to time events. We cursorily state *Nadi* principles if applicable.

Example #1

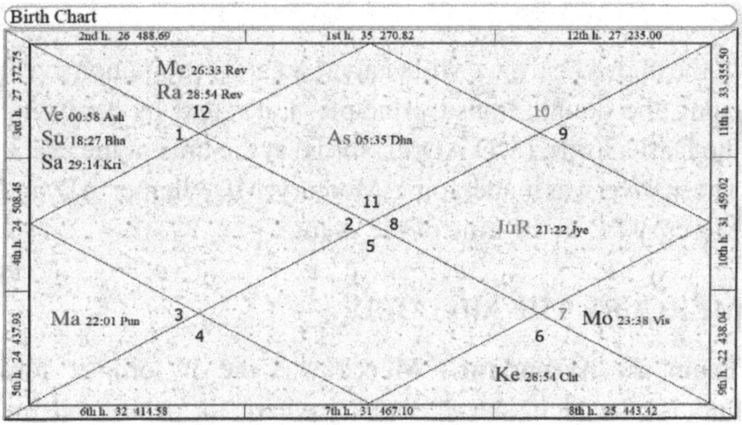

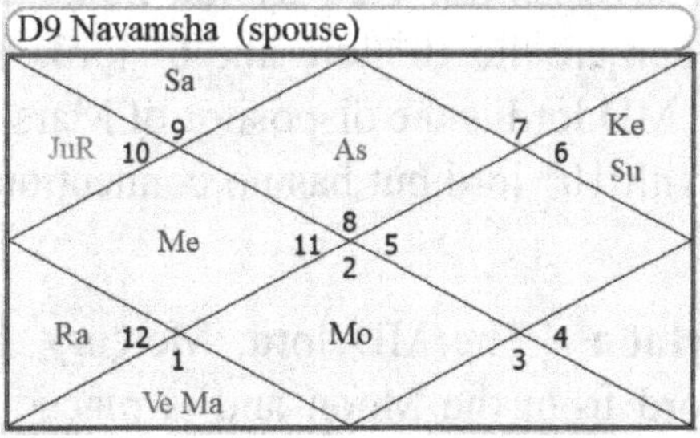

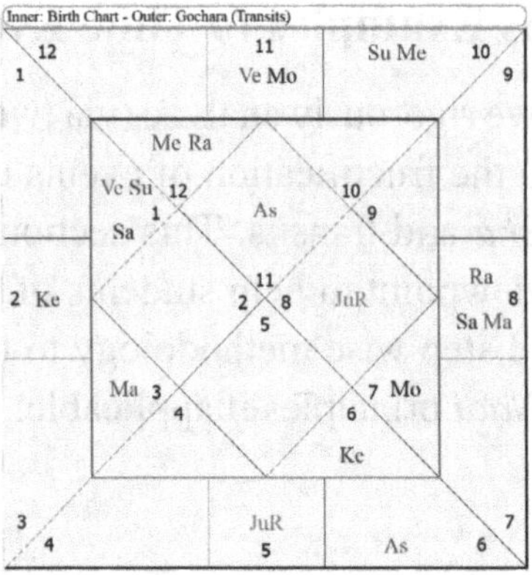

In the above chart, we will analyze a career promotion event using the double transit principle. Let's start by analyzing the Dasha lords, (MD/AD/PD lords) at the time of the event. The native was undergoing Mercury MD, Jupiter AD and Mercury PD at the time of the event.

MERCURY THE MD LORD:

From the Ascendant - Mercury is the 5th lord, 8th lord and is placed in the 2nd house, where its debilitated but gets *neechbhanga*; is aspected by the house lord, Jupiter. Mars and Moon are the 10th lord and 6th lords, respectively. Mercury, the MD lord is the dispositor of Mars and makes a connection with 10th lord but has no connection with the 6th lord.

From the Moon - The MD lord, Mercury, becomes the 9th and 12 lord from the Moon and is placed in 6th house from Moon. It's debilitated here and will likely promote the interests of 6th house (being the 9th lord; Moreover, Jupiter, the 6th lord and 3rd lord from Moon, aspects its own house). Moon is the 10th lord placed in Lagna.

In the *Navamsa* - The MD lord, Mercury, is in the 4th house aspecting the 10th house. It is aspected by *Karmadhipati*, Saturn, who is 3rd and 4th lord.

JUPITER THE AD LORD:

From the Ascendant - The AD lord, Jupiter is retrograde; the 2nd and 11th lord placed in 10th house. It influences the 6th house by aspect from 10th house and influences the 6th lord, Moon from Libra sign (being retrograde). Jupiter makes up for MD lord, Mercury not connecting with the Moon (6th lord).

From the Moon - The AD lord, Jupiter is the 3rd and 6th lord and aspects the 6th house and 10th house from the Moon and makes a connection with Moon (10th lord) via its retrograde position in Libra.

In the *Navamsa* - The AD lord, Jupiter is the 2nd and 5th lord; placed in 3rd house in debilitated and retrograde states. It aspects the 10th lord, Sun, the 6th lord, and the Lagna lord, Mars who is placed in 6th house and own house. This Mars guarantees a spectacular rise in service. Retro Jupiter makes a connect with Saturn in its own *rashi* Sagittarius.

MERCURY THE PD LORD

Mercury is the MD lord and has been discussed earlier.

THE DOUBLE TRANSIT

We will now look at the transit and analyze the double transit from all viewpoints.

From the Ascendant - Saturn, the *lagna lord* and the *karmadhipati* is transiting through the 10th house and is conjunct with 10th lord, Mars (forming a *raj yoga* in transit) and Rahu. It aspects the 7th lord Sun and retro Jupiter who is transiting through the 7th house. Jupiter, the *dharmadhipati* is retrograde and transiting through the 7th house and aspecting the 6th lord, Moon and aspecting Saturn from its retro position in 6th house in cancer *rashi*. It also aspects the 10th lord, Mars from this position. (T*he mutual aspect of Saturn, Jupiter and Jupiter's (AD Lord) influence on 6th house/ lord and lagna lord and Saturn influence on 10th house/lord promises overall good results*)

From the Moon - Saturn is transiting second from Moon and over the natal 6th lord from Moon, Jupiter. Jupiter is retrograde and can be said to be transiting from 10th house from Moon due to its retrograde motion. (*Saturn and Jupiter both make a connect with 6th/10th house/lords from Moon, thereby making a promise for high quality results)*

In the *Navamsa* - Saturn is transiting through the *lagna* of the *Navamsa.* It aspects the 10th house, 10th lord, Sun and transiting Jupiter. Jupiter is transiting through the 10th house and aspects the 6th house and 9th lord, Moon. Jupiter aspects the D9 *lagna,* transiting Saturn, Mars (6th lord) and Sun (10th lord) from its retro position from 9th house. (*Saturn and Jupiter, both connect with 6th and 10th house /lords, thereby promising excellent results in this transit*)

Now we will analyze the Dasha Lords in transit.

MD AND PD LORD MERCURY

From the Ascendant - Mercury is 5th and 8th lord and is transiting through the 12th house in Capricorn. It's in retrograde motion hence will influence from the 11th house and aspects the Natal 10th lord, Mars. (*The MD and PD lord, Mercury influences the 6th house and 10th lord)*

From the Moon - Mercury is transiting from the 4th house from the natal Moon and aspects the 10th house from natal Moon. (*The MD and PD lord, Mercury influences the 10th house*)

In the *Navamsa* - Mercury is transiting through the 3rd house and misses influencing or making a connect with 6th and 10th houses but does influence the Lagna lord, Saturn due to its retrograde motion. *(The MD and PD lord, Mercury misses to influence the 6th/10th houses and lords)*

AD LORD JUPITER

From the Ascendant - Jupiter is transiting through the 7th house, thereby influencing the *lagna* and influences the 10th house and 6th house and Saturn and 10th lord from its retrograde position in 6th house. *(This transit single handedly ensures an upsurge in the profession)*

From the Moon - Jupiter transits from the 11th house with respect to the natal Moon and aspects Moon (6th lord) and transits via the 10th house in retro motion and aspects the 6th lord, Jupiter and 6th house. *(This further creates a high probability of the fructification of the event)*

In the *Navamsa* - Jupiter is transiting from the 10th house and aspects Saturn, 6th lord (Mars) and the 10th lord (Sun), from its retrograde position in Cancer. (*The AD lord, Jupiter's transit in Navamsa further creates stellar conditions to fulfill the event)*

The fructification of the event can also be seen by applying *Nadi principles* on AD lord, Jupiter. Jupiter is transiting over trine 9th house in D9 and confirms wealth boost in form of career progression.

So, we see how the *Vimshottari dasha*, double transit and *Nadi principles* play a pertinent role for promising timing of any event.

Example # 2

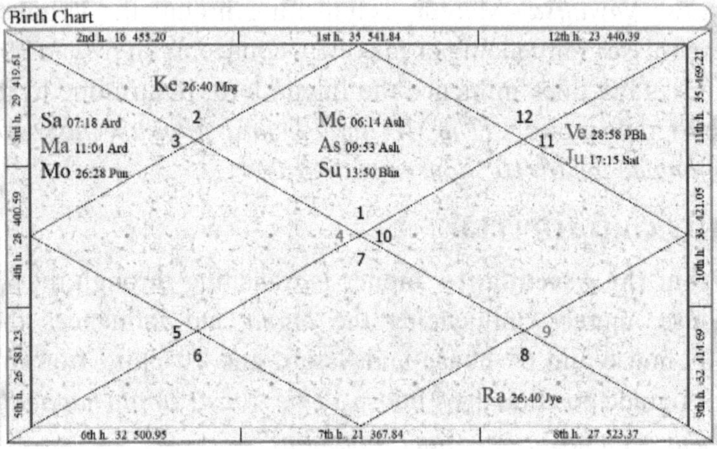

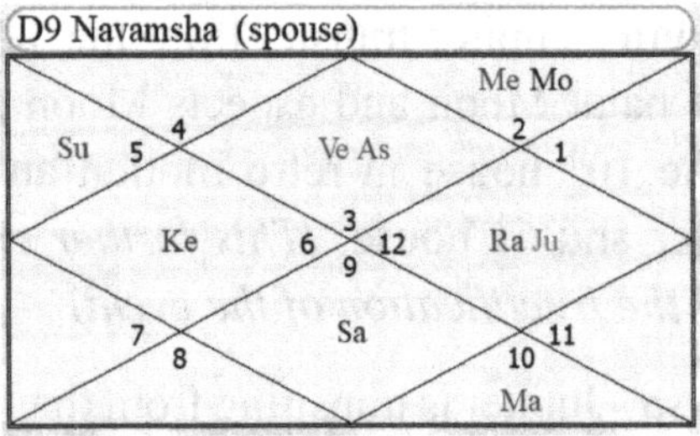

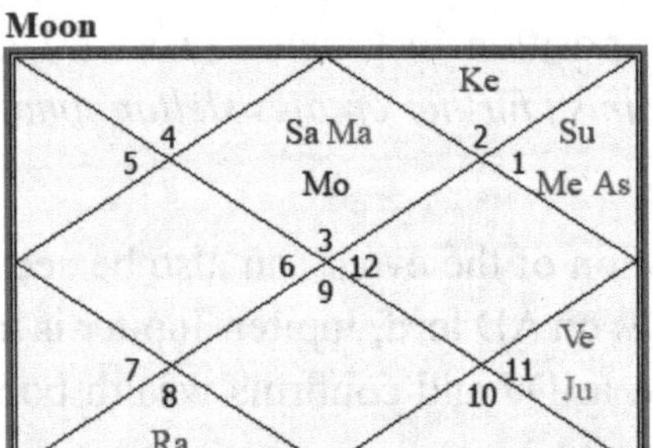

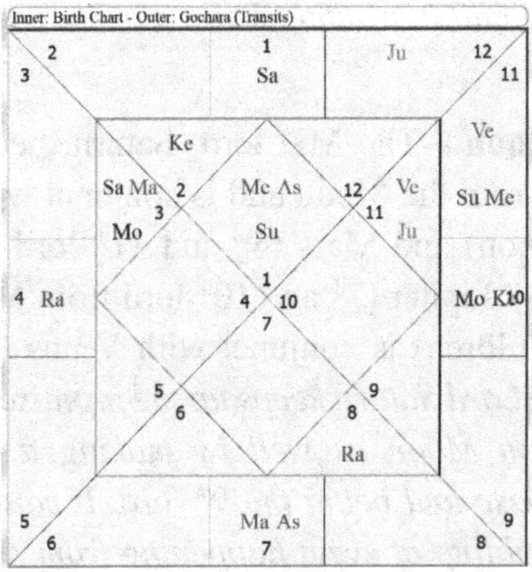

In the above chart, we will analyze a childbirth event using the double transit principle. Let's start by analyzing the Dasha lords, (MD/AD/PD lords) at the time of the event. The native was undergoing Saturn MD, Jupiter AD and Jupiter PD at the time of the event. We will consider involvement of Jupiter (the *karaka* of children), Lagna, 5th house, and 9th house (*bhavat bhavam* of 5th house and the *bhagya* house) while analyzing the event of childbirth.

SATURN THE MD LORD:

From the Ascendant – Saturn is the 10th lord and 11th lord and is placed in the 3rd house, and is conjunct with Lagna lord, Mars, and 4th lord, Moon. Its aspected by 9th and 12th lord, Jupiter. Saturn is the MD lord and is aspected by Jupiter who is the *karaka* of children. Saturn is the dispositor of Jupiter and Jupiter is placed in 11th house (conjunct with Venus, 2nd and 7th lord). MD lord is the dispositor of Jupiter and makes a connection with Jupiter who is *karaka* of children. (*It can be inferred that the MD Lord Saturn can deliver the event of childbirth as Jupiter (AD and PD lord* *and karaka of children) and Saturn make a connect in natal chart)*

From the Moon - The MD lord, Saturn, becomes the 8th and 9th lord from the Moon and is conjunct with Moon (2nd lord from Moon) and Mars (6th and 11th lord from Moon). Its aspected by Jupiter (7th and 10th lord from Moon). Jupiter (*karaka* of children) is conjunct with Venus (5th lord from Moon). (*MD Lord Saturn keeps up the promise of delivering the event from Moon as well by making a connect with Lagna, 5th house and being the 9th lord. It can be conferred that the probability of event happening from Ascendant and Moon is very high*)

In the *Navamsa* - The MD lord, Saturn, is in the 7th house aspecting the 9th house (*Bhagya* house, 9th house is also the *bhavat bhavam* of 5th house), Lagna of D9 and 4th house. It is aspected by Venus who is 5th and 12th lord in D9. (*The promise of MD Lord delivering the event further gets strengthened in Navamsa*)

JUPITER THE AD LORD:

From the Ascendant - The AD lord, Jupiter (who is the *karaka* of children) is 9th and 12th lord and is placed in 11th house and is conjunct with Venus (2nd and 7th lord). It influences the 3rd house, 5th house, and 7th house by aspect and influences Saturn (10th and 11th lord), Mars (Lagna lord and 8th lord) and Moon (4th lord). So, Jupiter, the karaka of children influences the 5th house, Lagna lord, Moon and the MD Lord, Saturn. (*The AD Lord looks promising for delivering the event being the karaka of children, 9th lord and aspect on lagna lord, 5th house, Moon and MD Lord)*

From the Moon - The AD lord, Jupiter is the 7th and 10th lord and aspects the Lagna, 3rd house, and 5th house from Moon. Its conjunct with 5th lord from Moon, Venus. So, the AD lord, Jupiter makes a connect with both, 5th lord, and 5th house from Moon and the *lagna*. (*The AD Lord keeps up the promise from Moon by its aspect on Lagna, 5th house, Moon and MD Lord)*

In the *Navamsa* - The AD lord, Jupiter is the 7th and 10th lord and placed in 10th house, conjunct with Rahu. Jupiter aspects 2nd, 4th and 6th houses.

JUPITER THE PD LORD

Jupiter is the AD lord and has been discussed earlier.

THE DOUBLE TRANSIT

We will now look at the transit and analyze the double transit from all viewpoints.

From the Ascendant - Saturn, the 10th and 11th lord is transiting through the Lagna (in its sign of debilitation but getting *neechbhanga,* because of aspect from Mars (who is transiting in Saturn's sign of exaltation)) and aspects the 3rd, 7th and 10th houses. It aspects the Lagna lord, Mars, who is transiting through 7th house and Moon who is transiting through the 10th house. Jupiter is transiting through the 12th house and aspects the 4th, 6th and 8th house. Sun (5th lord), Venus (2nd and 7th lord) and Mercury (3rd and 6th lord) are transiting through the 11th house and aspect the 5th house. MD Lord, Saturn is the dispositor of 11th house. *(The MD Lord, Saturn, being the dispositor of transiting 5th lord, Sun, makes an indirect connect with 5th house in transit; Sun (5th lord) aspects the 5th house in transit, thus blessing the possibility of event*)

From the Moon - Saturn is transiting 11th from Moon and over the natal Lagna lord (Mercury) and 3rd lord (Sun) from Moon, and aspects the 5th house from Moon. Saturn's dispositor, Mars (11th lord), is transiting through the 5th house. Jupiter is transiting through 10th house from Moon and aspects 2nd, 4th and 6th houses. (*Saturn makes a connect with Lagna and lagna lord, 5th house, thereby confirming possibility of event of childbirth;)*

In the *Navamsa* - Saturn is transiting through the 11th house of the *Navamsa* and aspects the *lagna,* 5th house, 8th house, and 11th lord, Mars. Jupiter is transiting through the 10th house and aspects the 2nd, 4th and 6th house. 5th lord, Venus is transiting through the trine 9th house and is conjunct with *lagna* lord (Mercury) and 3rd lord (Sun). (*Saturn (the functional 9th lord of D9) makes a connect with 5th house and lagna and Jupiter makes a connect with 2nd house.*)

Now we will analyze the Dasha Lords in transit.

MD LORD SATURN

We discussed this in double transit earlier

AD AND PD LORD JUPITER

We discussed this in double transit earlier

So, we see that even though Jupiter and Saturn do not mutually participate in the double transit, other aspects with respect to Lagna, 5th house, and 9th house, and house lords were so strong that it resulted in fructification of the event.

The fructification of the event can also be seen by applying *Nadi principles* on AD and PD Lord, Jupiter. Jupiter who is also the *putrakaraka* is transiting over natal Jupiter in D9 thus promising boost in happiness of native.

So, we see how the *Vimshottari dasha*, double transit and *Nadi principles* play a pertinent role for promising timing of any event.

8.6 – The *64th navamsa*

The most important and practical use of the 64th *navamsa* (in the D1 chart) is in relation to planetary transits. However, before we get there, it is imperative to be very clear about the definition and concept of the 64th *navamsa*.

8.6.1 Definition

The 64th *navamsa* (in reference to the D1 chart) lies in the 8th house (64 = 9x7 + 1) in order of sequence. As an example, say a planet is placed at 8d20' in Aries. This is the 3rd *navamsa* of the sign (as each *navamsa* spans 3d20'). Hence, the 64th *navamsa* to this planetary position will lie on Scorpio in the degree range 6d40' to 10d0', that is the 3rd *navamsa* of the Scorpio sign.

Now, one question that arises is: *what is the placement of this planet in the D9 chart?* To get an answer to this question note that the D9 chart has 12 houses and 64 divided by 12 gives 4 as remainder. Hence, the 64th *navamsa* from any planet (or ascendant) in the D1 chart is the 4th house (in the D9 chart) from the placement of the planet (ascendant) in that house in the D9 chart. As an **example**, if a birth ascendant in the D1 chart lies at 10d13' in Cancer, the placement of the ascendant in D9 is in the Libra ascendant. The 64th *navamsa* of the ascendant in D1 will lie in Capricorn in the D9 chart, as Capricorn is the 4th sign from Libra. As **another example**, if a planet lies on 8d30' in Aries in D1, it will be in the Gemini *navamsa* of D1 and in the D9 this planet will be placed in the Gemini sign. The 64th *navamsa* of this planet will lie in the Virgo sign in the D9 chart as Virgo is the 4th sign from Gemini.

8.6.2 Application Concept

It is quite evident that the 64th *navamsa* can mathematically bc applied to any point (i.e., planet, ascendant) in the D1 chart. However, from a predictive viewpoint, *which are the points that are the most important?* This is a question that has "confused" many over decades. It is obvious that the three most important reference points are the **birth ascendant, Moon ascendant and the Sun ascendant.** However, it is also a known fact that the 64th *navamsa* is primarily a transit application concept and **hence should be applied mainly from the natal Moon (along with the ascendant).** There is statistical establishment of this fact in the classics. The *Jataka Parijata* reckons the concept from the Moon; the *Brihat Parasara Hora Sastra* reckons it from the Moon and the birth ascendant; the *Prasna Marga* reckons it from the Moon, the birth ascendant, and the Sun. Hence amidst the variations, the Moon stands out as a common point of reference. Legendary astrologers such as *Vaidyanatha* and *Ganapati Muni* reckon the concept of the 64th *navamsa* (also known as a *khara navamsa*) from the Moon only. Richa Shukla, the *jyotish* guru of the author also reckons application of the 64th *navamsa* from the natal Moon. The **author assumes "equal" importance** between Moon ascendant and *lagna*.

8.6.3 Effects of Transits over the 64th navamsa

It is to be understood that the 64th *navamsa* is a sensitive point in a native's horoscope. Under specific conditions (to be discussed below), malefics transiting over the 64th *navamsa* can signal "death" of the native according to classics. However, the concept of "death" should be made very clear for the reader. The term "death" does not imply physical death, but one of the following: *shame, disease, sorrow, fear and grief, miseries, humiliation, calumny,* and *death*. These types of "death" can be experienced by a native when malefics transit the 64th *navamsa* – physical death a possibility when the lord of the 64th *navamsa* (from Moon, and *lagna*) and lord of the 22nd *drekkana* associate with one another and with other *maarakas*. The basic principles (not exhaustive) of transits over the 64th *navamsa* (from the Moon and ascendant) is summed up as follows:

(i) Transit of (slow-moving) malefics over the 64th *navamsa* give non-pleasant/surprising events which have long lasting effects, especially when a malefic is placed in that sign occupied by the 64th *navamsa* (or the sign in the D9 that the *navamsa* occupies). Rahu and Ketu are malefics that are slow-moving planets. The transit of fast-moving planets over sensitive points such as the 64th *navamsa* produce events of small magnitude. Transit effects get worse if a malefic planet is placed in the sign of the 64th navamsa.

(ii) When the *navamsa* lord of that occupied by Moon is inimical or friendly to the lord 64th *navamsa* from Moon, the person will have short or long life, respectively.

(iii) A natural malefic placed in the 64th *navamsa* from any planet brings harm to the significations of that planet. As an example, if natural malefics are placed in the 64th *navamsa* from Venus, spouse can be negatively impacted.

iv) Moon is the Lagna Lord of D1 - please refer to earlier analysis on Lagna lord in (ii).

(v) When the lord of 22nd *drekkana* from the *lagna* and the 64th *navamsa* from Moon is the same planet and it transits a sign deprived of *bindu* in the *ashtakvarga* then (physical) death is unavoidable, or a death like experience will result upon the native. If the two planets are different, then both transiting the sensitive point gives a (physical) death-like experience to the native.

(vi) The death of a close relative is possible when Rahu transits the 64th *navamsa* either from the ascendant or from the Moon.

(vii) When the lord of the 64th *navamsa* (from the ascendant or Moon) is placed in 6, 8, 12 houses, and is in conjunction with Saturn, a person can die of poisoning. On the other hand, when this lord of the 64th *navamsa* is placed in 6, 8, 12 houses and is conjunct Rahu/Ketu then death is possible by execution. Please note that *sthan, kaal, vaatavaran* needs to be duly applied when dealing with this rule.

Overall Disclaimer – It is to be much emphasized that the transit rules mentioned above **only** applies when the *dasha* periods favor the event. It is also to be emphasized that benefic/negative PAC associations of planets need to be duly considered before arriving at any predictive inference.

8.6.4 Application Examples on the 64th *navamsa*

We provide a few examples of transit applications of the 64th *navamsa*. In these applications, events have taken shape when the 64th *navamsa* has been taken from the *lagna*, and *dasha* periods have shown promise of the fructification of the event.

Example #1

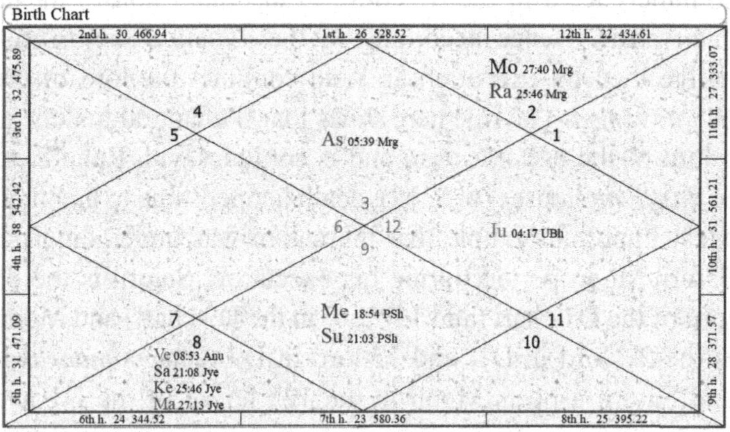

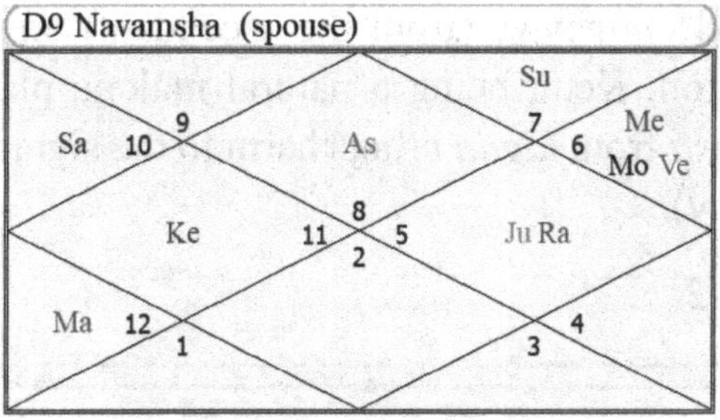

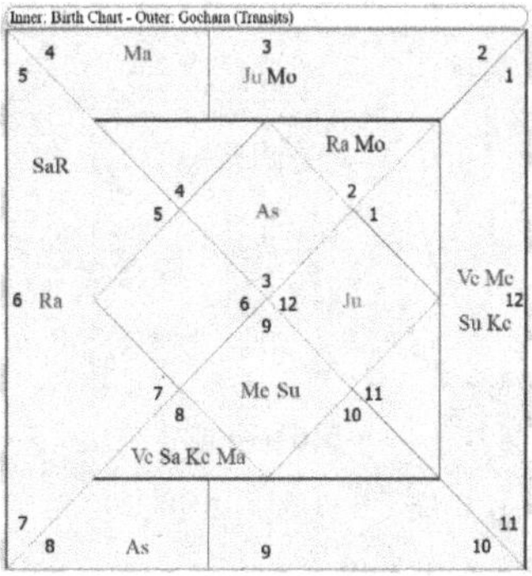

Transit chart on execution day

The native has the 64th *navamsa* from the birth ascendant (denoting physical body) in Aquarius (4th sign from Scorpio that hosts the D9 *lagna*). Saturn is the lord of Aquarius that conjuncts Ketu in the 6th house (a *dusthana house*) in the natal chart. Hence according to the *Jataka Parijata*, the native died by execution as Ketu conjunct the lord of the 64th *navamsa*. The rule here states that if a natural malefic is a lord of the 64th *navamsa* and is conjunct with Rahu/Ketu in *dusthana* houses (6, 8, 12), death happens due to hanging. Most importantly, note that the native was undergoing the Saturn/Moon period during his execution. Saturn is the 8th lord of the D1 chart (and 12th lord in the D9 chart) and Moon is the 2nd lord in D1, and 7th lord in D9 (acts as *maaraka*) and Saturn aspects Moon in the 12th house of the D1 and is also conjunct Ketu in the 6th house. Ketu was transiting over the 64th *navamsa* (from the ascendant) on the day of the execution. Ketu, being a natural malefic placed in the 64th *navamsa* from *lagna* brings harm to the significations of *lagna* (body).

Example #2

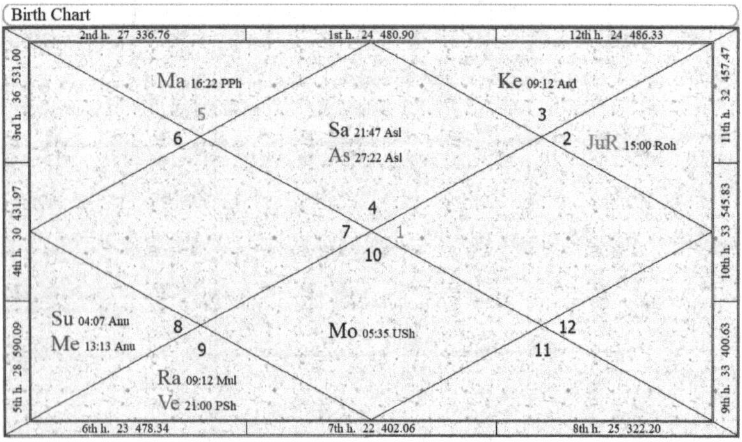

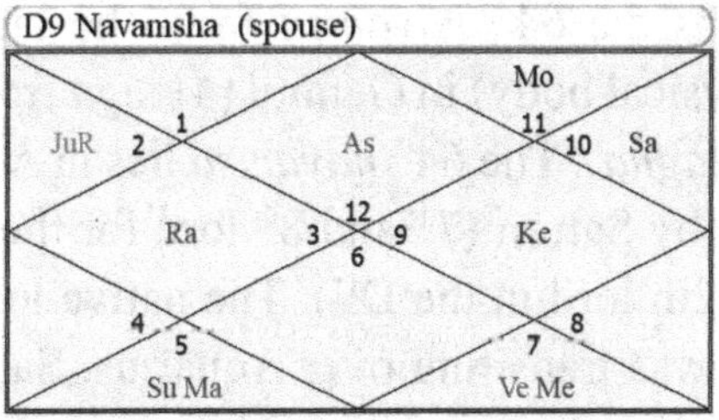

Transit chart on day of losing mother

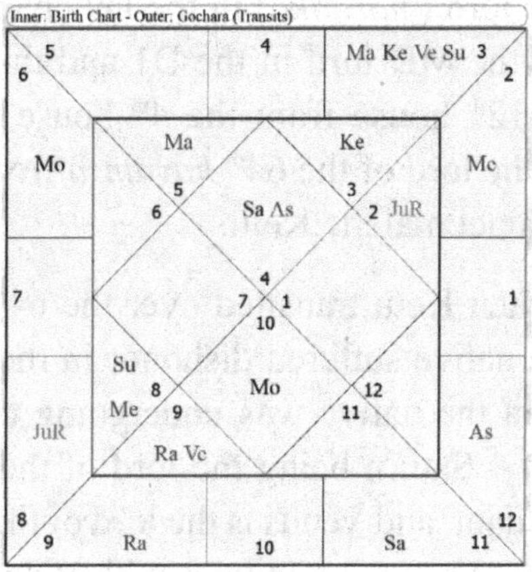

Transit chart on a day of career dishonor

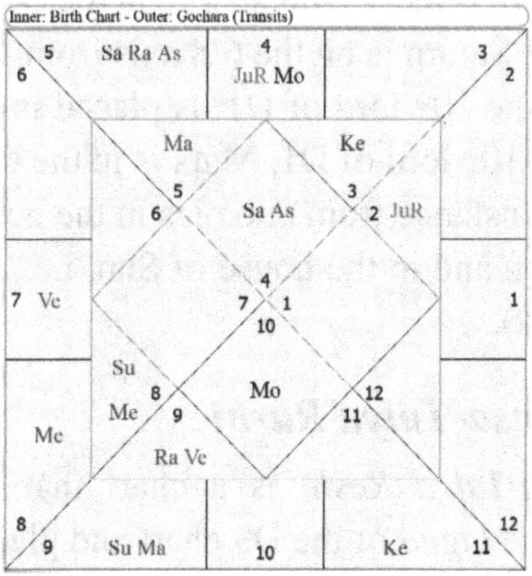

The native has the 64th *navamsa* from the birth ascendant (denoting physical body) in Gemini (4th sign from Pisces that hosts the D9 *lagna*). The 64th *navamsa* lies in Aquarius in D1 that is lorded by Saturn (7th and 8th lord for the native in the D1 and the 12th lord in the D9). The native lost her mother when Saturn was transiting over Aquarius. Saturn in transit aspected MD lord Mars, in the D1, and in the D9 aspects MD lord Mars that directly aspects Moon in the 12th house. Mars is the 2nd lord (*maraaka*) in the D9 chart. Moon is the 12th lord from the MD lord in the D1 and the D9. Moon is transiting the 12th house from the 4th house on the day of death. Venus, the lord of the 64th *navamsa* from the Moon is transiting conjunct malefic Ketu.

In addition, when Ketu transited over the 64th *navamsa* for the native, the native suffered dishonor in their career. This happened when the native was undergoing the Saturn MD and Venus AD – Saturn being the lord of the 64th *navamsa* from the ascendant, and Venus is the lord of the 64th *navamsa* from the Moon. Venus is conjunct with Rahu in D1 that is placed in the *nakshatra* of Ketu that is transiting over the 64th *navamsa*. Saturn is the 7th and 8th lord in the D1 and is the 12th lord in the D9. Saturn is on the 6/8 axis from AD lord Venus in D1. Mars, the 10th lord of D1, is placed in the *nakshatra* of Venus. The 10th lord of D1, Mars is in the 6th house of D9 (facing stiff resistance from enemies in the government as it is conjunct Sun and in the house of Sun, i.e., Sun is 6th lord in the D9 chart).

8.7 – *Navamsa-Tulya Rashi*

The *Navamsa-Tulya Rashi* is a chart that is created by maintaining the *lagna* of the D9 chart and placing planets in the D1 chart on the D9 chart. However, the **best application** of the *Navamsa-Tulya Rashi* chart is when we maintain the *lagna* of the D9 chart and **place transiting planets on the D1 chart** in the D9 chart. Why? Because it is well-known in Vedic astrology that if a planet is transiting the D1 chart in a sign, it will influence that particular sign in all divisional charts (including the D9 chart).

For example, if Saturn is transiting Gemini, it will influence Gemini in all divisional charts (including the D9). Atop this if someone has Moon in Gemini or Taurus and Cancer, the Saturn *saade-saati* effects will be felt in all the divisional charts (including the D9) with respect to the matters of the chart.

We first take an example of a static application of the *Navamsa-Tulya Rashi* and then follow it up with a transit application of the *Navamsa-Tulya Rashi*.

***Example #1* (Static Assessment)**

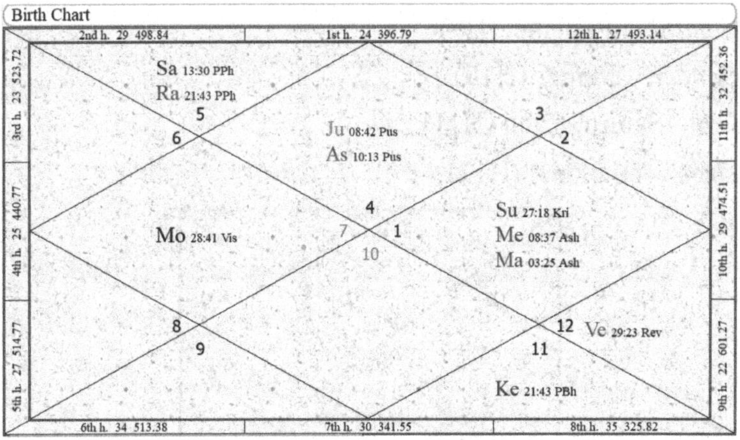

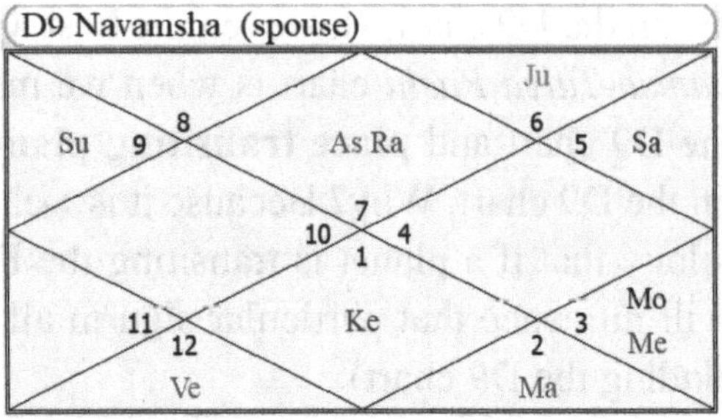

The *Navamsa-Tulya Rashi* placement of planets for the native is as follows (and shown in chart below):

Libra – Lagna, Moon (H1)

Scorpio – no planet (H2)

Sagittarius – no planet (H3)

Capricorn – no planet (H4)

Aquarius – Ketu (H5)

Pisces – Venus (H6)

Aries – Sun, Mars, Mercury (H7)

Taurus – no planet (H8)

Gemini – no planet (H9)

Cancer – Jupiter (H10)

Leo – Saturn, Rahu (H11)

Virgo – no planet (H12)

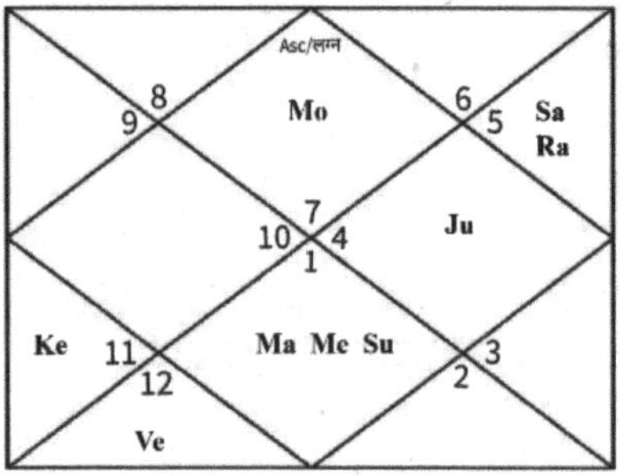

The *Navamsa-Tulya Rashi* chart in static mode shows the **inherent and true potential and promise of a horoscope.** Let us consider the career aspect of the native as an example. The native has the 10th lord placed in the first house and aspected by the 11th lord, 2nd lord, 7th lord, 9th lord, and the 12th lord. The native promises to be a very work-driven individual who is motivated by honors (*pada-praapti*), gains and academic wealth, and in addition enjoys working in foreign environments. The 7th house (*bhavat bhavam* of the 10th house) is loaded with exalted Sun (11th lord), own house Mars, and 9th lord and 12th lord Mercury, and is aspected by 10th lord Moon. The native has the potential to earn great fame and honors in his career from government and authorities in the field of defense/cyber (due to Mars influence) and via writing efforts (due to Mercury influence). The native will earn these honors in the role of a guru/teacher/philosopher (and/or in the field of philosophy/astrology) as Jupiter (placed in the 10th house) and Venus are in trines in *moksha rashis*. The 3rd lord, Jupiter, is in the 10th house and is exalted thereby showing great courage/hard work/passion to pursue a career choice in a teaching/advisor role. *Gajakesari yoga* is formed by planet Jupiter placed in the 10th house with Moon. Multiple *raja yogas* are formed due to connection between trine and *kendra* lords. Multiple *dhana yogas* are formed due to connection of 2, 5, 9, and 11 lords. In summary, there is a great amount of **inherent and true potential and promise in the horoscope on career front.**

Transit Application (Dynamic Assessment)

The *Navamsa-Tulya Rashi* chart is used for transits.

Let us take **one example** to make the application clear. Let us take the principle of *Nadi* astrology. According to the

Chandra Kala Nadi, the transit of Saturn in the sign identical with the D9 sign occupied by the lord of the 8th house from a given *bhava*/house (in the D1 chart) or a trine thereof will destroy the good effect due to that *bhava*.

Say, for example, Saturn is transiting Gemini in D1. In the Gemini sign in the D9/*Navamsa* chart, say Sun is placed. Assume now that Sun happens to be the 9th lord in a native's D1 chart (hence, the native is of Sagittarius ascendant) and hence Sun is the 8th lord from the 2nd house of family and wealth. Thus, Saturn's transit in Gemini would adversely affect the matters of the 2nd house (wealth, savings) – this was indeed the outcome of this transit on a particular native. The native's father's health also suffered due to the transit as the Sun is the *karaka* of father and is the 9th lord for the native. It is assumed that *dasha* was favorable for the fructification of such events.

Now take **another example** application for the same native. Say Saturn is transiting Aries in the D1. In the D9 chart, Jupiter and Saturn (debilitated) are placed in Aries. Hence Jupiter and Saturn also placed in Aries in D1. Jupiter is the D1 Lagna lord for the native and is also the 4th lord of the birth chart. Hence, Jupiter becomes the 8th lord from 9th house and from the 6th house respectively. It was during this transit that the native's work (6th house matter) started troubling him the most. In addition, the native's father's health was also adversely affected.

In both these above examples, note the *Navamsa-Tulya-Rashi* chart consists of planets in transit in the D1 chart (the dynamic snapshot), along with the planets in the D1 chart (the static configuration) with the D9 *lagna* acting as the first house.

Part 3

Navamsa Case Study Workbook

CHAPTER 9

Case Study Practice Workbook

In this chapter, we lay down a practice workbook of case studies from various areas of a native's life. The purpose is for students and enthusiasts to self-practice to build confidence in analyzing cases using the D1 and the D9 charts. These case studies also serve as instructional and examination material for teachers of Vedic astrology.

The reader is provided some hints after mostly every case study on how to proceed with analyzing the study. It is not necessary to stick to the hints provided but a correct PAC analysis is a must to derive the correct outcome. Based on the *Navamsa* concepts and their detailed worked out applications showcased in the previous chapters, **we expect the student/reader to analyze these case studies in a similar logical and pointwise manner to gain strength in analysis.** It is but obvious that there are shortcuts to every chart to arrive at the right conclusion – but these shortcuts should only be used by the expert/instructor for their own use, and not for the purpose of exposition.

We divide our suite of case studies into five topics: **(i) education, (ii) career, (iii) marriage and relationships, (iv) wealth and fortune,** and **(v) children**. We provide a problem statement, the D1, the D9, and additional birth details (if applicable) for every chart as sufficient material for analysis.

Case Study E1 (Education)

Problem Statement – The native got his doctorate on the 17th of January 1984. **Analyze using the D1 and the D9 why this event occurred.** You may calculate transits (if needed) based on birth data. *Hint:* Use *dasha*/transit ideas discussed in Chapter 7, 8.

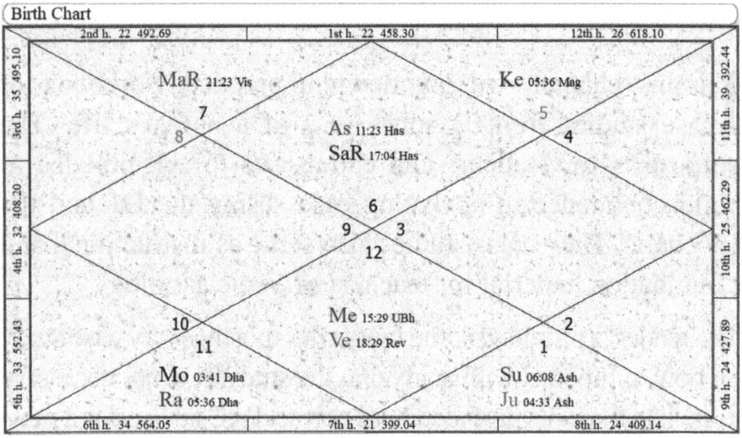

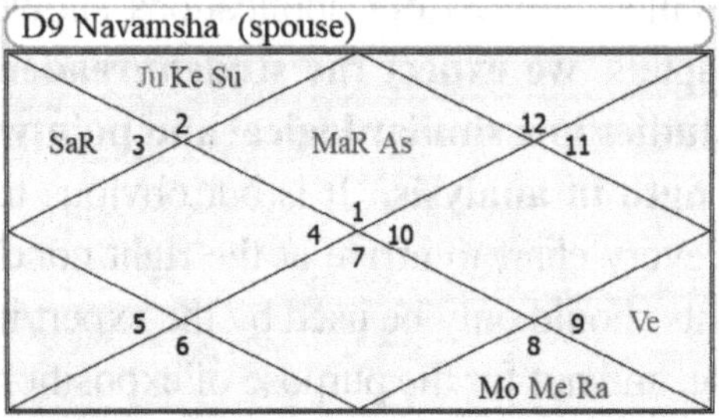

Birth Details: 19th April 1952, 16:52, New Delhi, India

Case Study E2 (Astrology Education)

Problem Statement – The native started his astrology education when he was undergoing the Sun MD. **Analyze using the D1 and the D9 why this event occurred, and whether he would continue in the field of Vedic astrology.** *Hint:* Use *dasha* analysis ideas discussed in Chapter 7.

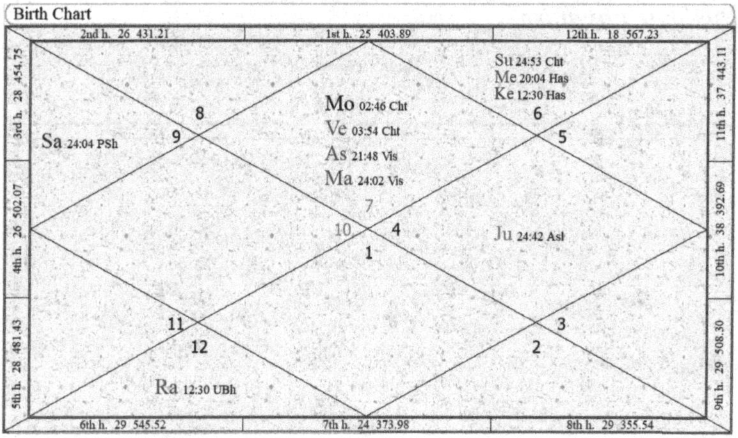

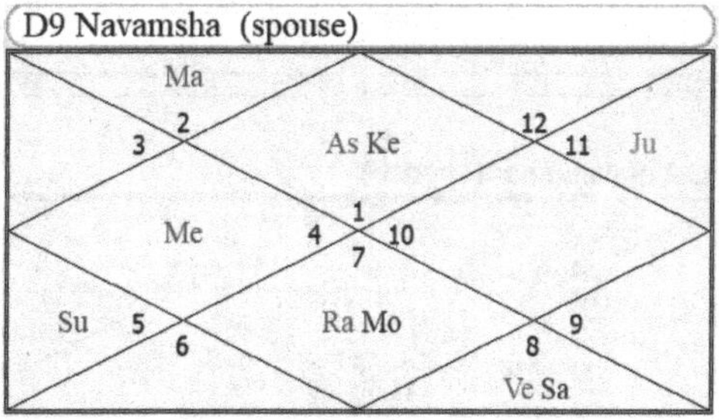

Birth Details: 12th October 1931, 07:53, Machilipatnam, India

Case Study E3 (Education)

Problem Statement – The native has a sharp mind but could not do well in his basic school education when he was undergoing the Rahu MD. **Analyze using the D1 and the D9 why this happened.** *Hint:* Use *dasha* analysis ideas discussed in Chapter 7, in addition to the concept of the *Pushkar navamsa*.

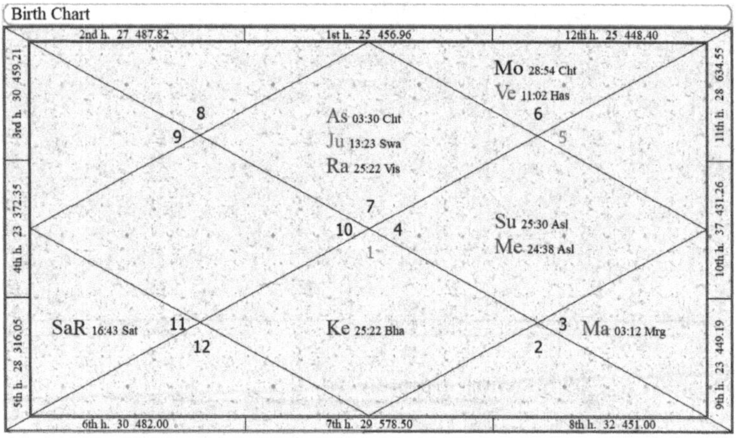

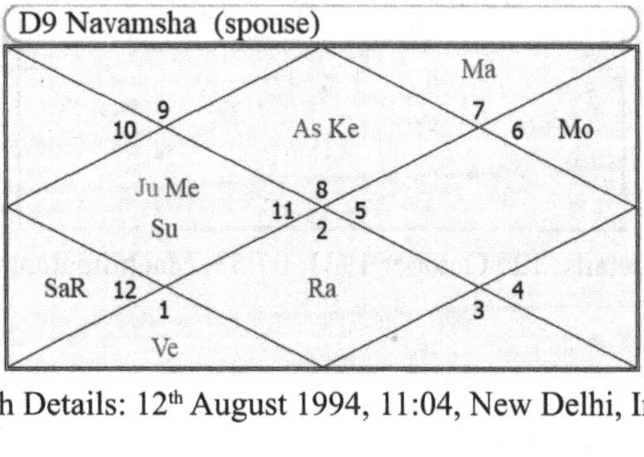

Birth Details: 12th August 1994, 11:04, New Delhi, India

Case Study E4 (Education)

Problem Statement – The native is currently a well-known logician. However, he relatively struggled with logic and memory in basic school education when he was undergoing the Saturn MD. **Analyze using the D1 and the D9 why this happened.** *Hint:* Use *dasha* analysis ideas discussed in Chapter 7.

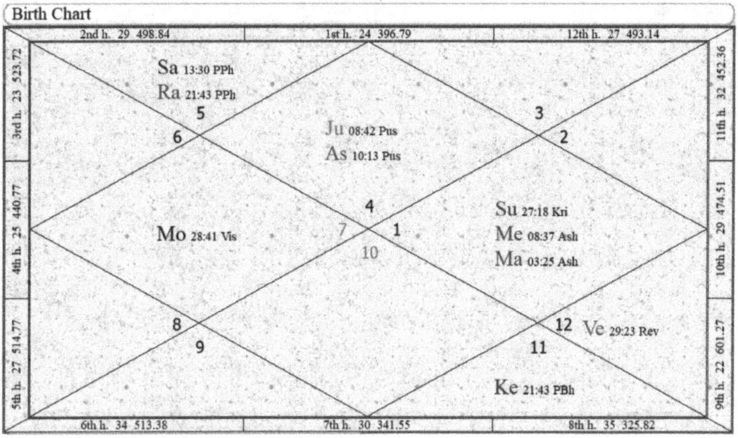

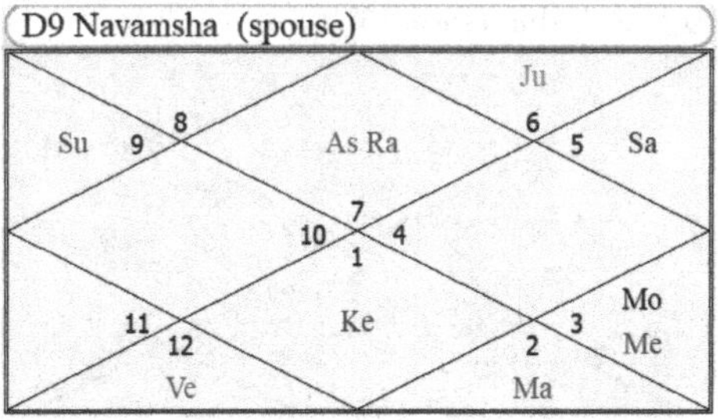

Birth Details: 12th May 1979, 10:10, Kolkata, India

Case Study E5 (Education)

Problem Statement – The native had a very rough time in his school education, especially during his Ketu MD, but showed his genius in higher education when he was undergoing Venus MD. **Analyze using the D1 and the D9 why this happened.** *Hint:* Use *dasha* analysis ideas discussed in Chapter 7.

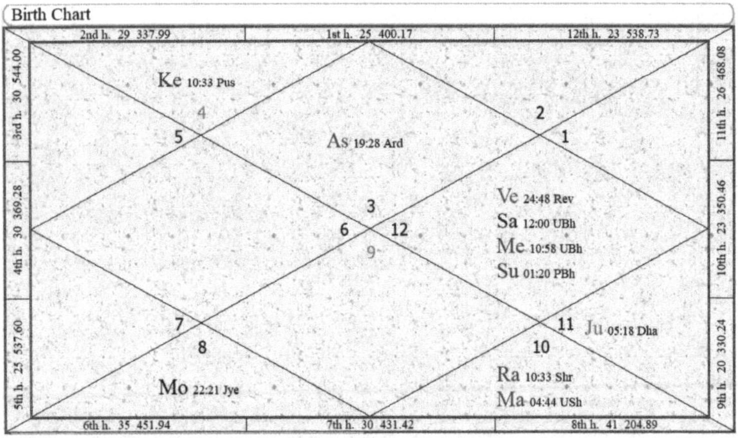

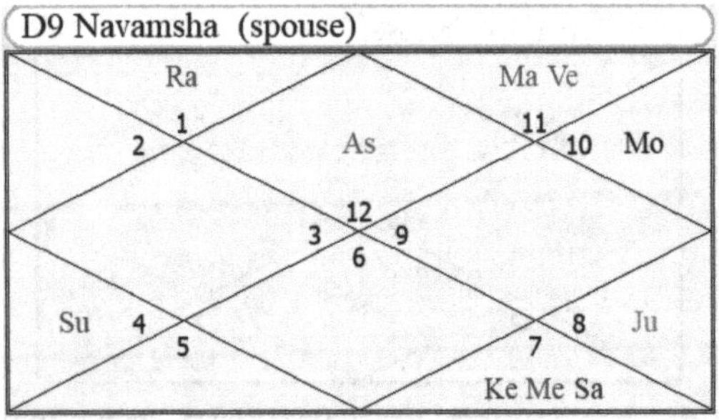

Birth Details: 14th March, 1879, 11:30, Ulm, Germany

Case Study C1 (Career)

Problem Statement – The native got a very high boost in his career as a civil servant and ranked in the competitive examination when he was undergoing the Mercury/Mercury period. The native got this boost on 8th July, 1994. **Analyze using the D1 and the D9 why this happened.** *Hint:* Use *dasha*/transit analysis ideas discussed in Chapters 7 and 8.

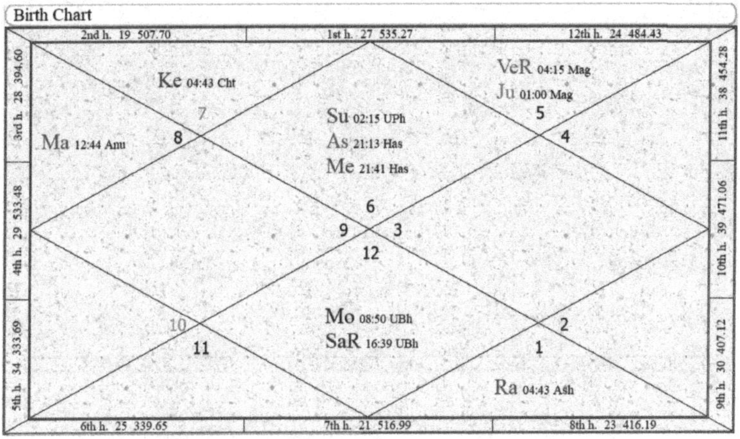

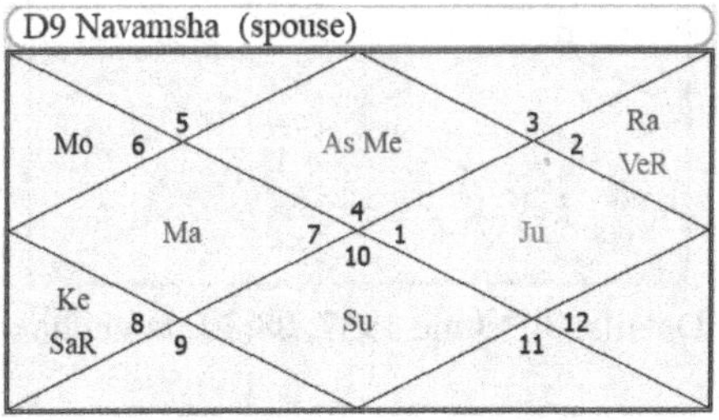

Birth Details: 19th September 1967, 08:15, Brussels, Belgium

Case Study C2 (Career)

Problem Statement – The native is a war officer. **Justify the military career of the native using the D1 and the D9 charts.** The native started his career in the Mercury/Mercury period and became a general in the Venus MD. **Justify this career progress using the D1 and the D9 charts.** *Hint:* Use *dasha* analysis ideas discussed in Chapter 7.

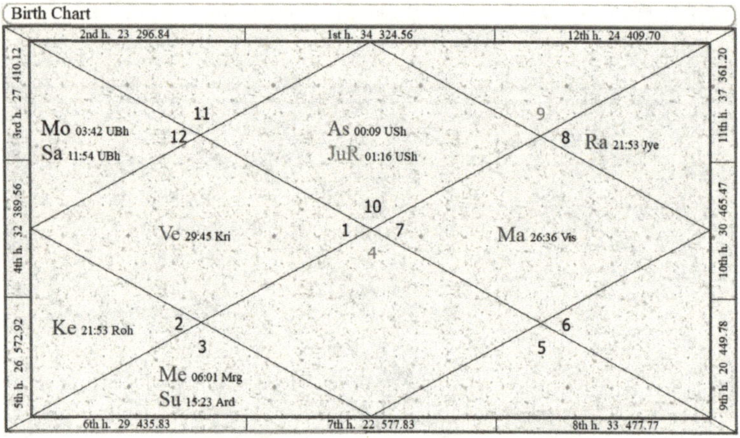

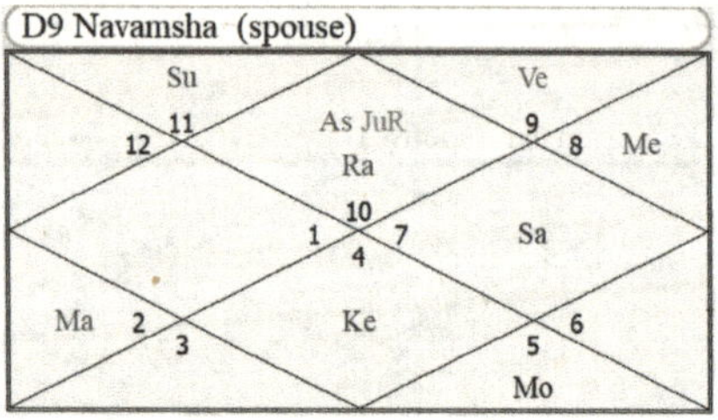

Birth Details: 30th June 1937, 08:30, Jalandhar, India

Case Study C3 (Career)

Problem Statement – The native is a state leader (politician). **Justify the political career of the native using the D1 and the D9 charts.** The native became a Governor in 1986. **Justify using the D1 and the D9.** The native loses a major election in 1989 but remained undefeated between 1990 and 1997. **Justify this career down and up from the D1 and the D9**. *Hint:* Use *dasha* and transit analysis.

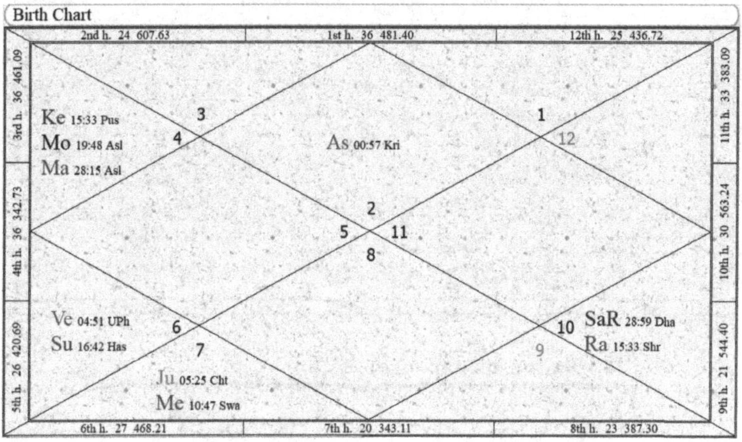

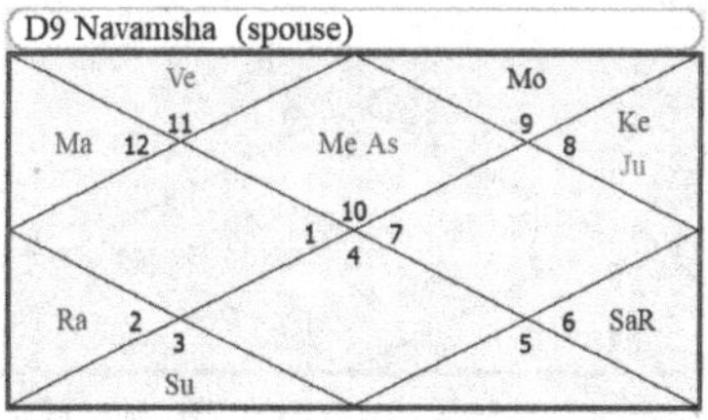

Birth Details: 3rd October 1934, 20:00, Sibsagar, India

Case Study C4 (Career)

Problem Statement – The native is a businessman. **Justify business as a career for the native using the D1 and the D9 charts.** *Hint:* Apply principles of career assessment from Sun, Moon, and Lagna.

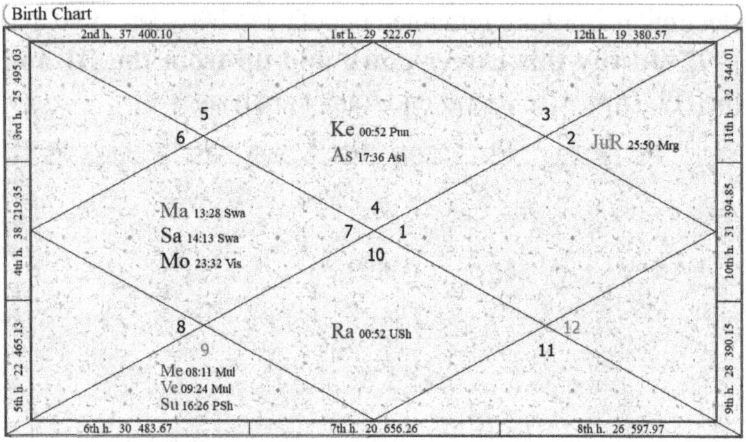

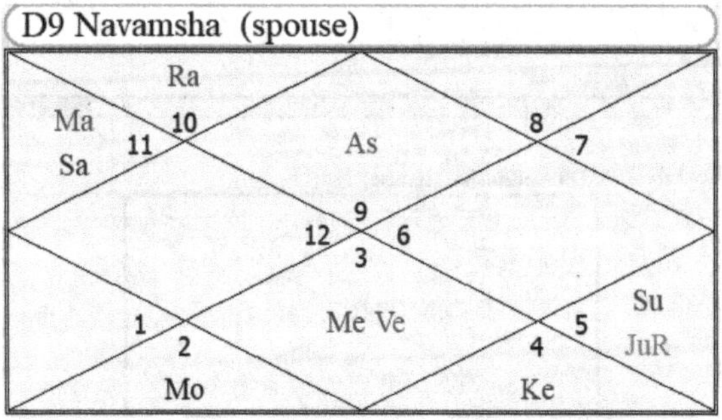

Birth Details: 31st December 1953, 20:28, Bombay, India

Case Study C5 (Career)

Problem Statement – The native is a journalist. **Justify journalism as a career for the native using the D1 and the D9 charts.** *Hint:* Apply principles of career assessment from Sun, Moon, and Lagna.

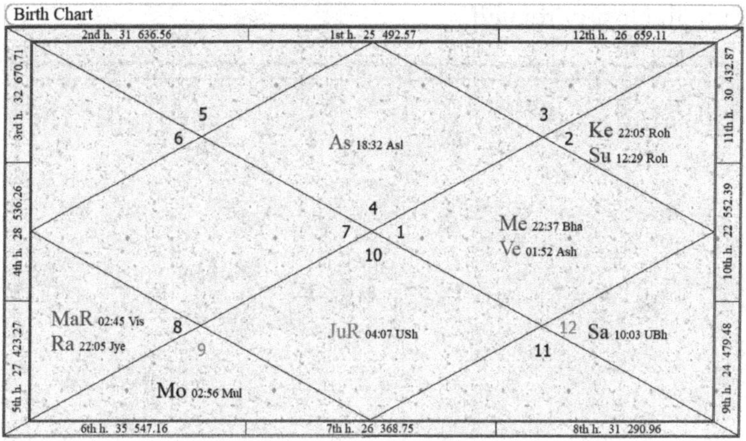

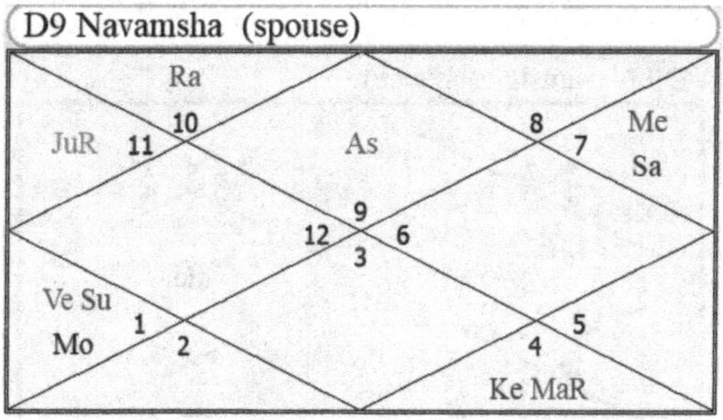

Birth Details: 27 May 1937, 10:13, Garhwal, India

Case Study C6 (Career)

Problem Statement – The native has a transferrable job in the government. **Justify this career trait for the native using the D1 and the D9 charts.** Hint: A transfer in job is different from transfer to different locations for a living – though closely related.

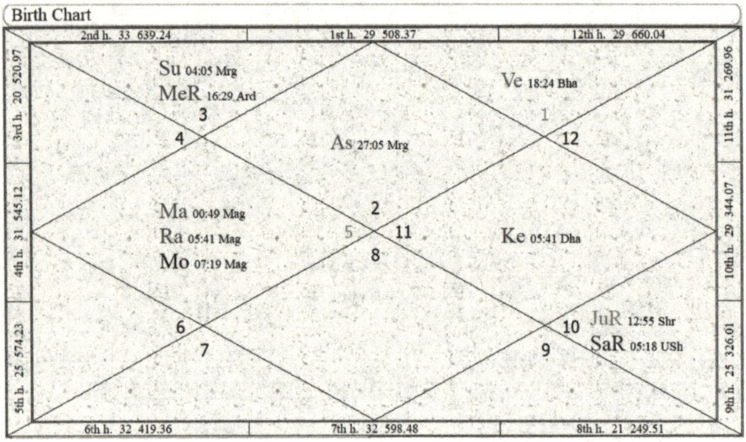

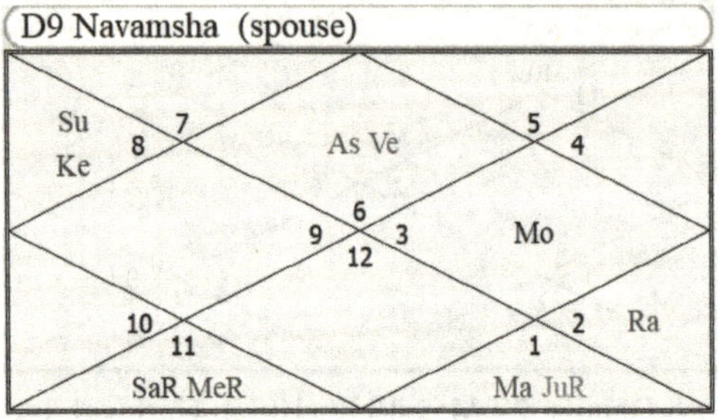

Birth Details: 19 June 1961, 04:00, Tezpur, India

Case Study C7 (Career)

Problem Statement – The native has a transferrable job in a government transport sector. **Justify this job trait using the D1 and the D9 charts.** The native got a transfer in the Rahu/ Venus period. **Justify this transfer in his career using a *dasha* analysis on the D1 and the D9 charts.**

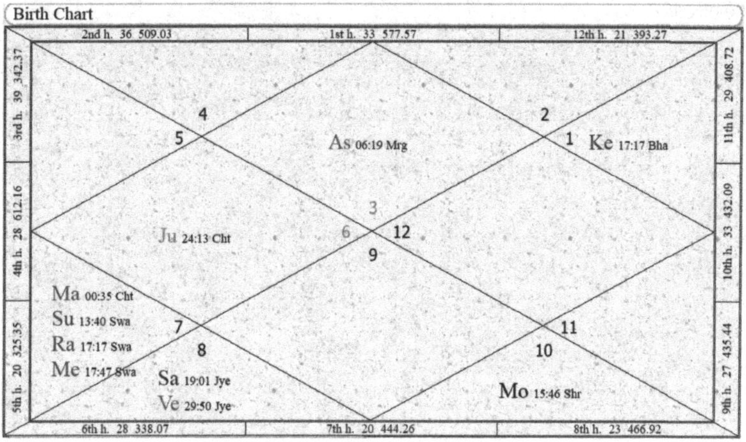

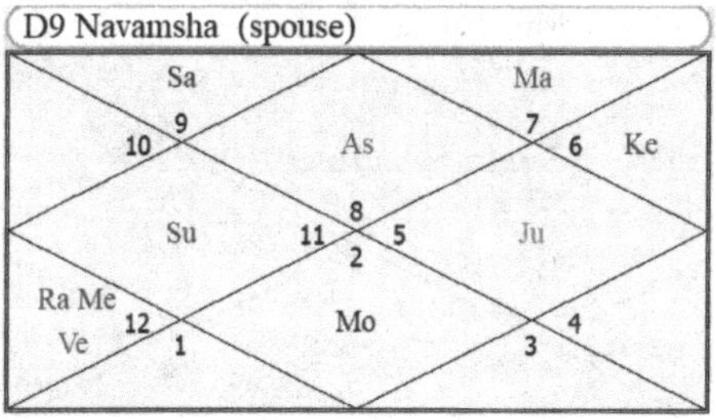

Birth Details: 30 October 1957, 20:50, Agra, India

Case Study C8 (Career)

***Problem Statement* – Justify the career of this native using the D1 and the D9 charts.** How did his career progress take a turn on June 10, 1967, and on October 1, 1973. **Justify this progress in his career using a *dasha* and transit analysis on the D1 and the D9 charts.**

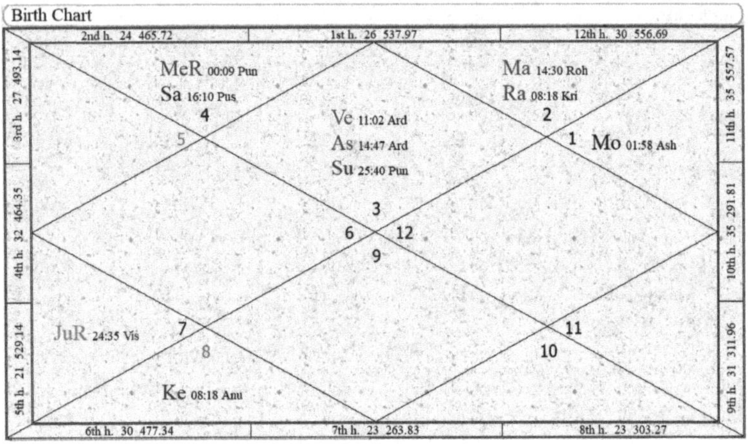

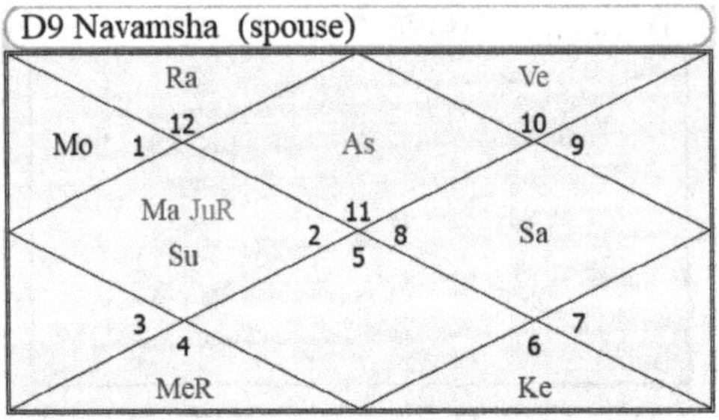

Birth Details: 12 July 1947, 04:50 Lahore, Pakistan

Case Study W1 (Wealth)

Problem Statement – The native got a big financial boost on the 2nd of November 1994 in the Rahu/Mercury period. **Justify this financial fortune gain using the D1 and the D9 charts.** You may use the placement of the Indu and Hora *lagnas* for the purpose of analysis. The details are on the next page. One may also use *upagraha* placements for analysis.

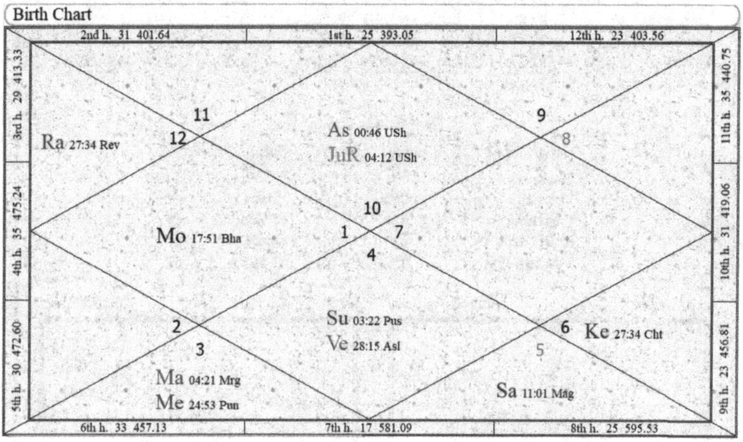

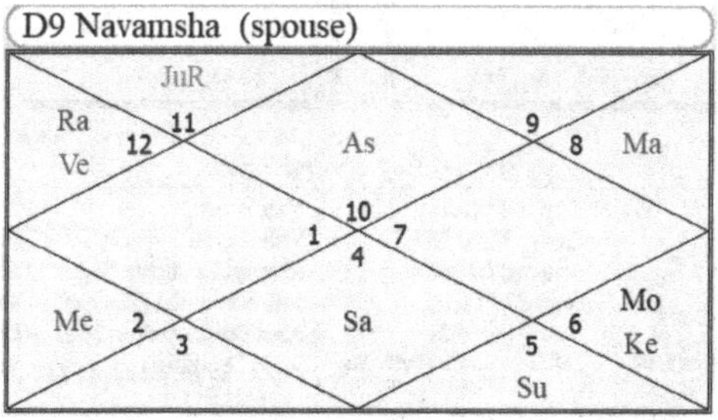

Birth Details: 19th July 1949, 19:11, Shimla, India

W1 ॐ Sub-Planets

Upagrahas or Sub-planets

Gulikaadi Group

Birth between mid-day and sun-set • Sunrise-Sunset : 05:34-19:20 • Astrological Weekday : Tuesday

Upagraha	Lord	Duration of Upagraha	Beginning (Parashara Method)				Ending (Kalidasa method)			
			Sign	Degree	Nakshatra	P	Sign	Degree	Nakshatra	P
Kaalavela	Sun	14:10-15:53	Lib	23:02:09	Vishakha	1	Sco	14:48:34	Anuradha	4
Paridhi	Mon	15:53-17:37	Sco	14:48:34	Anuradha	4	Sag	07:33:39	Moola	3
Mrityu	Mar	05:34-07:17	Can	02:50:09	Punarvasu	4	Can	24:34:38	Ashlesha	3
Ardhaprahara	Mer	07:17-09:00	Can	24:34:38	Ashlesha	3	Leo	16:32:49	P.Phalg.	1
Yamakantaka	Jup	09:00-10:43	Leo	16:32:49	P.Phalg.	1	Vir	08:51:47	U.Phalg.	4
Kodanda	Ven	10:43-12:27	Vir	08:51:47	U.Phalg.	4	Lib	01:08:14	Chitra	3
Gulika	Sat	12:27-14:10	Lib	01:08:14	Chitra	3	Lib	23:02:09	Vishakha	1

Dhoomadi Group

Upagraha	Lord	Sign	Degree	Nakshatra	Pd.
Dhooma	Mar	Sco	16:42:38	Jyeshtha	1
Vyatipata	Rah	Leo	13:17:22	Magha	4
Parivesha	Mon	Aqu	13:17:22	Satabhi.	2
Inderchapa	Ven	Tau	16:42:38	Rohini	3
Upaketu	Ket	Gem	03:22:38	Mrigashi	4

Upagraha Chart (Beginning Time)

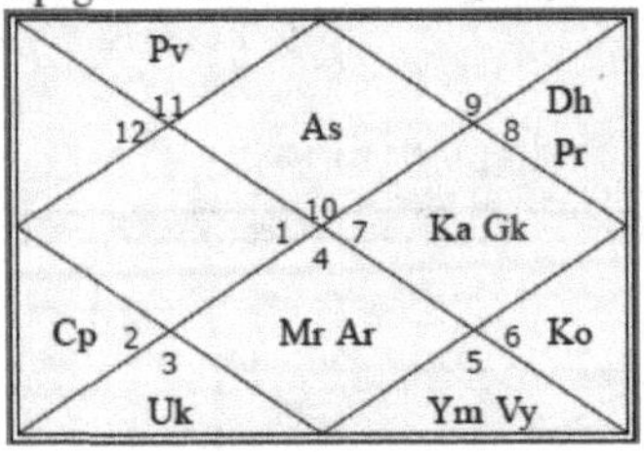

Upagraha Chart (Ending Time)

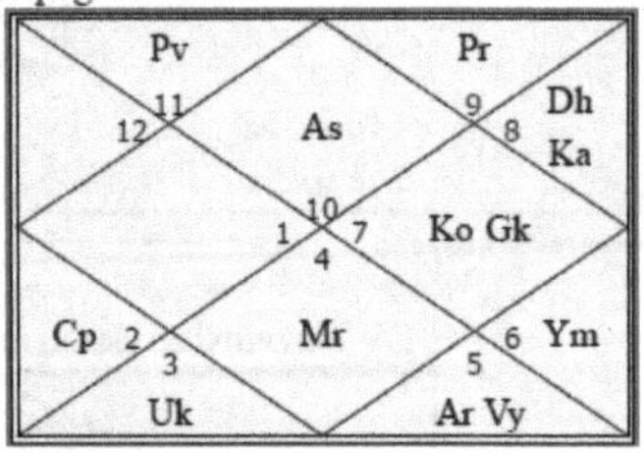

Special Lagnas and Points

Bhava Lagna	Cap	27:05:16	Yogi Point	24:33:51 Lib
Hora Lagna	Leo	21:20:23	Yogi	Ju
Ghatika Lagna	Tau	04:05:46	Avayogi/Duplicate Yogi	Su/Ve
Indu Lagna	Vir	15:00:00	64th Navamsha (Mo/As)	Sagittarius/Aries
Beeja Sphuta	Leo	05:50:21	22nd Dreshkana (As/Mo)	Leo/Pisces
Birth chart/Navamsha	odd/even 50% (medium)		Sarpa Dreshkana	VeRa

Hint: Look at the *arth*/gain houses from Hora and Indu *lagnas*.

Case Study W2 (Wealth)

Problem Statement – The native was blessed with great wealth and fortune that he made by himself. **Justify this financial fortune using the D1 and the D9 charts.** You may use the placement of the Indu and Hora *lagnas* for the purpose of analysis. The details are on the next page. One may also use *upagraha* placements for analysis.

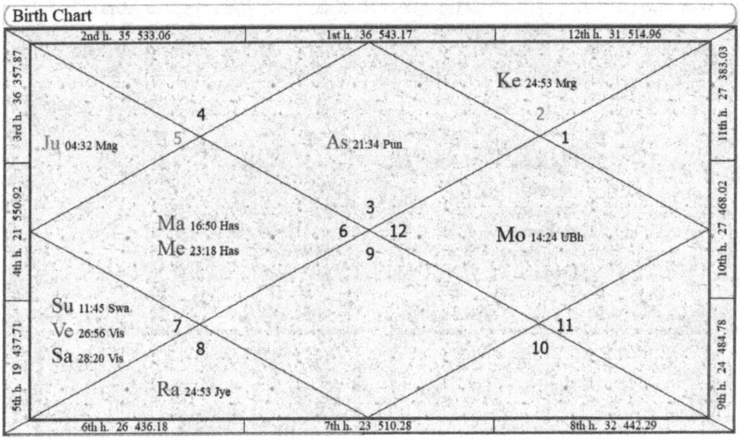

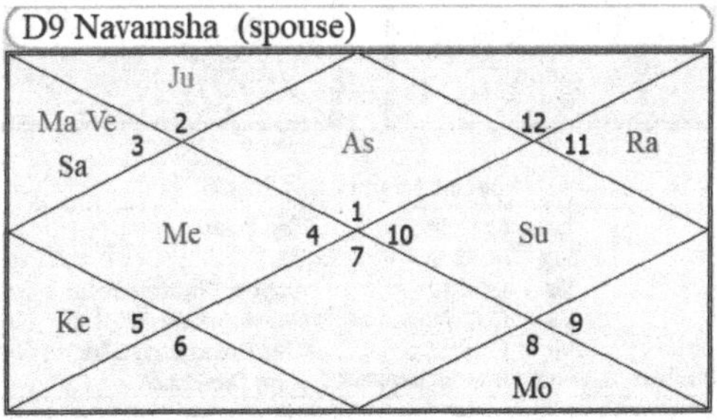

Birth Details: 28th October 1955, 20:58, Seattle, USA

W2 ॐ Sub-Planets

Upagrahas or Sub-planets

Gulikaadi Group

Birth between sun-set and midnight • Sunrise-Sunset : 06:51-16:53 • Astrological Weekday : Friday

Upagraha	Lord	Duration of Upagraha	Beginning (Parashara Method)				Ending (Kalidasa method)			
			Sign	Degree	Nakshatra	P	Sign	Degree	Nakshatra	P
Kaalavela	Sun	01:38-03:23	Leo	14:05:20	P.Phalg.	1	Vir	03:28:09	U.Phalg.	3
Paridhi	Mon	03:23-05:08	Vir	03:28:09	U.Phalg.	3	Vir	22:53:01	Hasta	4
Mrityu	Mar	16:53-18:38	Ari	11:34:55	Ashwini	4	Tau	18:55:17	Rohini	3
Ardhaprahara	Mer	18:38-20:23	Tau	18:55:17	Rohini	3	Gem	14:26:58	Ardra	3
Yamakantaka	Jup	20:23-22:08	Gem	14:26:58	Ardra	3	Can	05:22:33	Pushya	1
Kodanda	Ven	22:08-23:53	Can	05:22:33	Pushya	1	Can	24:50:30	Ashlesha	3
Gulika	Sat	23:53-01:38	Can	24:50:30	Ashlesha	3	Leo	14:05:20	P.Phalg.	1

Dhoomadi Group

Upagraha	Lord	Sign	Degree	Nakshatra	Pd.
Dhooma	Mar	Aqu	25:05:09	P.Bhadra.	2
Vyatipata	Rah	Tau	04:54:51	Krittika	3
Parivesha	Mon	Sco	04:54:51	Anuradha	1
Inderchapa	Ven	Leo	25:05:09	P.Phalg.	4
Upaketu	Ket	Vir	11:45:09	Hasta	1

Upagraha Chart (Beginning Time)

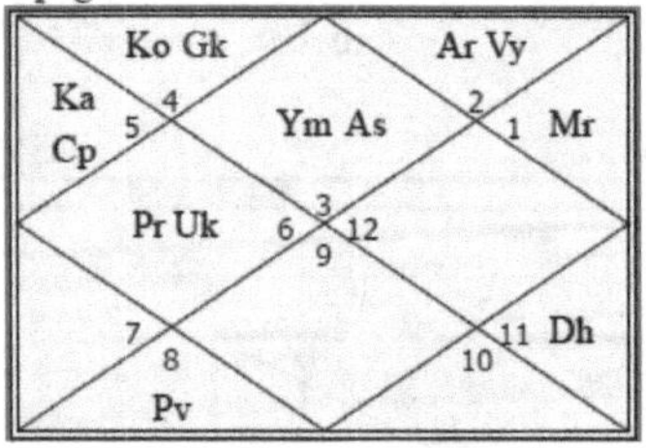

Upagraha Chart (Ending Time)

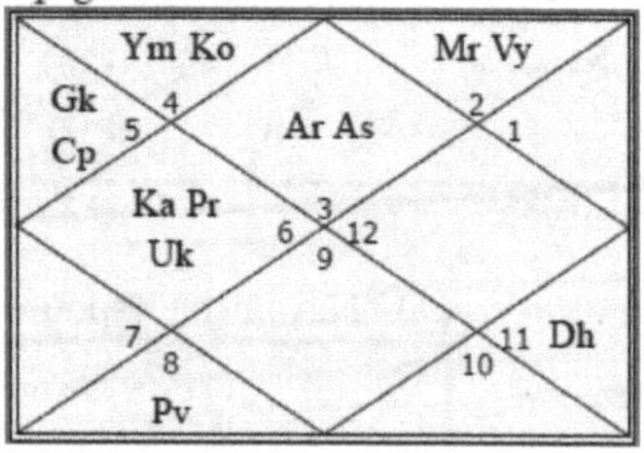

Special Lagnas and Points

Bhava Lagna	Tau	12:43:24	Yogi Point	29:29:10 Sag
Hora Lagna	Sag	14:16:51	Yogi	Su
Ghatika Lagna	Vir	18:57:12	Avayogi/Duplicate Yogi	Sa/Ju
Indu Lagna	Vir	15:00:00	64th Navamsha (Mo/As)	Aquarius/Cancer
Beeja Sphuta	Vir	13:13:12	22nd Dreshkana (As/Mo)	Virgo/Aquarius
Birth chart/Navamsha	even/odd 50% (medium)		Sarpa Dreshkana	

Hint: Look at the *arth*/gain houses from Hora and Indu *lagnas*.

Case Study W3 (Wealth)

Problem Statement – The native maintained and increased on the great wealth and fortune that he was blessed with through a family lineage. **Justify this financial fortune using the D1 and the D9 charts.** You may use the placement of the Indu and Hora *lagnas* for the purpose of analysis. The details are on the next page.

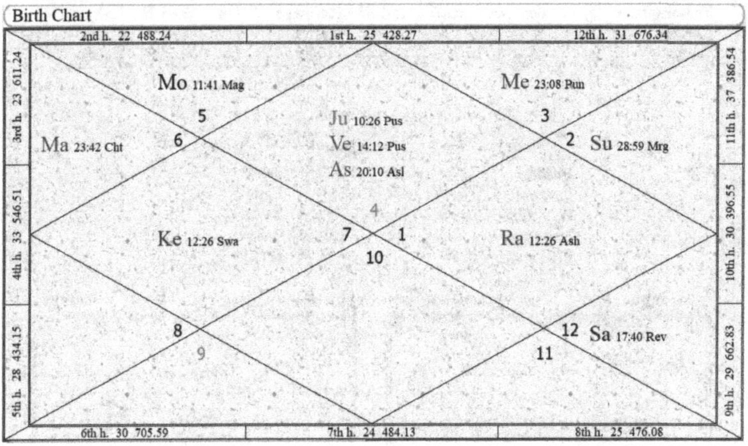

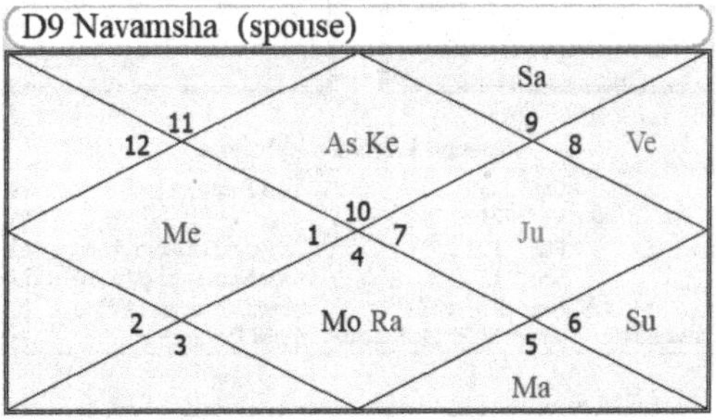

Birth Details: 14th June 1967, 08:45, Kolkata, India

W3 Sub-Planets

Upagrahas or Sub-planets

Gulikaadi Group

Birth between sun-rise and mid-day • Sunrise-Sunset : 04:55-18:17 • Astrological Weekday : Wednesday

Upagraha	Lord	Duration of Upagraha	Beginning (Parashara Method)				Ending (Kalidasa method)			
			Sign	Degree	Nakshatra	P	Sign	Degree	Nakshatra	P
Kaalavela	Sun	11:36-13:16	Leo	29:04:53	U.Phalg.	1	Vir	22:15:34	Hasta	4
Paridhi	Mon	13:16-14:57	Vir	22:15:34	Hasta	4	Lib	15:01:35	Swati	3
Mrityu	Mar	14:57-16:37	Lib	15:01:35	Swati	3	Sco	07:12:04	Anuradha	2
Ardhaprahara	Mer	04:55-06:35	Tau	28:50:47	Mrigashi	2	Gem	21:41:55	Punarvasu	1
Yamakantaka	Jup	06:35-08:15	Gem	21:41:55	Punarvasu	1	Can	13:45:27	Pushya	4
Kodanda	Ven	08:15-09:56	Can	13:45:27	Pushya	4	Leo	06:06:52	Magha	2
Gulika	Sat	09:56-11:36	Leo	06:06:52	Magha	2	Leo	29:04:53	U.Phalg.	1

Dhoomadi Group

Upagraha	Lord	Sign	Degree	Nakshatra	Pd.
Dhooma	Mar	Lib	12:19:56	Swati	2
Vyatipata	Rah	Vir	17:40:04	Hasta	3
Parivesha	Mon	Pis	17:40:04	Revati	1
Inderchapa	Ven	Ari	12:19:56	Ashwini	4
Upaketu	Ket	Ari	28:59:56	Krittika	1

Upagraha Chart (Beginning Time)

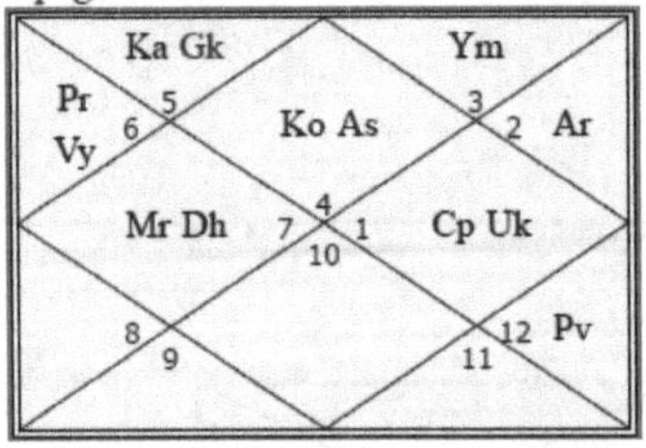

Upagraha Chart (Ending Time)

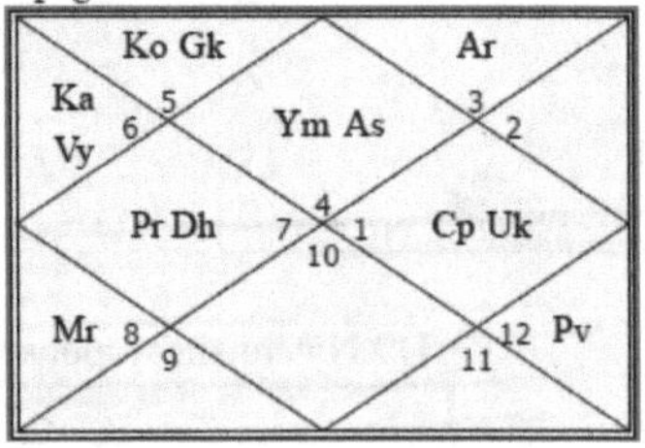

Special Lagnas and Points

Bhava Lagna	Can	26:15:12	Yogi Point	14:01:42 Cap
Hora Lagna	Vir	23:39:38	Yogi	Mo
Ghatika Lagna	Pis	15:52:53	Avayogi/Duplicate Yogi	Me/Sa
Indu Lagna	Sco	15:00:00	64th Navamsha (Mo/As)	Libra/Aries
Beeja Sphuta	Sag	23:38:07	22nd Dreshkana (As/Mo)	Libra/Cancer
Birth chart/Navamsha	odd/even 50% (medium)		Sarpa Dreshkana	JuVe

Hint: Look at the *arth*/gain houses from Hora and Indu *lagnas*.

Case Study W4 (Wealth)

Problem Statement – The native is a businessman who earned who earned his wealth with lots of courage. **Justify this point with the D1 and the D9 charts.** The native made lots of wealth in the Jupiter, Moon, Sun, and Venus periods. **Justify with the D1 and the D9 charts.** You may use the placement of the Indu/Hora *lagnas* for the purpose of analysis.

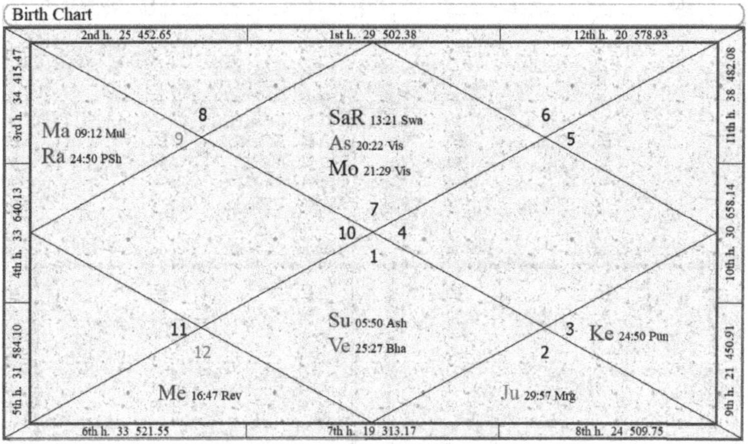

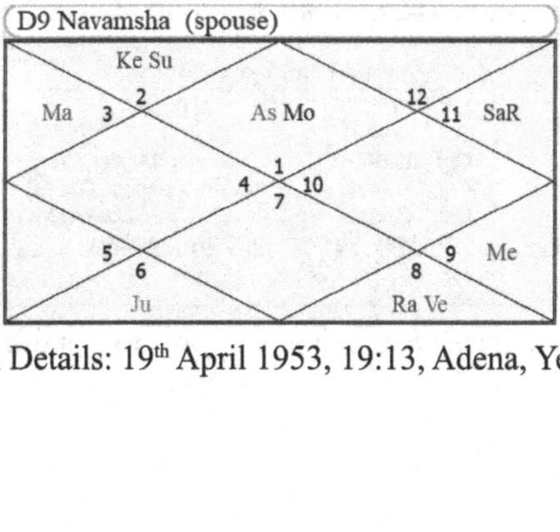

Birth Details: 19th April 1953, 19:13, Adena, Yemen

W4 Sub-Planets

Upagrahas or Sub-planets

Gulikaadi Group

Birth between sun-set and midnight • Sunrise-Sunset : 05:49-18:11 • Astrological Weekday : Monday

Upagraha	Lord	Duration of Upagraha	Beginning (Parashara Method)				Ending (Kalidasa method)			
			Sign	Degree	Nakshatra	P	Sign	Degree	Nakshatra	P
Kaalavela	Sun	21:06-22:33	Sco	16:17:55	Anuradha	4	Sag	06:06:32	Moola	2
Paridhi	Mon	22:33-00:00	Sag	06:06:32	Moola	2	Sag	26:42:18	U.Shad.	1
Mrityu	Mar	00:00-01:27	Sag	26:42:18	U.Shad.	1	Cap	19:04:24	Shravana	3
Ardhaprahara	Mer	01:27-02:54	Cap	19:04:24	Shravana	3	Aqu	13:46:44	Satabhi.	3
Yamakantaka	Jup	02:54-04:22	Aqu	13:46:44	Satabhi.	3	Pis	10:09:41	U.Bhadra.	3
Kodanda	Ven	18:11-19:38	Lib	05:47:39	Chitra	4	Lib	26:22:43	Vishakha	2
Gulika	Sat	19:38-21:06	Lib	26:22:43	Vishakha	2	Sco	16:17:55	Anuradha	4

Dhoomadi Group

Upagraha	Lord	Sign	Degree	Nakshatra	Pd.
Dhooma	Mar	Leo	19:10:15	P.Phalg.	2
Vyatipata	Rah	Sco	10:49:45	Anuradha	3
Parivesha	Mon	Tau	10:49:45	Rohini	1
Inderchapa	Ven	Aqu	19:10:15	Satabhi.	4
Upaketu	Ket	Pis	05:50:15	U.Bhadra.	1

Upagraha Chart (Beginning Time)

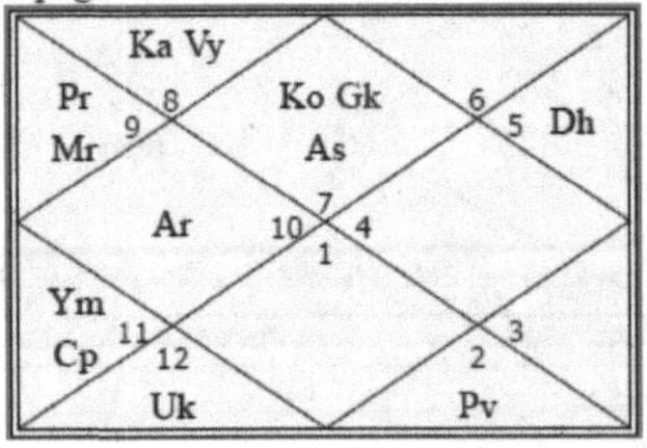

Upagraha Chart (Ending Time)

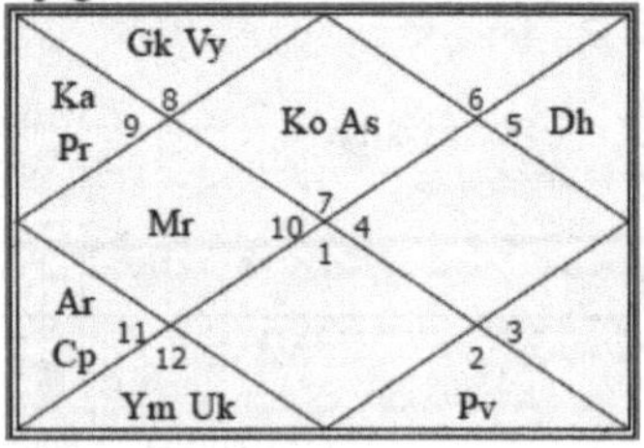

Special Lagnas and Points

Bhava Lagna	Lib	26:02:53	Yogi Point	00:39:35 Aqu
Hora Lagna	Tau	16:48:11	Yogi	Ma
Ghatika Lagna	Cap	19:04:04	Avayogi/Duplicate Yogi	Ke/Sa
Indu Lagna	Cap	15:00:00	64th Navamsha (Mo/As)	Cancer/Cancer
Beeja Sphuta	Can	01:15:02	22nd Dreshkana (As/Mo)	Capricorn/Capricorn
Birth chart/Navamsha	even/even 0% (poor)		Sarpa Dreshkana	

Hint: Look at the *arth*/gain houses from Hora and Indu *lagnas*.

Case Study W5 (Wealth)

Problem Statement – The native is in the entertainment world and earned a lot of reputation and wealth. **Justify this point with the D1 and the D9 charts.** The native took a big hit in his wealth base between the Mercury/Venus period to the Me/Mars period. **Justify this point with the D1 and the D9 charts.** You may use the placement of the Indu/Hora *lagnas* for the purpose of analysis.

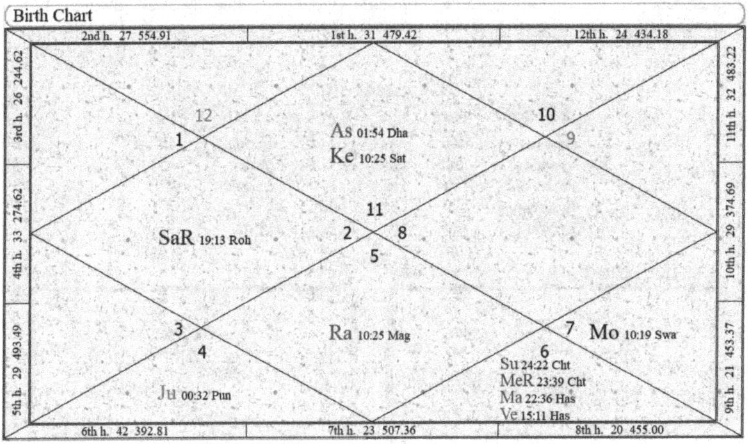

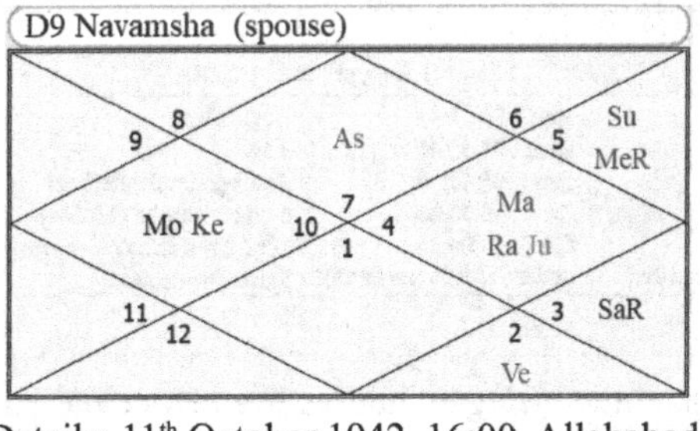

Birth Details: 11th October 1942, 16:00, Allahabad, India

W5 Sub-Planets

Upagrahas or Sub-planets

Gulikaadi Group

Birth between mid-day and sun-set • Sunrise-Sunset : 07:02-18:36 • Astrological Weekday : Sunday

Upagraha	Lord	Duration of Upagraha	Beginning (Parashara Method)				Ending (Kalidasa method)			
			Sign	Degree	Nakshatra	P	Sign	Degree	Nakshatra	P
Kaalavela	Sun	07:02-08:29	Vir	24:00:44	Chitra	1	Lib	13:18:55	Swati	2
Paridhi	Mon	08:29-09:56	Lib	13:18:55	Swati	2	Sco	02:13:53	Vishakha	4
Mrityu	Mar	09:56-11:22	Sco	02:13:53	Vishakha	4	Sco	21:05:07	Jyeshtha	2
Ardhaprahara	Mer	11:22-12:49	Sco	21:05:07	Jyeshtha	2	Sag	10:38:22	Moola	4
Yamakantaka	Jup	12:49-14:16	Sag	10:38:22	Moola	4	Cap	02:03:15	U.Shad.	2
Kodanda	Ven	14:16-15:42	Cap	02:03:15	U.Shad.	2	Cap	26:38:21	Dhanish.	1
Gulika	Sat	15:42-17:09	Cap	26:38:21	Dhanish.	1	Aqu	24:48:59	P.Bhadra.	2

Dhoomadi Group

Upagraha	Lord	Sign	Degree	Nakshatra	Pd.
Dhooma	Mar	Aqu	07:42:53	Satabhi.	1
Vyatipata	Rah	Tau	22:17:07	Rohini	4
Parivesha	Mon	Sco	22:17:07	Jyeshtha	2
Inderchapa	Ven	Leo	07:42:53	Magha	3
Upaketu	Ket	Leo	24:22:53	P.Phalg.	4

Upagraha Chart (Beginning Time)

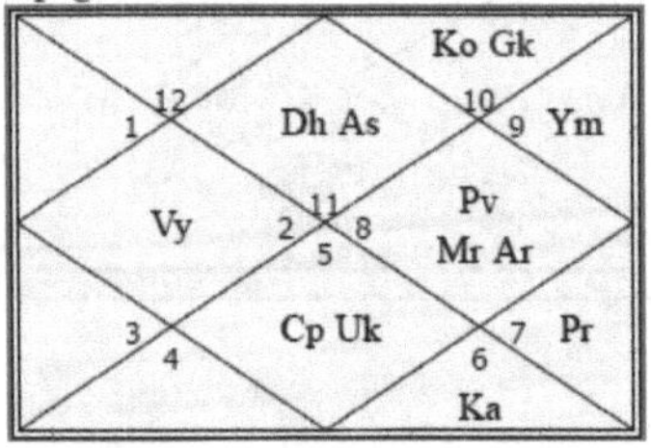

Upagraha Chart (Ending Time)

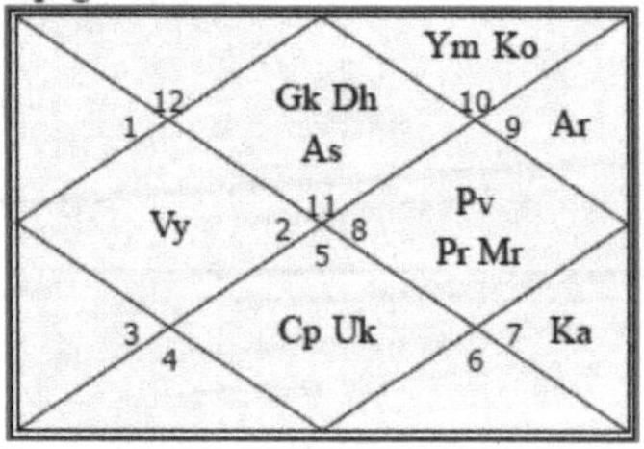

Special Lagnas and Points

Bhava Lagna	Aqu 08:21:45	Yogi Point	08:01:54 Can
Hora Lagna	Gem 22:42:46	Yogi	Sa
Ghatika Lagna	Leo 05:45:50	Avayogi/Duplicate Yogi	Mo/Mo
Indu Lagna	Tau 15:00:00	64th Navamsha (Mo/As)	Aries/Capricorn
Beeja Sphuta	Gem 10:06:30	22nd Dreshkana (As/Mo)	Virgo/Virgo
Birth chart/Navamsha	odd/even 50% (medium)	Sarpa Dreshkana	

Hint: Look at the *arth*/gain houses from Hora and Indu *lagnas*.

Case Study W6 (Wealth)

Problem Statement – The native is in the entertainment world and earned a lot of reputation and wealth. However, he started from very humble beginnings. **Justify this rise of wealth starting the Rahu/Venus period and extending till the Jupiter MD, with the D1 and the D9 charts.** You may use the placement of the Indu/Hora *lagnas* for the purpose of analysis.

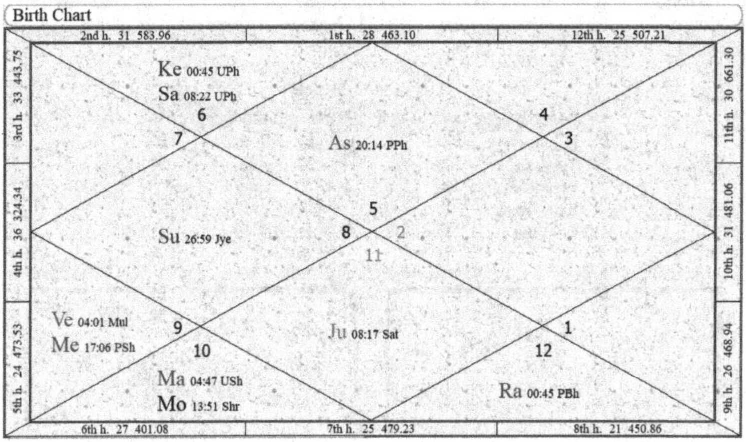

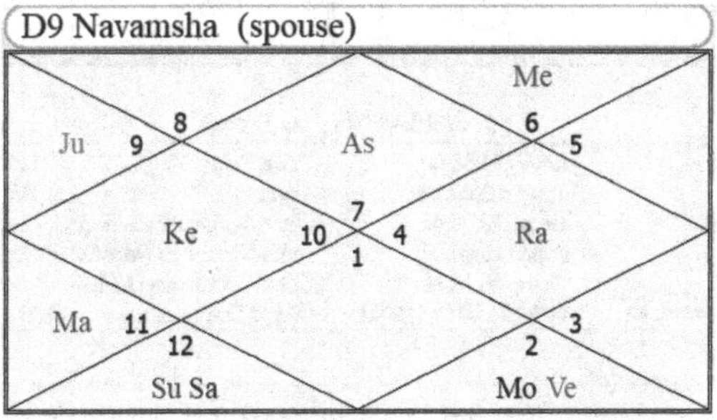

Birth Details: 12th December 1950, 23:49, Bangalore, India

W6 Sub-Planets

Upagrahas or Sub-planets

Gulikaadi Group

Birth between sun-set and midnight • Sunrise-Sunset : 06:35-17:50 • Astrological Weekday : Tuesday

Upagraha	Lord	Duration of Upagraha	Beginning (Parashara Method)				Ending (Kalidasa method)			
			Sign	Degree	Nakshatra	P	Sign	Degree	Nakshatra	P
Kaalavela	Sun	19:26-21:02	Gem	18:45:21	Ardra	4	Can	10:30:44	Pushya	3
Paridhi	Mon	21:02-22:37	Can	10:30:44	Pushya	3	Leo	02:55:52	Magha	1
Mrityu	Mar	22:37-00:13	Leo	02:55:52	Magha	1	Leo	26:15:53	P.Phalg.	4
Ardhaprahara	Mer	00:13-01:49	Leo	26:15:53	P.Phalg.	4	Vir	19:59:19	Hasta	3
Yamakantaka	Jup	01:49-03:24	Vir	19:59:19	Hasta	3	Lib	13:14:05	Swati	2
Kodanda	Ven	03:24-05:00	Lib	13:14:05	Swati	2	Sco	05:33:15	Anuradha	1
Gulika	Sat	17:50-19:26	Tau	26:44:21	Mrigashi	2	Gem	18:45:21	Ardra	4

Dhoomadi Group

Upagraha	Lord	Sign	Degree	Nakshatra	Pd.
Dhooma	Mar	Ari	10:19:38	Ashwini	4
Vyatipata	Rah	Pis	19:40:22	Revati	1
Parivesha	Mon	Vir	19:40:22	Hasta	3
Inderchapa	Ven	Lib	10:19:38	Swati	2
Upaketu	Ket	Lib	26:59:38	Vishakha	3

Upagraha Chart (Beginning Time)

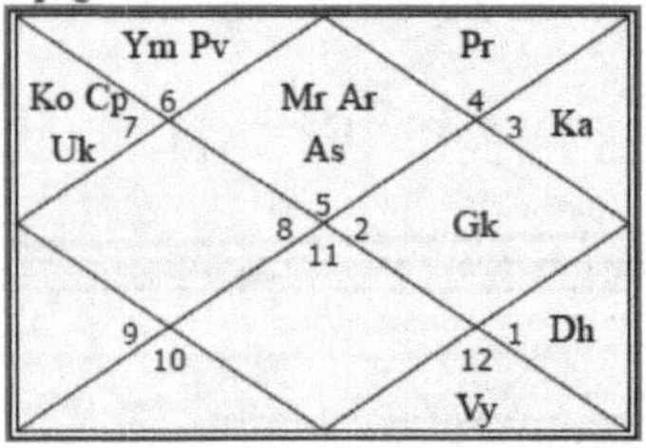

Upagraha Chart (Ending Time)

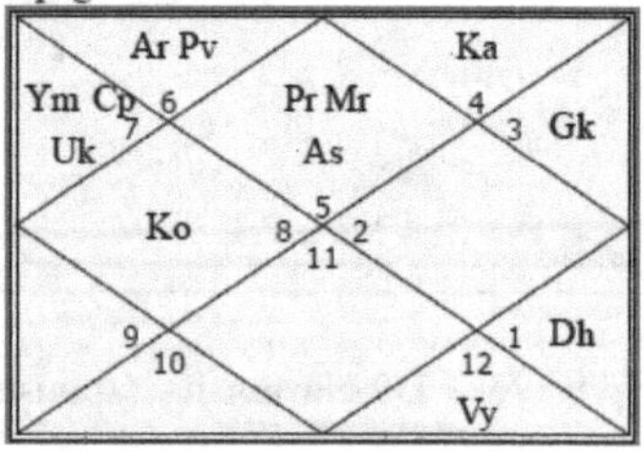

Special Lagnas and Points

Bhava Lagna	Leo 14:38:00	Yogi Point	14:11:27 Sag
Hora Lagna	Tau 03:00:10	Yogi	Ve
Ghatika Lagna	Gem 28:06:40	Avayogi/Duplicate Yogi	Ju/Ju
Indu Lagna	Aqu 15:00:00	64th Navamsha (Mo/As)	Leo/Capricorn
Beeja Sphuta	Gem 09:18:30	22nd Dreshkana (As/Mo)	Scorpio/Sagittarius
Birth chart/Navamsha	odd/odd 100% (good)	Sarpa Dreshkana	

Hint: Look at the *arth*/gain houses from Hora and Indu *lagnas*.

Case Study M1 (Marriage)

Problem Statement – Will the native get married? **Answer this question in view of the D1 and the D9 charts.** *Hint:* Use a point approach to see how many of the necessary conditions for marriage (taught in multiple courses globally) are satisfied in D1 and the D9 and make an assessment (correct answer – Yes).

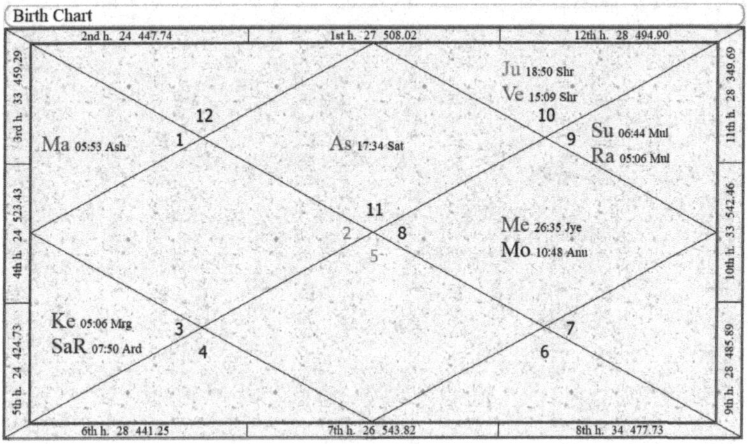

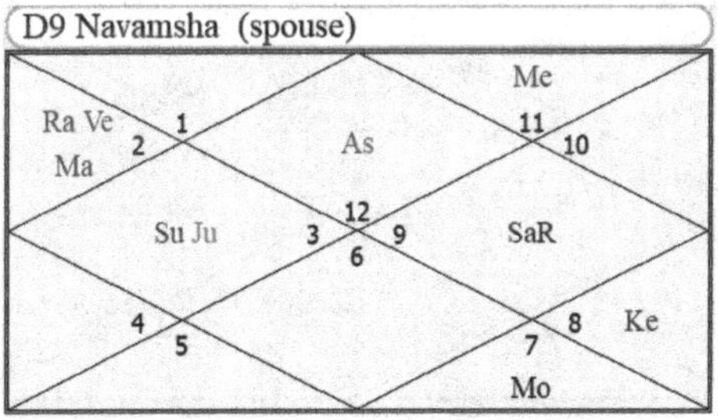

Birth Details: 22nd December 1973, 11:25, Delhi, India

Case Study M2 (Marriage)

Problem Statement – This native had a delayed marriage. **Justify this fact in view of the D1 and the D9 charts.** *Hint:* Use a point approach to see how many of the necessary conditions for marriage delay (taught in multiple courses globally) are satisfied in D1 and the D9 and do an analysis.

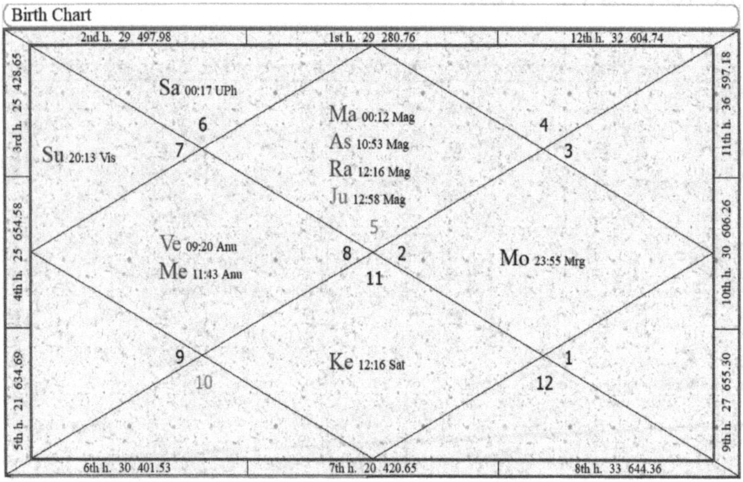

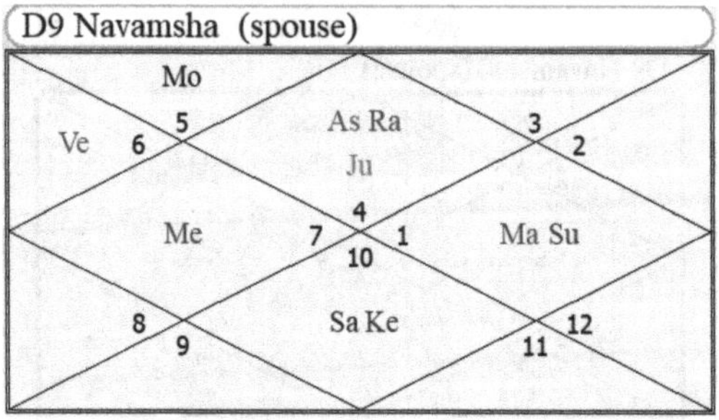

Birth Details: 7th November 1979, 01:23, Delhi, India

Case Study M3 (Marriage)

Problem Statement – This native had an early marriage. **Justify this fact in view of the D1 and the D9 charts.** *Hint:* Use a point approach to see how many of the necessary conditions for early marriage (taught in multiple courses globally) are satisfied in D1 and the D9 and do an analysis.

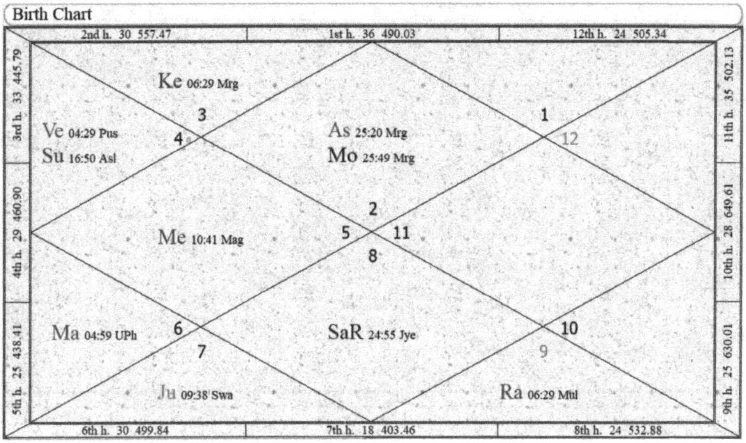

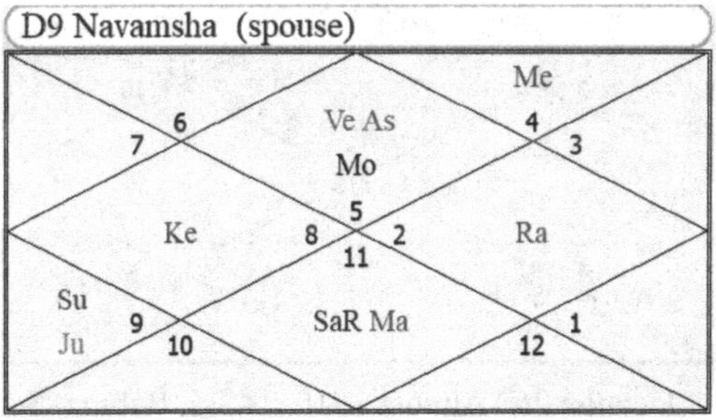

Birth Details: 2nd August 1899, 01:45, Delhi, India

Case Study M4 (Marriage)

Problem Statement – This native did not marry. **Justify this fact in view of the D1 and the D9 charts.** *Hint:* Use a point approach to see how many of the necessary conditions for no marriage (taught in multiple courses globally) are satisfied in D1 and the D9 and do an analysis.

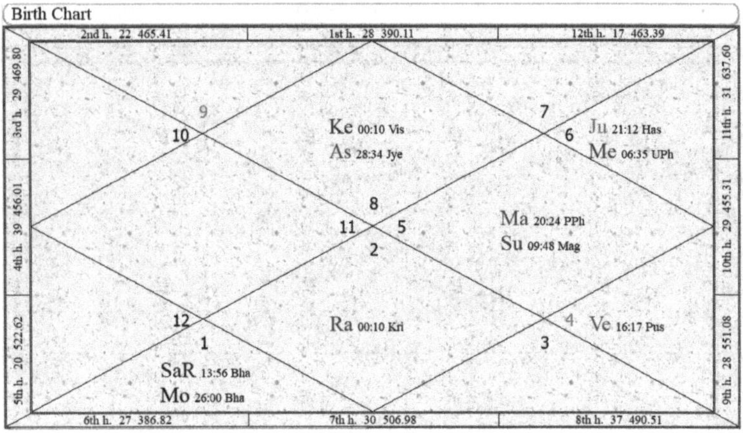

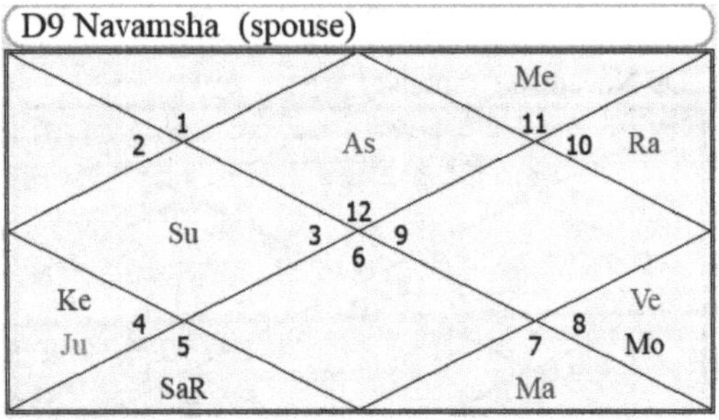

Birth Details: 26th August 1910, 14:25, Babina, Serbia

Case Study M5 (Marriage)

Problem Statement – This native married on 26-2-1968. **Justify this event in view of the D1 and the D9 charts.**

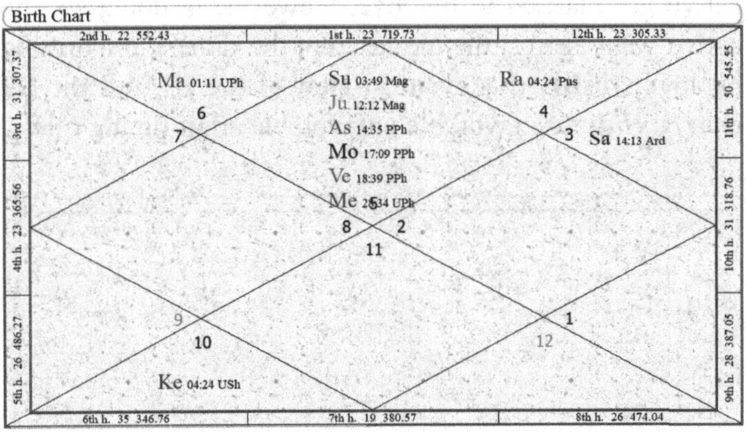

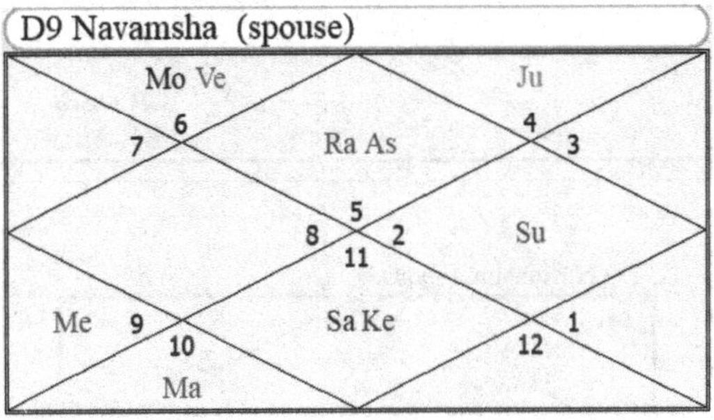

Birth Details: 20th August 1944, 08:11, Bombay, India

Case Study M6 (Marriage)

Problem Statement – This native fell in love with a young woman. The parents opposed the affair, however later the native got married to his love. However, in doing so, the native went against the mother (not the father) in marrying his love. **Justify this event in view of the D1 and the D9 charts.** *Hint:* use favorable/unfavorable affair timing rules.

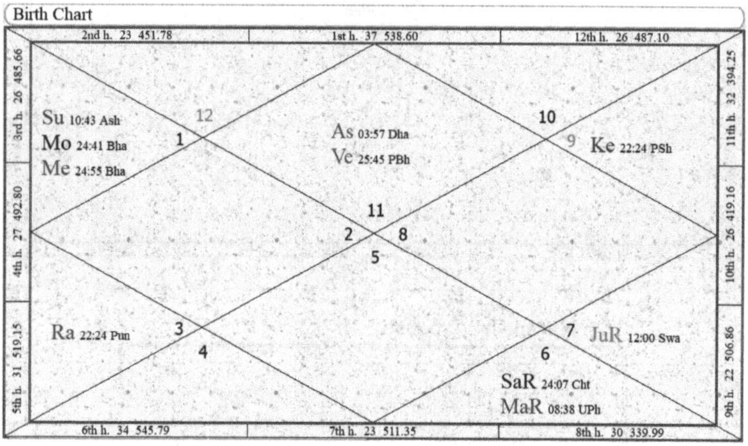

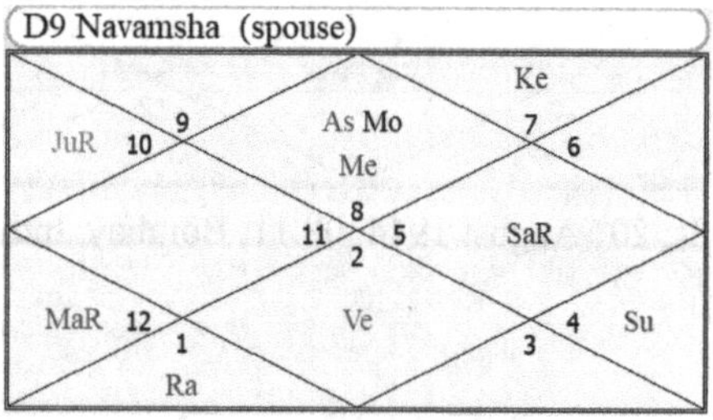

Birth Details: 25th April 1982, 02:20, near Delhi, India

Case Study M7 (Marriage)

Problem Statement – This native had a normal marriage. i.e., marriage within own relations (caste). **Justify this event in view of the D1 and the D9 charts.** *Hint:* use principles of intra-caste marriages.

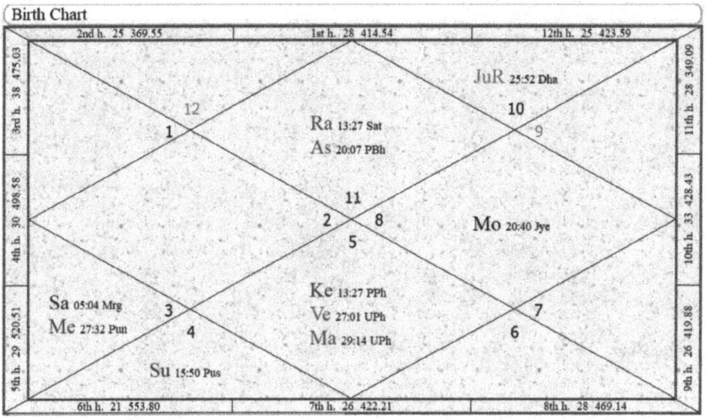

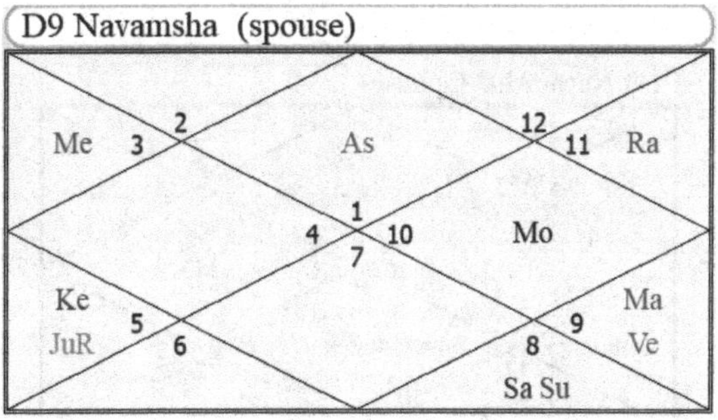

Birth Details: 1st August 1914, 20:55, Delhi, India

Case Study M8 (Marriage)

Problem Statement – This native had an inter-caste/inter-religion love marriage. **Justify this event in view of the D1 and the D9 charts.** *Hint:* use principles of inter-caste marriages.

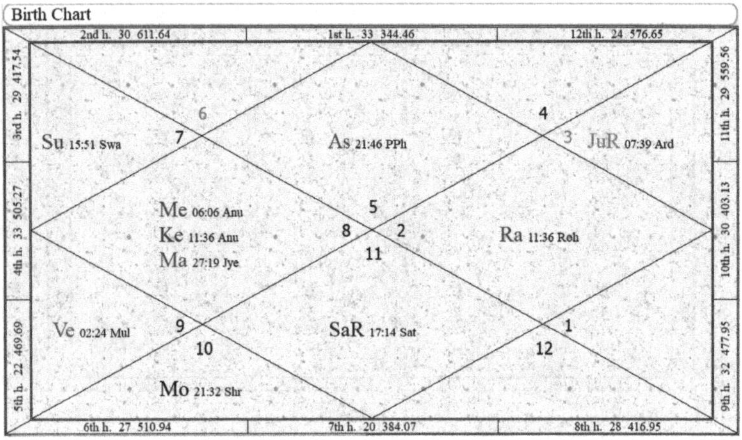

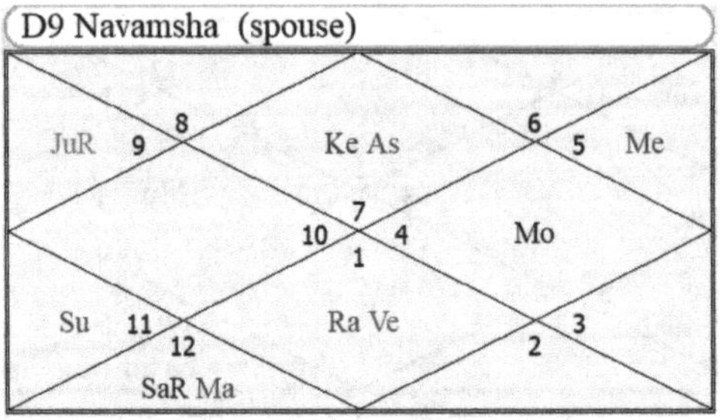

Birth Details: 2nd November 1965, 02:30, Delhi, India

Case Study M9 (Marriage)

Problem Statement – This native had an extra-marital affair post marriage in the Jupiter/Venus period. **Justify this event in view of the D1 and the D9 charts.** *Hint:* use principles of *dasha* analysis.

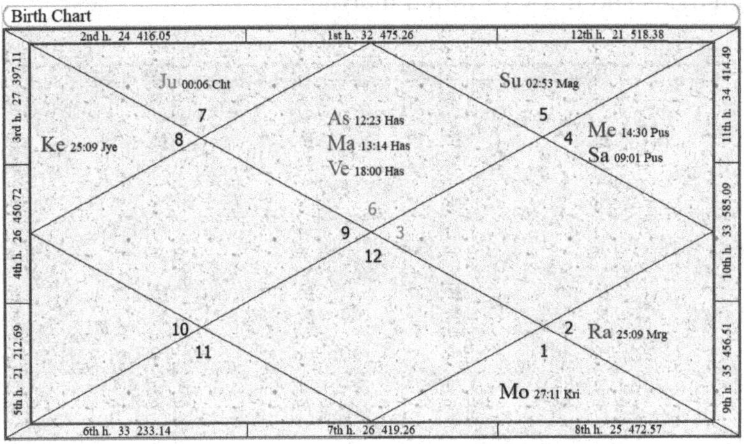

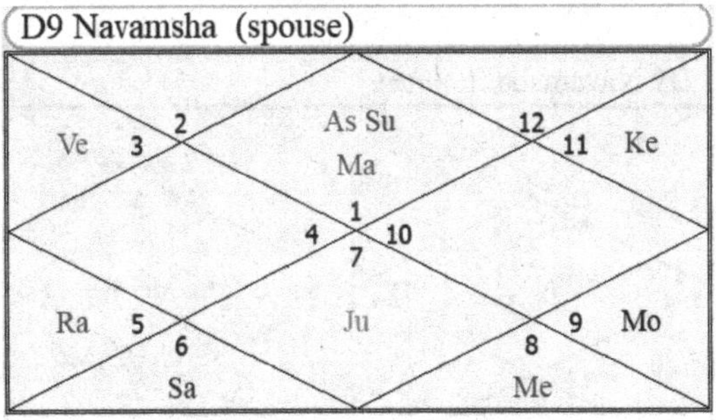

Birth Details: 19th August 1946, 08:51, Arkansas, USA

Case Study M10 (Marriage)

Problem Statement – This native had failed first marriage in the Mercury/Jupiter period and is also facing problems in the second marriage. **Justify these married life events in view of the D1 and the D9 charts.** *Hint:* use principles of *dasha* analysis and those of failed marriages.

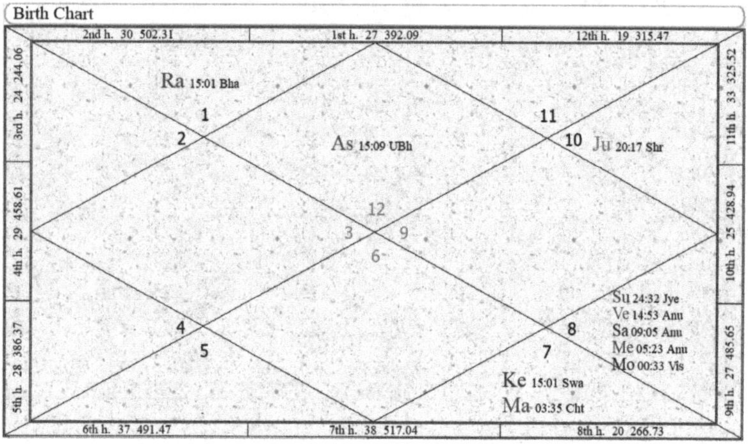

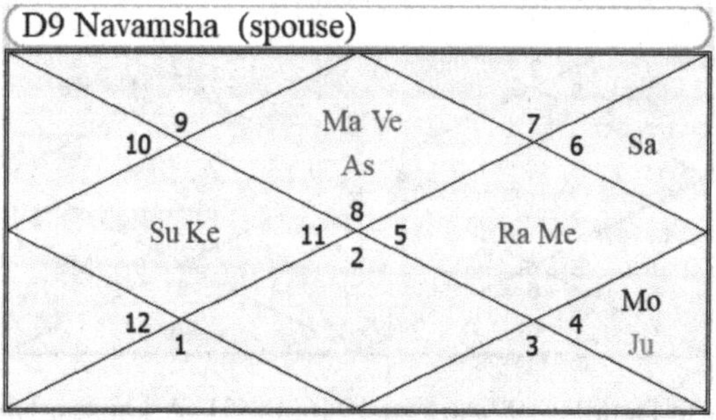

Birth Details: 10th December 1985, 13:30, Delhi, India

Case Study M11 (Marriage)

Problem Statement – This native married atleast three times. **Justify these married life events in view of the D1 and the D9 charts.** *Hint:* use principles of multiple marriages in the D1 and the D9 charts, as taught in any Vedic astrology course.

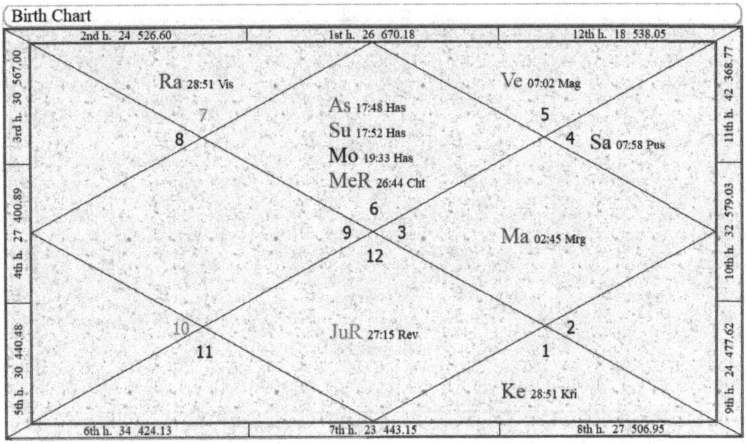

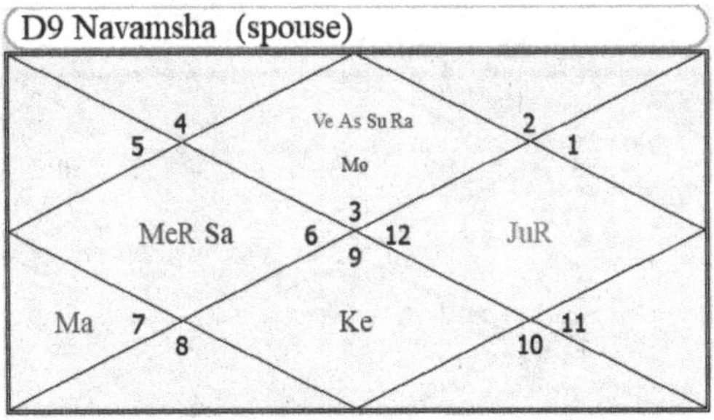

Birth Details: 5th October 1975, 07:15, Reading, UK

Case Study M12 (Marriage)

Problem Statement – This native married in the Rahu/ Mercury/Mercury period. **Justify this marriage event in view of the D1 and the D9 charts.** *Hint:* use principles of *dasha*-based marriage time in the D1 and the D9 charts, as taught in any Vedic astrology course.

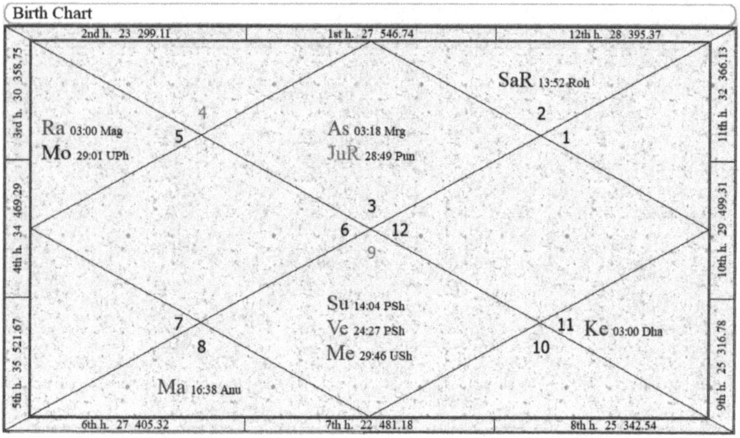

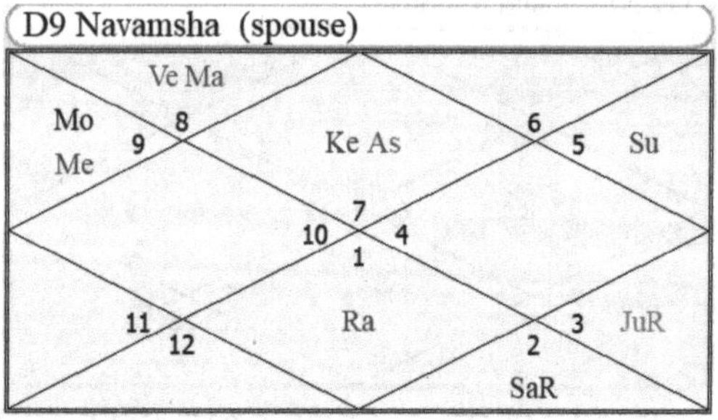

Birth Details: 29th December 1942, 18:05, Burewala, Pakistan

Case Study CH1 (Children)

Problem Statement – This native faced anxiety, grief, pain, and suffering from children. **Justify this in view of the D1 and the D9 charts.**

Birth Chart

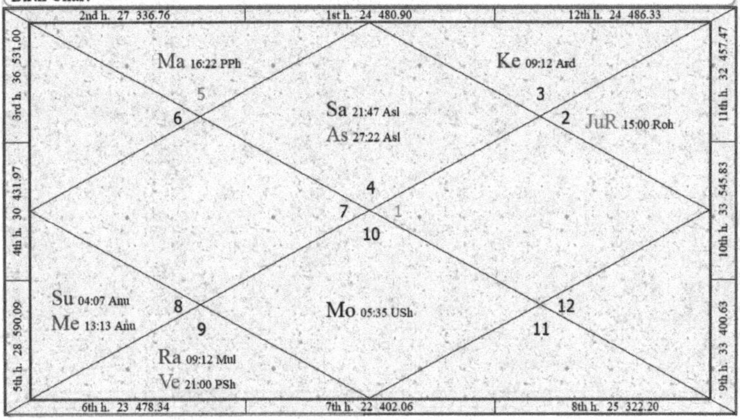

D9 Navamsha (spouse)

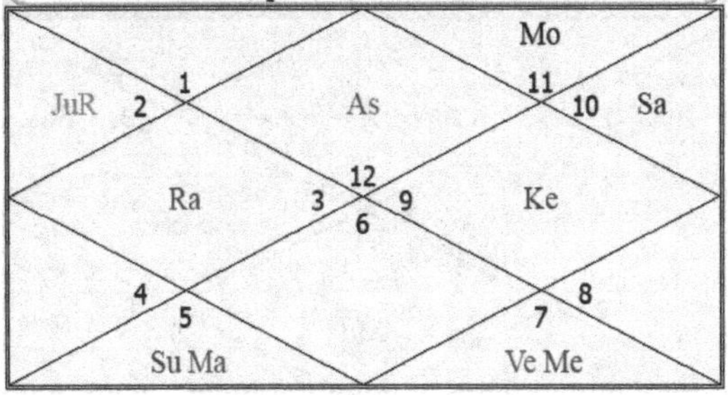

Birth Details: 19th November 1917, 23:11, Allahabad, India

Case Study CH2 (Children)

Problem Statement – This native had children who were independent and increased the socio-economic status of the native. **Justify this in view of the D1 and the D9 charts.**

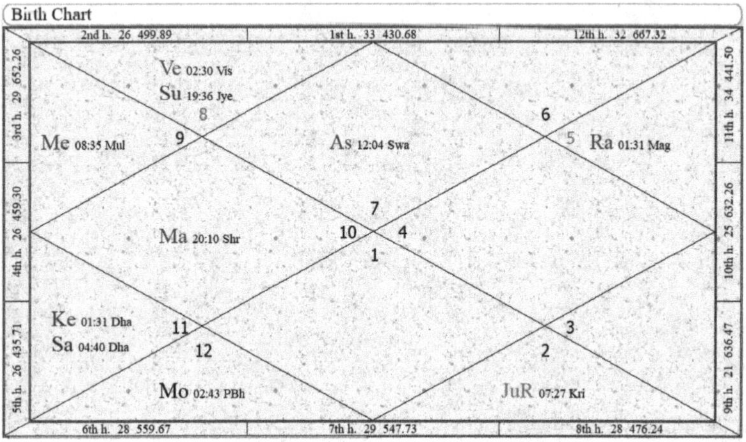

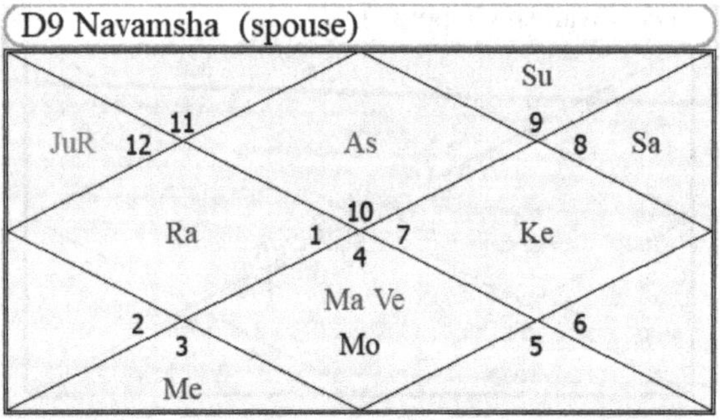

Birth Details: 5th December 1905, 04:15, Srinagar, India

Case Study CH3 (Children)

Problem Statement – This native had a child born on February 27, 1990. **Justify this event in view of the D1 and the D9 charts, along with transits.** Hint: Use *dasha* and transit analysis on the D1 and the D9.

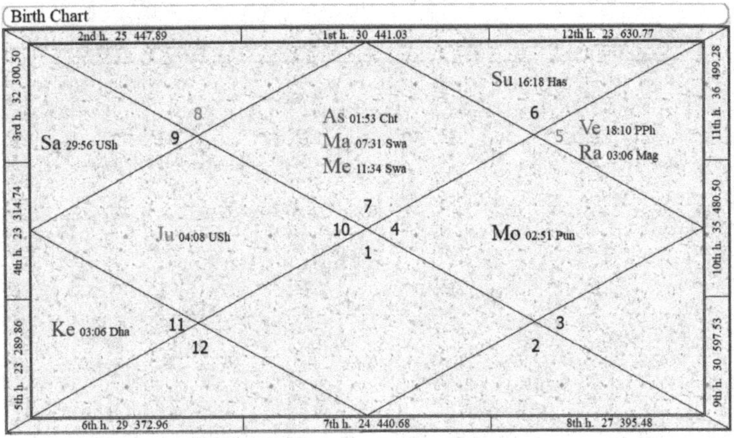

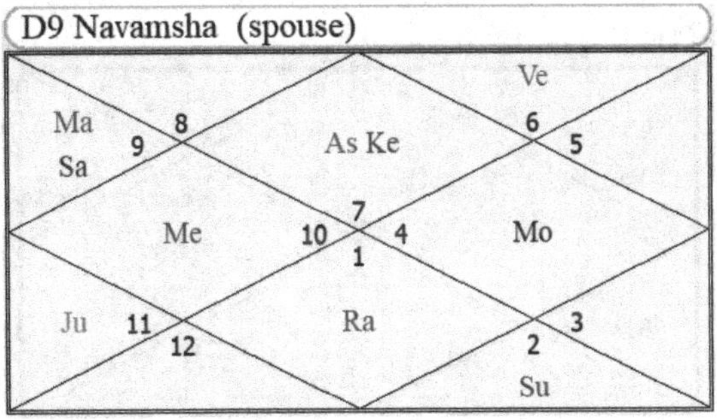

Birth Details: 3rd October 1961, 07:30, Delhi, India

Case Study CH4 (Children)

Problem Statement – This native had a child born on July 30, 1985. **Justify this event in view of the D1 and the D9 charts, along with transits.** Hint: Use *dasha* and transit analysis on the D1 and the D9.

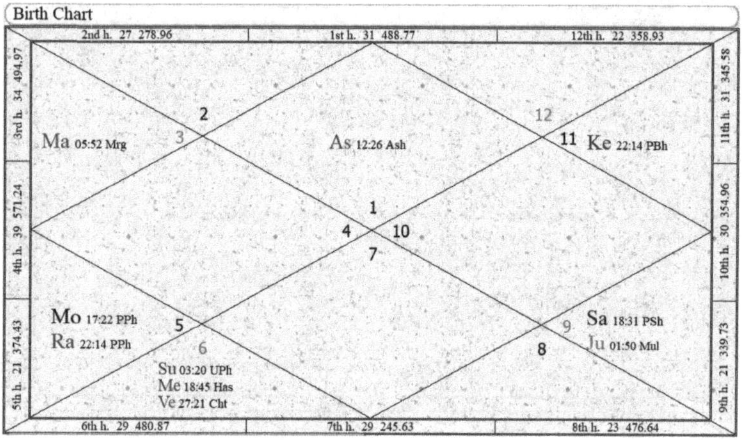

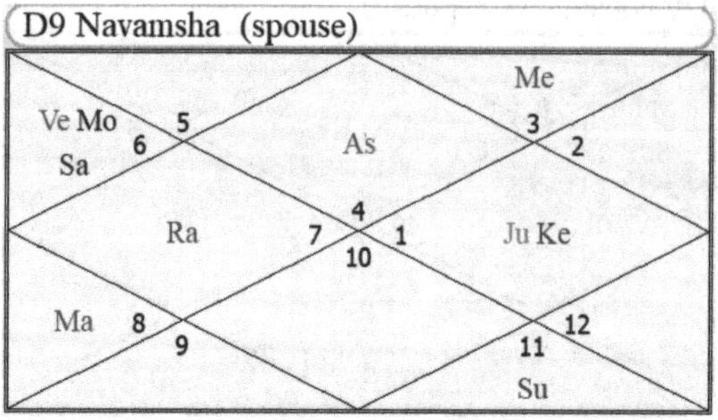

Birth Details: 19th September 1960, 20:11, Delhi, India

Case Study CH5 (Children)

Problem Statement – This native had a child born on 19th November 1917, when he was running the Venus/Moon period. **Justify this event in view of the D1 and the D9 charts.** Hint: Use *dasha* and transit analysis on the D1 and the D9.

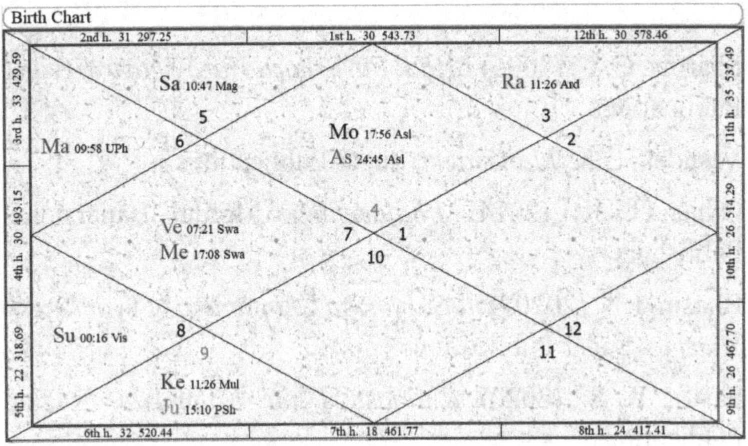

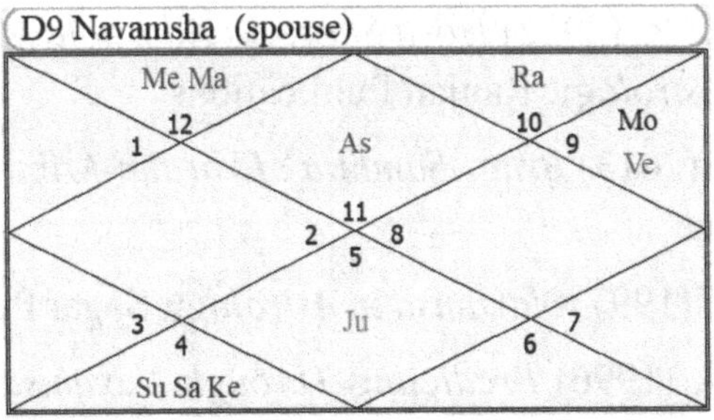

Birth Details: 14th November 1889, 23:11, Allahabad, India

Bibliography

Sharma, G. C. (2006) *Brihat Parashara Hora Shastra.* Sagar Publications

Vasudev, P. K. *Manasagri*. Sagar Publications

Ojha, G. K. (2014) *Phaldeepika.* Motilal Banarsidass Publishers

Bhasin, J. N. (2020) *The Sarvartha Chintamani of Vyankatesh Sharma.* Sagar Publications

Sastri, P. S. (2020) *Kalidasa Uttar Kalamrita.* Ranjan Publications

Santhanam, R. (2012) *Hora Sara: An Adorable Masterpiece of Hindu Astrology.* Ranjan Publications

Iyer, N. C. (2013) *Brhat-Samhita of Varaha-Mihira.* Parimal Publications

Patel, C. S. (1997) *Navamsa in Astrology.* Sagar Publications

Patel, C. S. (1996) *Predicting Through Navamsa and Nadi Astrology.* Sagar Publications

Goel, V. P. (2017) *Predict with Navamsa.* Sagar Publications

Goel, V. P. (2017) *Comprehensive Predictions by Divisional Charts.* Sagar Publications

Poddar, S. (2024) *The Vargas.* Notion Press

Khushu, P. L. (2023) *Navamsa and its Importance in Vedic Astrology.* Sagar Publications

Iyer, H. R. S. (1963) *New Techniques of Predictions. Volumes 1 and 2.* Janapriya Prakashan

Kumar, K. (2002) *Secrets of Vargas.* Alpha Publications

Vasan, T. S. (2018) *Navamsha: An Essential Tool for Predictive Astrology.* Indian Council of Astrological Studies

Aditya, V. (2022) *Splendour of Vargas.* Indian Council of Astrological Studies

Rath, S. (1998) *Varga Chakra.* Sagar Publications

Sastri, P. S (2013) *Brihat Jatak.* Ranjan Publications

Vasudev, G. D. (2011) *The Art of Interpreting Horoscopes.* Motilal Banarsidass International

Raman, B. V. (1995) *How to Judge a Horoscope Volume 1.* Motilal Banarsidass Publishers

Raman, B. V. (1995) *How to Judge a Horoscope Volume 2.* Motilal Banarsidass Publishers

Santhanam, R. (2004) *Deva Keralam. Volumes 1-3.* Sagar Publications

Satyacharya. (2018) *Satya Jatakam.* Ranjan Publications

Raman, B. V. (1999) *Prasna Marga Volumes 1 - 5.* Motilal Banarsidass Publishers

Mishra, S. C. (2021) *A Textbook of Nakshatra Jyotisha.* Vedic Astro India

Bagal, N. N. (1965) *Formulas for Astrology and Horoscopes in India*, Sanskrit Pustak Bhandar

Gaur, A. K. (2015) *Professions: Inclination, Fructification, and Career Profile.* Alpha Publications

Biography

Dr. Ranjan Pal has been into *jyotisha* analysis and philosophy since 2000. His recent and first book "*Can Rahu Give Spiritial Ethos: An Argumentative Analysis in Jyotish*" has been published by Motilal Banarsidass International in 2025. In his professional work sphere, Ranjan is a computer scientist, decision scientist, and applied mathematician at the Massachusetts Institute of Technology, USA and serves on the faculty of the MIT Sloan School of Management. He conducts and leads research at the MIT Sloan School of Management in the field of cybersecurity; consults for Fortune 100 Global MNCs; and is an invited member of a World Economic Forum working group. Ranjan has an M.S. and a Ph.D. in computer science. Prior to joining MIT, Ranjan held cybersecurity research positions at Princeton University, USA and the University of Cambridge, UK. He was a faculty member of the University of Michigan, USA, and a visiting faculty of Indian Institute of Management Ahmedabad, Indian Institute of Management Calcutta, Indian Institute of Technology Delhi, the Indian School of Business, and the All India Institute of Medical Sciences. Ranjan has given more than 45 invited talks around the globe on his academic research. He has been schooled in Vedic astrology first by his late father (as part of a 150-year family tradition) who was a faculty member and Acting Director of the Indian Institute of Management (IIM) Calcutta. He was then schooled by Dr. Richa Shukla – a professional astrologer based in Gurgaon. Ranjan's goal is to make the exposition of Vedic astrology a simple, structured, and logical task for the student mass studying the subject. Besides Vedic astrology, he is an ardent follower of the reasoning behind the Vedic Advaita philosophy.